Disk Mince
p. 232
PowerNap i88

Mac OS X
Illustrated

A Design Graphics Field Guide

D E S I G N G R A P H I C S

WILEY

Wiley Publishing, Inc.

Mac® OS X Illustrated Panther Edition

A Design Graphics Field Guide

Published by

Wiley Publishing, Inc.

111 River Street

Hoboken, NJ 07030

www.wiley.com

ISBN: 0-7645-4397-0

Manufactured in the United States of America

10 9 8 7 6 5 4 3 2 1

1K/TQ/RS/QS/IN

Published by Wiley Publishing, Inc., Indianapolis, Indiana

Published simultaneously in Canada

For general information on our other products and services or to obtain technical support, please contact our Customer Care Department within the U.S. at 800-762-2974, outside the U.S. at 317-572-3993 or fax 317-572-4002.

Wiley also publishes its books in a variety of electronic formats. Some content that appears in print may not be available in electronic books.

Library of Congress Cataloging-in-Publication Data

 is a trademark of Wiley Publishing, Inc.

Mac OS X Illustrated Panther Edition
A Design Graphics Field Guide

Conceived and produced by DG Books Pty Ltd
2 Sherbrooke Road
Sherbrooke VIC 3789
Australia

DG Books is a member of the Xandia group of companies.

From the Xandia Group, Design Graphics publishes:

Design Graphics magazine (monthly)
Art & Design Education Resource Guide (annual)
Oz Graphix (annual)

*INSTALLING applications
P 98 . ADMINISTRATOR needs PASS WORD
MAYbe I have NONE*

DESIGN GRAPHICS

Acknowledgements

Mac OS X Illustrated Panther Edition
A Design Graphics Field Guide

Concept and Art Direction
Colin Wood

Project Editor and Design Coordinator
Colleen Bate

Writers
Colleen Bate
Stephen Withers

Designers
Steve Page
Carly Goodwin

Pre-production
Steve Page

Cover design
Colin Wood

Contents summary

Contents

1   Where things are

Finding old favorites

Mac OS innovations

2   Getting started

3   Basic system management

4   Mac OS finder

5 The digital hub

6 Quick tour of Mac OS X

This is a guide for people who don't read manuals. Apple's Mac OS X is a significant leap forward in operating systems and is the biggest change for users in the history of the Macintosh.

This guide aims to make your transition to OS X as painless as possible. It should also increase your levels of fun and productivity as you bring out the best in you and your Mac. There are loads of new features and new ways of doing things. Some things will be familiar; some won't. Some things have moved and are not where you'd expect them to be.

This guide will help you find all your favorites and introduce you to all the new features. Find out how to make your Mac a digital hub and use all the new apps and utilities. Let 'Mac OS X Illustrated' be your constant companion as you settle in and get comfortable with your new working environment.

How to use this guide

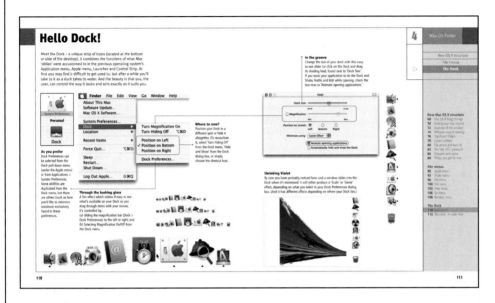

Browse
Before you get stuck into details, browse through the book. You'll be surprised what you'll pick up.

Subject groups
The book is divided into six *subject groups*. (See the Contents summary on page 6.)

Chapters
Chapters are grouped within the six *subject groups*. (See page 6.)

Macro subjects
Each chapter contains related *macro subjects*. Macro subjects contain several *individual subjects*.

Individual subjects
So that you're not swamped with too much information at once, each spread is devoted to a single subject. Related subjects may be nearby.

Contents summary
The contents summary shows the six *subject groups* with their chapters. (See page 6.)

Contents
Every subject is listed, together with page numbers. (See page 8.)

Start with the easy stuff
The front part of the guide has the easy stuff. We've placed the more technical subjects at the back.

Index
See page 272 for the comprehensive index.

Chapter name

List of contents
Your first stop should
be the list of contents
starting on page 8.

Chapter number

4

Mac OS Finder

Chapter colour tab

New OS X structure

File menus

The Dock

Subject indicator

▷

Macro subjects

The **macro subjects**
within a chapter are
listed in the order they
appear in the guide.

The **current macro
subject** is highlighted
with a darker grey bar
and a subject indicator
arrow.

Navigation
An important aspect
of navigating your
way through this
guide is the ease
with which you can
find related
subjects.

The **other subjects**
in the current chapter
are listed with their
page numbers.
Thus you can see
what related subjects
are nearby.
Once again, the
current subject is
highlighted with a
darker gray bar.

Helpful hints
Along the way you'll find
helpful hints in the 'Tech
Tip' boxes.

TECH TIP

THAT BELONGS WHERE?
Simply select and drag a document
onto the application icon of choice
in the Dock, and watch how it
automatically launches the
document and application together.

Things you get for free

Not too long ago the most you could hope for when buying a new operating system were a few utilities. Now Mac OS X provides iPhoto, iDVD, iMovie, iTunes, GarageBand, iChat, iCal, iSync, Mail, Address Book and QuickTime. Plug in your new Mac and can download and organize your digital photos, edit your digital video, create interactive DVDs, manage your MP3 collection, make music, manage contacts and time, synchronize calendars and contacts with PDAs or mobile phones, chat online, manage email and control 'spam'. Extra cost: $0.

iPhoto www.apple.com/ iphoto/	**iMovie** www.apple.com/ imovie/	**iDVD** www.apple.com/ idvd/	**iTunes** www.apple.com/ itunes/	**iCal** www.apple.com/ ical/	**GarageBand** www.apple.com/ garageband/
Connect digital still cameras via USB or FireWire.	Connect digital video cameras via FireWire	Create interactive DVDs featuring digital video.	Manage your MP3 music collection.	Schedule/share calendars on web or your devices.	Create, record and mix your own music.
Shipped with Mac OS X 10.3: Version 2.0	**Shipped with Mac OS X 10.3:** Version 3.0.3	**Shipped with Mac OS X 10.3:** N/A	**Shipped with Mac OS X 10.3:** Version 4.0.1	**Shipped with Mac OS X 10.3:** Version 1.5	**Shipped with Mac OS X 10.3:** N/A
Latest version via iLife '04 and Software Update: 4.0.1	**Latest version via iLife '04:** 4.0	**Latest version via iLife '04 and Software Update:** 4.0.1	**Latest version via Software Update:** 4.2	**Latest version via Software Update:** 1.5.2	**Latest version via iLife '04 and Software Update:** 1.0.1
Ships free with: • All models	Ships free with: • All models	Ships free with: • All SuperDrive-equipped systems.	Ships free with: • All models • Online at www.apple.com/itunes/	Ships free with: • All models • Online at www.apple.com/ical/	Ships free with: • All models

Five superb tools with iLife

iLife comes free with every new Mac you purchase, running Mac OS X 10.3. The collection includes iPhoto, iMovie, iDVD, iTunes and GarageBand. Don't despair if you already own a Mac, however—the latest versions are available on CD-ROM at a modest price.

iSync www.apple.com/ isync/	**iChat AV** www.apple.com/ ichat/	**Mail** www.apple.com/ mail/	**Address Book** www.apple.com/ macosx/	**QuickTime** www.apple.com/ quicktime/
Synchronize PDAs, or Bluetooth mobile phones.	Chat client compatible with AOL's AIM.	Email client with anti-spam and .Mac integration.	Email client with anti-spam and .Mac integration.	Movie player with MPEG-4 support.
Shipped with Mac OS X 10.3: Version 1.2	**Shipped with Mac OS X 10.3:** Version 2.1	**Shipped with Mac OS X 10.3:** Version 1.3.7	**Shipped with Mac OS X 10.3:** Version 3.1.1	**Shipped with Mac OS X 10.3:** Version 6.0.3
Latest version via Software Update: 1.4	**Latest version via Software Update:** 2.1	**Latest version via Software Update:** 1.3.4	**Latest version via Software Update:** 3.1.1	**Latest version via Software Update:** 6.5
Ships free with: • All models • Online at www.apple.com/ isync/download/	Ships free with: • All models	Ships free with: • All models	Ships free with: • All models	Ships free with: • All models

Pro users
(www.apple.com/powermac/)
But wait, there's more. With the Power Mac G4 or G5, professional customers also get: Safari, Sherlock, DVD Player, Classic environment, Acrobat Reader, Art Directors Toolkit, EarthLink, FAXstf, FileMaker Pro Trial, GraphicConverter, Microsoft Internet Explorer, Microsoft Office v. X Test Drive, OmniGraffle, OmniOutliner, QuickBooks for Mac New User Edition, Zinio Reader, and Developer Tools.
(May vary by model and in different geographies.)

Consumers (www.apple.com/imac/)
With their iMac or iBook purchase, Apple customers also get:
Sherlock 3; DVD Player; AppleWorks 6; Quicken Deluxe; World Book
Encyclopedia; Sound Studio; Tony Hawk's Pro Skater 4; Deimos Rising;
Microsoft Internet Explorer, Microsoft Office v.X Test Drive; and Mac OS X

The pro choice

For creative professionals, free applications will only take you so far. Apple offers a wide range of industrial-strength solutions for: editing digital video with Final Cut Pro or Final Cut Express; high-quality DVDs using DVD Studio Pro; file and web sharing with the UNIX-strength Mac OS X 10.3 Server; movie compositing with Shake; Digital video authoring and playback with QuickTime Pro; Web application development with WebObjects; and remote control of Macs over Ethernet, AirPort or the Internet with Apple Remote Desktop.

Images courtesy of **Apple**

Final Cut Pro HD
Create professional digital video productions complete with high-end effects and controls.

Final Cut Express 2
Prosumer digital video editing: more capable than iMovie, less expensive than Final Cut Pro.

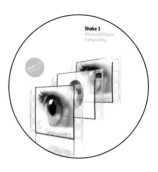

Shake 3
High-performance compositing software designed for large format film productions

DVD Studio Pro 3
A DVD authoring tool for full-featured DVD video discs including Dolby Digital 5.1 encoding.

QuickTime Pro
Author MPEG-4 content and export as most common formats including a number of Web streaming presets. See pages 116-119.

QuickTime MPEG-2 Playback
Convert MPEG-2 video content into other formats, for the Web, CD-ROM, or DV tape. See pages 116-119.

Mac OS X Server 10.3
A platform for delivering scalable workgroup and network services with a solid UNIX foundation.

WebObjects
A tool to develop and deploy Java server applications as standards-based Web services.

Apple Remote Desktop
Remotely manage other Macs on a local network, AirPort wireless network or across the Internet.

Glossary

A

Active window
Current modal or document window (brought forward above other windows.) Active windows display distinctive details and are affected by users actions.

Administrator
The person with the privileges to administer users to the computer network. The administrator can create new users and organises privileges for each document or folder for each user.

Advanced memory management
The Mac OS X capability to automatically assign the correct amount of memory to an application. It puts an end toout-of-memory messages, as well as the need to manually adjust application memory.

AirPort
Apple's wireless networking technology using IEEE 802.11. Available in desktop, iMac, iBook and PowerBook G4s.

Alias
Alias allows files and folders to be multi-referenced without making multiple copies of these items.

Always-on Internet
A connection to the Internet that is always connected. Classed as DSL, ISDN or Cable Internet, the download speeds can vary between 8Kb to as fast as 500Kb per second.

Anti-aliasing
A technique used on a greyscale or colour bitmap display to make diagonal edges appear smoother. In the Classic environment, text smoothing is an option of the Appearance control panel.

Apple Desktop Bus (ADB)
This is the name for the superseded mechanism for connecting the mouse and keyboard to the Apple computer. It has since been replaced by USB.

Apple key
Also called the Command key, it is situated next to the space bar on most keyboards.
It has the Apple logo and cloverleaf or propeller pattern.

AppleTalk
Suite of network protocols standard on Macintosh computers. Can be integrated with other network systems, such as the Internet.

Application
Another name for programs such as Microsoft Word, Adobe Photoshop or FileMaker. In the mainframe environment, this refers to a process whereby many programs and databases are utilised for a final result.

Application Programming Interface (API)
The means by which application programs take advantage of operating system features.

Aqua
The new, more intuitive Mac OS X interface. Aqua includes expressive icons, vibrant colour, and fluid motion, as well as innovative features to help users navigate and organize their system.

B

Bandwidth
The transmission capacity of the frequency interval used by a communications channel.

Beta
The status of a product that has already been extensively alpha and field tested. Available for public download but generally not guaranteed to be 'bug-free'.

Bit
A binary digit, the smallest information entity bitmap. A dot-by-dot description of an electronic image, with each dot represented by a binary digit (bit) that is 'on' (1) or 'off' (0).

Bitmap
Data structure representing positions and states of a corresponding set of pixels.

Boot
Booting, re-booting the computer refers to when the computer system is started. The computer runs through some internal checks and then loads its operating system from its main designated disk.

Browser
Application that allows users to see the contents of a Web server.

BSD (Berkeley System Distribution):
A version of UNIX developed by the Computer Systems Research Group of the University of California at Berkeley.

Attachment
One or more files that can be attached to emails, so it can be viewed at the other end. Some ISPs limit the size allowable to send.

C

Cache memory
Hardware device used to store the most frequently accessed data in memory. Used in conjunction with disk drives and meant to reduce access time by eliminating the rotational delay and seek time.

Carbon
A set of Mac OS X programming interfaces that allows software developers to update or 'tune up' applications to run in Mac OS X. Carbon applications take advantage of new Mac OS X features such as the advanced Darwin foundation, Quartz graphics, and the Aqua user interface.

CD-ROM
Compact Disc Read Only Memory. A version of the Compact Disc for storage of 'Read'Only Memory' digital data. User capacity is usually in excess of 600Mb.

Channel
In a QuickTime Player, a channel delivers interactive QuickTime TV content, which can include streaming video, streaming audio, and links to related information on the Web.

Classic
A software compatibility environment that allows you to run thousands of Mac OS 9 applications in Mac OS X. Mac OS 9.2 is the basis for the Classic environment, allowing previous versions of Macintosh software to

Byte
Eight bits makes one byte. It takes one byte to produce one character, such as the letter A, on the monitor.

work just as they do in Mac OS 9. They look like Mac OS 9 applications with the 'Platinum' user interface, and they do not make use of new Mac OS X features.

Clipboard
Also known as the pasteboard, the clipboard enables the transfer of data between applications and the Finders. It contains data that the user has cut or copied and is implemented using Core Foundation Pasteboard Services or the Cocoa NSPasteboard class.

Cocoa
The native programming language of Mac OS X. Cocoa is an application programming interface (API) that runs advanced, object-oriented applications. It is the fastest and most powerful way for developers to create new applications for Mac OS X. Like Carbon applications, Cocoa applications take advantage of all the advanced features of Mac OS X.

Compositing
In image editing, the process of combining several images or specific portions of images into one overall image.

Configuration
Group of settings for a particular networking component such as AppleTalk or TCP/IP.

ColorSync
Industry-standard architecture for reliably reproducing colour images on operating systems and devices such as scanners, video displays and printers.

Contextual menu
The convenient menu that

appears when you Control+Click on an item.

D

Darwin
The UNIX-based core operating system that is the foundation of Mac OS X, Darwin evolved from a joint effort by Apple engineers and programmers in the open source software community. UNIX and Linux software developers will appreciate the ease of porting existing UNIX applications to Mac OS X using Darwin.

Database
A collection of interrelated data items readable and searchable using keywords. It can either be a basic level structure or be relational, which stipulates that there may be many-to-one, one-to-many or many-to-many relationships to records in other linked files.

Disk
The hardware that holds data in the computer. Internal drives that you never actually see, but external hard disks can also connect via a network.

Disk image
This file represents a disk volume. The Disk Copy utility mounts any disk image after you double click on the file. A removable disk icon for the disk image appears on the desktop. Use the Finder to navigate to folders on the disk image just as you would navigate to find a file on a physical hard disk.

Directory
A folder, single level or root level of a disk. It displays a list of items enclosed in that area. Possibly includes navigational guides to surrounding levels.

Domain
An area of the file system reserved for software, documents and resources. There are four domains: user, local, network and system.

DOS
The operating system for PCs which precedes more recent versions of Microsoft Windows.

Download
The moving of a file from one computer to another, either through an intranet, WLAN or the Internet.

Dock
The bar that appears at the bottom of the Mac OS X desktop screen. The Dock contains icons for launching applications. You also can minimise an open file and windows to an icon on the Dock, then click the icon on the Dock to reopen the window.

Drag
Holding the mouse button down and rolling the mouse, moving the cursor and an item, perhaps a folder or icon on the screen.

Driver
A file that provides extra functionality to your system such as a file needed to enable Mac OS X to use a particular printer or camera.

DSL
An addition to the standard telephone service that allows a constant internet service over a standard telephone line.

Dual-booting
Mac OS X supports dual booting, which means that Mac OS X users can choose to start up their system using either Mac OS X or Mac OS 9.x.

DVD
Stands for Digital Versatile Disc, a form of optical disc that holds upwards of 4.7Gb of data. The DVD supports disks with capacities of from 4.7Gb to 17Gb and access rates of 600Kbps to 1.3Mbps. One of the best features of DVD drives is that they are backward-compatible with CD-ROMs. This means that DVD players can play old CD-ROMs, CD-I disks, and video CDs, as well as new DVD-ROMs.

E

Ethernet
This one of the most common LAN standards in networking. A newer version of Ethernet, called 100Base-T (or Fast Ethernet), supports data transfer rates of 100 Mbps. And the newest version, Gigabit Ethernet supports data rates of one gigabit (1,000 megabits) per second.

Encryption
A form of scrambling of files into un-readable form. This secures the contents for specific readers only. Decoding of the files can then be regulated.

Extensions
Small applications that run behind the scenes of the desktop, which can display and control timing, mail, fax reception, monitor calibration as well as many other house-keeping duties on the computer.

Extensions manager
An extra application that controls the activity and administration of the many extensions that start up and run alongside the operating system.

External hard drive
A box connected by USB or FireWire to the main computer body. This hard drive may be used as a scratch disk or an extra area of storage for large files and applications.

Email Rule
A specification telling the email client how to deal with incoming traffic, such as instantly deleting a message from a source that sends junk mail.

F

Favorite
In the Finder or Microsoft Internet Explorer, this is an alias of a folder, file or page that you use frequently and can double click to open, wherever it may be.

File
The named document that you create in an application.

Firewall
Software (or computers running such software) that prevents unauthorised access to a network and therefore unauthorised spread of data.

Folder
Named after a physical folder, this is the place that you store files on a computer hard drive. It may have a name, and a colour, to classify the contents.

G

Gb
A gigabyte is exactly 1,000,000,000-bytes of data.

GUI
The Graphic User Interface, which includes folders, files, icons, pull-down menus and a point-and-click cursor system. As this is based on a system able to be seen, it is widely considered to be a more user friendly system that command-line interfaces.

H

Hacker
A hacker is considered to be a person with an intense interest in computers and also considered to be using this knowledge with malicious intent.

Hang
To have an application or the operating system stop responding to input for some reason. No movements or mouse-clicks will restore the desktop. In Mac OS X, only the offending application needs to be Force-quit to regain control.

Help Viewer
An application that helps you browse for help in Mac OS X.

HFS (Hierarchical File System)
Mac OS file-system format. Files are represented as a hierarchy of directories or folders, in turn containing files or folders.

Home folder
A folder set up to store files for your user name within a multi-user environment in Mac OS X.

HTML (Hypertext Markup Language)
Text file prepartion method to ensure that contents are displayed and link to other files on the World Wide Web.

Glossary

I

Icon view
A finder window, depicting each file and folder as an icon.

Insertion point
In a graphical application or text box, the point where the cursor sits flashing.

Internal hard disk
As the name suggests, it is the hard disk inside the computer. Named accordingin to your preference, this is the primary area where applications and files can be run from start-up.

Internet service provider (ISP)
Someone or a company who provides the necessary service for connection to the Internet.

iTunes
An audio application that enables Mac users to play audio CDs, create MP3 files, and build playlists.

K

Kernel
This is the pivotal component of the operating system. The kernel handles most of the interaction between the operating system and the hardware.
The Darwin core kernel is based on Mach 3.0 from Carnegie Mellon University and FreeBSD 3.2 (derived from the University of California at Berkeley's BSD 4.4 Lite), a core technology from two widely acclaimed operating system projects.

Keyboard repeat rate
The rate controls how rapidly the system duplicates the character.

L

Linux
An implementation of the UNIX kernel, originally written from scratch, with no proprietary code. The kernel as a whole is available under the GNU General Public License.

Login
Entering your name and password to gain access to Mac OS X after you start up the system.

M

Mach
Lowest level of the Mac OS X kernel. It provides basic services such as threads, tasks, ports, and interprocess communication (IPC), etc.

Magnification
A Dock feature in Mac OS X that increases icon size when the cursor is rolled over it.

Memory protection
System of memory management in Mac OS X where programs are prevented from being able to modify or corrupt the memory partition of another program. (Note: Mac OS 8 and 9 do not have memory protection).

Menu bar
The strip of commands that can be pulled down from the top of the screen with the mouse-click when an application is open.

Mount
When Disk Copy opens a disk image file, an icon is created for the application on the desktop.

Multitasking
The ability to carry out multiple programs concurrently.
Mac OS X uses pre-emptive multitasking while Mac OS 8 and 9 use cooperative multitasking.

N

Networking
Mac OS X offers UNIX-based networking with built-in support for PPP, AirPort, and Ethernet. Users benefit from quick and easy access to Internet service providers, as well as seamless local area network integration.

NeXT
A company called NeXT Software was founded by Steve Jobs in 1986. It created hardware that took advantage of object oriented technologies. NeXT Software was sold to Apple in 1997.

NeXTSTEP
NeXTSTEP is based on an operating system called Mach to which NeXT has added a UNIX interface. You can use the UNIX command-line if you like, but unlike your average UNIX system, NEXTSTEP is easier to use.

O

OpenGL
Contributing to the incredible graphics offered by Mac OS X, OpenGL is the world's most widely used 3D technology.

Optical disk
A platter-shaped disk coated with optical recording material on which information is read and written using a laser light, focused on a single line of material.

P

Pane
An alternate word for a window in a Macintosh desktop interface.

Password
A secret word or group of characters that you enter to login to Mac OS X and some web sites. Passwords limit access to authorised users only.

Pasteboard
Another name for the Clipboard.

PDA
Abbreviation for a Personal Digital Assistant, as introduced by the Palm and Handspring group of companies.

PDF (Portable Document Format)
File format for viewing documents independently of the original software, hardware, and operating system used to create them. A PDF file can contain any combination of text, graphics, and images.

Permission
Each user in the Mac OS X has their own list of folders and areas where they are permitted to enter. They have permission to use the contents of these folders.

Pixel
Basic logical unit of programmable color on a computer display or in a computer image. The size of a pixel depends on the resolution of the display screen.

Plug-in
External module of code and data separate from a host (i.e. an application, operating system or other plug-in) that can add features without needing access to the source code of the host.

Pointer
The little black arrow that is the point of interaction on the screen. Also named the cursor.

PostScript
Industry standard for printing and imaging, this language describes the appearance of a printed page and is an ouput format of Quartz.

PPP (Point-to-Point Protocol)
The Internet standard for transmitting network data, such as IP packets, over serial point-to-point links.

Pre-emptive multitasking
A Mac OS X function that prioritizes tasks according to their importance. You can do things such as check email, write a letter, or surf the web, and your Mac will continue to respond, even when executing processor-intensive tasks such as compressing a movie file.

Preferences
Files generated by every application as they are run. Each preference file holds API instructions and scripts that ensure relevant and constant application behaviour at each launch. System Preferences hold instructions for System start-up and housekeeping procedures.

Print Center
The Mac OS X application that enables you to install and control printers.

Privileges
Within Mac OS X, there are many areas that users are not able to enter unless they are also the administrator and owner of the machine. These are

the regulated privileges with the system.

Propeller key
Another name for the Apple Command key, first key to use in a combination command, like Command-Q for quit.

Protected memory
Mac OS X isolates each application in its own memory space, so if an application does crash, Mac OS X shuts it down without affecting anything else on your computer. You can continue working or playing on your Mac without interruption and without restarting your computer.

Public folder
This holds documents and files which are meant to be visible and useable by all users of the Mac OS X system on any computer in question. There are no privileges attached.

Q

Quartz
A powerful, high-performance new 2D graphics system developed by Apple. Quartz features on-the-fly rendering, anti-aliasing, and compositing of PDF for pristine, high-fidelity graphics. It even allows you to save as PDF in Mac OS X applications.

R

RAM
Random-access memory and one which a microprocessor can read or write to.

Removable disk
A removable drive which is attached with FireWire or USB if it is an External drive. Possibly ATA/100 if it is an internal drive.

Rendering
The conversion of a data-based description into a graphical image for display.

Resolution
Number of pixels contained on a display monitor.

S

Script
Series of statements that instruct an application or operating system to perform operations. Normally written in a scripting language such as AppleScript or Perl.

Server
Process that provides services to other clients in the same or other computers.

Sheet
Dialog associated with a specific window that appears to slide out from beneath the window title.

Shutdown
Under the Apple Menu. This can be used to close Mac OS X and power down your Macintosh.

Startup disk
The settings pane in the System Preferences application that lets the user set system and alert volumes, and choose the disk from which the Mac starts. This can also be used to select between the Mac OS X and older Mac environments.

Symmetric multiprocessing
A real boon for dual-processor Power Mac G4 systems. This feature allows Mac OS X to automatically assign both processors to handle operations and applications that are more

processor-intensive. With Mac OS X installed on a dual-processor system, certain operations run nearly twice as fast.

System Preferences
An application that, in part, replaces the Control Panels folder. It offers direct access to Mac OS X System Preferences, such as for date and time, monitor resolution and network configuration.

T

TCP/IP
Transmission Control Protocol/Internet protocol. A suite of protocols designed to allow Protocol/Internet communication between networks regardless of the technologies implemented in each network.

Terminal
A Mac OS X application used to access the UNIX command-line interface.

Toolbar
A row of icons or buttons that when clicked once, activate a specific command in a program.

U

Unicode
16-bit character set that assigns unique character codes to characters in a wide range of languages. (There are approximately 65 000 distinct Unicode characters that represent unique characters used in many languages.)

UNIX
The first non-proprietary operating system written in the C language, and the first open operating system that can be improved or enhanced by anyone. Darwin, the

foundation of Mac OS X, is based on UNIX.

URL
Uniform Resource Locator. This signifies a www. hypertext link, representing nearly every Internet link or service.

USB
Universal Serial Bus. A plug-and-play peripheral standard developed by Intel for keyboard, mouse, digital cameras, drives and printers. The high speed variation is USB 2.0 and its biggest competition is FireWire.

Utilities
Small applications that facilitate housekeeping tasks indirectly. Examples include system usage. File maintenance, disk copying etc.

V

Virtual memory
The method used to extend the memory available to your Mac by allocating part of the hard drive as a swap file. When built-in memory is not sufficient to meet operating system or program needs, Mac OS X uses the file to swap unneeded data. Beginning with Mac OS X, the memory needs of an application are established dynamically as needed.

Volume
A storage device or portion of that device that is formatted to contain folders and files of a particular file system.

W

Wireless Internet
Technologies that bring wireless connections to

the Internet by receiving satellite transmissions or fixed beams of signal.

Web page
A single document for display on the web.

Web site
A location on the Web that contains a selection of Web pages.

X

X
Signifies the numeral ten and is the system adopted by Apple for leveraging the Apple platform onto a UNIX base.

Y

Yahoo
One of the more successful web 'Search engine-turned-everything' companies. Having survived the dot.com crash, Yahoo has gone on to be one of the largest Web-based mail/chat/retail hubs.

Z

ZIP
A compression tool from PKWARE that works on PCs, Macs and UNIX computers. These compressed files are usually sent across the net as they can self-check for consistency while the file is being expanded. Aladdin Stuffit Expander (www.aladdinsys.com) can decode ZIP archives.

Zip drive
A removable storage device developed by Iomega Corporation, which can store up to 250Mb of data. The portable storage ability was a new feature.

On your marks ...

Finding old favorites

	OS 9		OS X	
 **About this Mac**	In OS 9 if you need to find out how much memory your Mac has and how much it is using, you simply go to the Apple	menu and select 'About this Mac' to see available memory and how it is utilized.	You will still find 'About this Mac' in the Apple menu in OS X, but it has a different function – it will display the amount of memory available on your	system as well as provide you with processor information, a comprehensive system profile, software update, serial and build numbers.
Aliases		Make an alias by pressing Command+ Option and drag or Command+M (shortcut File Menu > Make Alias.)	Make an alias by pressing Command+Option and drag or Command+L (shortcut File Menu > Make Alias.)	
AppleScript		AppleScript can be found in System Folder > Extensions.	AppleScript has been enhanced and dwells in the Applications folder in OS X as well as in AppleScript Studio on the Developer Tools CD.	
Application information 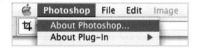	To view basic information on a current OS 9 application, go to the Apple menu. 'About this Mac' changes to 'About [Application Name]'.		To view basic information on a current OS X application, go to the Finder menu. 'About this Mac' changes to 'About [Application Name]'.	
Application menu 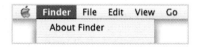	In Mac OS 9 this menu is located in the right hand corner of the screen.		This menu no longer exists in OS X, but you can select the new Finder menu to hide/show applications, or go to the Dock to monitor running	applications and/or items. Alternatively, bring up the Application Switcher by holding down Command and pressing Tab.
Applications running 	All applications currently running in OS 9, will be listed in the Applications menu.		You can view running applications, preferences and/or minimized documents on the Dock, indicated by a small black triangle pointing	towards your application icon. A quick alternative is to hold Command and press Tab to activate the Application Switcher.

Where they were, where they are now

OS 9		OS X	
Chooser	Go to the chooser to select a printer or activate AppleShare in OS 9.	The Chooser is no longer a feature of Mac OS X, the alternatives are: • Print Center to select network printers; and	• Connect to Server (Go>Connect to Server) to connect to a server or shared folder.
Contextual menus	Contextual menus are available in OS 9 (while holding down the Control key, point to an item and click). 	Contextual menus are still available in OS X, accessed by holding down the Control key. These capabilities extend	to the Dock – select any icon in it while holding Control and a contextual menu will also appear!
Control Panels	Control Panels are found in your System folder in OS 9. 	Many Control Panels in OS 9 have undergone a facelift and been moved to the System Preferences in OS X. These include • Appearance: some of these can be found in Personal; • Date & Time; • Energy Saver; • Internet; • Keyboard – keyboard layouts Script moved to 'International'; • Monitors: renamed 'Displays' in Mac OS X; • Keyboard & Mouse; • Multiple Users: renamed 'Setup' in Accounts in Mac OS X; • Numbers: absorbed into 'International' in OS X; • QuickTime Settings: renamed 'QuickTime'; • Software Update; • Sound; • Speech; and	• Startup Disk: this is where you will select whether to start up in Classic or OS X. Control Panels no longer in OS X include: • Apple Menu Options; • Control Strip; • Launcher; • Memory; • Text; and • General Controls. Control Panels absorbed into Internet and Network System Preferences include: • AppleTalk; • Configuration Manager; • DialAssist; • Extensions Manager; • File Exchange; • File Sharing; • Location Manager; • Modem; • Remote Access; • TCP/IP; • USB Printer Sharing; and • Web Sharing. Keychain Access and ColorSync Control panels are now located in Utilities in OS X.

Personal

Appearance   Desktop & Screen Saver   Dock   Exposé   International   Security

Hardware

CDs & DVDs   Displays   Energy Saver   Keyboard & Mouse   Print & Fax   Sound

Internet & Network

.Mac   Network   QuickTime   Sharing

System

Accounts   Classic   Date & Time   Software Update   Speech   Startup Disk   Universal Access

Finding old favorites

	OS 9	OS X
Desk Accessories	Calculator, Key Caps and Stickies are convenient desk accessories that live in the System Folder > Apple Menu Items in OS 9. 	In OS X, Calculator and Stickies have moved to Applications. Key Caps can be accessed in the Edit menu (now called Special Characters) or via the 'International' System Preference (Go to the Input Menu button and Check 'keyboard viewer' box in the list of input names).
Desktop 	The OS 9 desktop consists of disk icons and a trash can. The current date, international settings and Applications menu are located to the top right of the screen. The Apple menu to the far left of the screen is represented by a colored Apple icon.	In OS X, disk icons may or may not be visible, depending on what you have selected in Finder preferences. The Date & Time, Monitor and Sound settings are located on the top right of the screen. Although the menus are to the left, the Special menu is gone and there's a new menu – Finder. At the far left, the Apple menu is represented as typically aqua by a translucent blue Apple icon. The new Dock may or may not be visible, and if so, it may be located to the left, bottom or right of the screen – again, depending on the Finder preferences you have selected.
Dock	Mac 'oldies' used the Application menu, Apple menu, Launcher, Chooser and Control strip to share files, quickly launch applications, identify and toggle between currently running applications, open recent documents and gain fast access to items such as Remote Access, Finder, printer/s, general settings and utilities.	The Dock combines the functions of OS 9's Application menu, Launcher, Chooser and Control strip. It contains a unique strip of icons that can be uniquely controlled, and easy-to-see triangles below or beside the icons (depending on Dock placement) show you what applications are running at a glance.

	OS 9	OS X
Finder 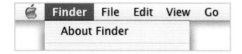	Finder is located in the Applications menu in OS 9. (When toggling between applications it navigates from desktop to other windows.)	In Mac OS X the term Finder refers to quite a variety of different items. • the finder window that appears when you have selected Finder on the Dock; • Mac OS X's new-look windows; and • the all-new Finder menu.

OS 9	OS X

Finder windows

Windows are not known as finder windows in Mac OS 9. Typically, they contain:
- two gray buttons (to the top right) – to adjust the height or width of the window; and
- one gray button (to the left) used for closing the window. Clicking on a window's title bar minimizes it so that only the title bar can be seen.

To see a window in list, icon or view, go to Finder > View menu. OS 9 windows are not equipped with a toolbar.

Finder Windows refer to the new-look windows in OS X. Attractive, customizable and easy-to-use, they consist of:
- Toolbar, with:
- 3 colored buttons to the left of the window. These close (red), minimize, move to dock (yellow) and adjust (green) the window.
- View panel: choose from Icon view, List view, and the all-new Column view, which displays folders in multiple levels, providing thumbnails of icons and photos;

- a Back and Forward button for ease of navigation.
- Show/hide button at the top right to display or hide the toolbar.
- Search facility
- Places sidebar which lets you instantly check and link to available hard drives, media and servers.
- Embossed effect triangle on bottom right of window for resizing.

Folders

To make a new folder, select Command+N or go to File > New. The concept of spring-loaded folders was introduced in OS 9.

Making a new folder still available from the File menu but the shortcut is now Apple+Option+N. Note: spring-loaded folders were re-introduced

in Jaguar, available in Icon, List and Column view. (This feature was omitted in early versions of OS X.)

Fonts

Fonts can be found in the Fonts folder, in the System Folder on your hard disk in OS 9. The Fonts folder consists of individual fonts, stored in folders and font suitcases, which may contain sets of related fonts or font families.

Mac OS X's all-new Font Book lets you enable and disable fonts, individually or in groups. It allows you to shorten the list of fonts to the ones you use regularly. The Font Panel, available in any application that uses fonts, provides

advanced typographic features and a Character Palette for quick and easy character previews. A handy feature is the ability to search for fonts by family and typeface name within Font Book.

29

Finding old favorites

	OS 9	OS X	
Force Quit 	Command+Option+Esc causes you to Force Quit an application when it's giving you trouble. This does not always isolate the problem and often you have to restart your computer anyway.	You can still press Command+Option+Esc to Force Quit an application. However, you can also go to the Apple Menu > Force Quit, or hold down the Option key and press the application icon in the Dock. Force Quit also works differently in Mac OS X. Darwin allocates a unique	memory space for each application. This means that if something goes wrong, your computer won't need to be restarted. When Force Quit is selected, OS X simply shuts down the troublesome application without harming other applications or the system itself.
Getting information 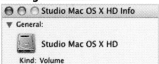	For details on your selected icon, go to File > Get Info (Command+I). An application's memory can be adjusted using Get Info.	Get Info was changed to Show Info in OS X, and reverted to Get Info in OS X 10.2. The File Menu and shortcut key command remain	unchanged, but you can no longer adjust memory in OS X using this option – it is no longer necessary (see also pre-emptive multi-tasking).
Labels 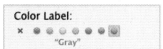	View > Labels is a nifty feature in OS 9 that allows you to assign text labels and colors to files for easy identification.		The Labels feature was omitted in earlier versions of Mac OS X, but reintroduced in Panther.
Networking 	In Mac OS 9, use: • the Internet Control Panel to enter settings such as your email address, preferred email application and Web browser; • the AppleTalk, Modem, Remote Access, and TCP/IP Control Panels to set up network connections;	In Mac OS X use: • the Internet Connect application to connect to the Internet, dial your ISP establish a PPP connection over Ethernet, connect to an Airport network, etc.. • the Network pane in System Preferences for network settings.	(AppleTalk, Modem, Remote Access, and TCP/IP settings have been consolidated here.)

	OS 9		OS X	
Pre-emptive multi-tasking  Image courtesy of **Apple**	In Mac OS 9, it's often necessary for a user to set preferred memory requirements for each application (See also 'Getting information') Because applications are actually sharing the system's processing time,	it's common to have to quit the application and increase the amount of memory assigned to it. Not only this but complex tasks fully consume the processor until complete, forcing other tasks to be put on hold.	In OS X there's no more quitting an application so that others can run. Thanks to Darwin, memory for each application is automatically adjusted and whenever more memory is needed, it allocates exactly the amount required. Darwin also knows	how to give priority to your primary application, but still crunch away at other jobs in the background. With Mac OS X pre-emptive multitasking, the system remains responsive, so you can do a whole bunch of other things while processing the task in the background.
Printing Windows	File > Print Window is a handy feature in OS 9 that lets you print out information on the content of your Finder windows.		File > Print Window is not featured in OS X.	
Recent Applications, Documents and Servers 	In OS 9 you can go to the most recent applications, documents and servers by selecting Apple Menu Items > Recent Applications.	To select recent applications, documents or servers in OS X, go to Recent Items in OS X's Apple menu. Choose	Recent Folders from the available from the Go menu to choose those folders you worked on most recently.	
Sherlock	Sherlock is located in the Applications folder on OS 9. (Command+F) provides a quick alternative to launching it.	This personal search detective had a radical makeover in OS X 10.2. Located in the Applications folder, it can no longer be accessed	by Command+F. (Instead, this shortcut command now launches Mac OS X 10.2's Find command (Finder menu).	
Special menu	This well-used menu carries out regulars tasks such as emptying trash, ejecting and erasing a disk and	burning a CD. The Sleep, Restart and Shut Down commands can also be found in the Special menu .	This is no longer a feature of OS X. Instead, Sleep, Restart and Shut Down are located in the Apple menu. Burn disc	has moved to the File menu, Empty Trash has moved to the Finder menu and Eject has moved to the File menu.

Finding old favorites

	OS 9		OS X	
System Folder		In OS 9, the System Folder is easily located on your hard disk. Many items in the System Folder can be modified to keep the operating system running smoothly.	OS X does not have the kind of System Folder you got used to in its previous systems. The folder named 'System'	has more files than it did in OS 9 and is not accessible unless you are logged on as root user.
Trash		The OS 9 trash can serves many purposes: • trash items in OS 9 by dragging them to the trash can or selecting the Move to Trash or Put Away options. (Found in the File menu or on a contextual menu when Control is pressed); • choose whether or not you would like to be	warned before emptying the trash by clicking on the trash can and selecting the File > Get Info menu option. • The trash can is also used as a medium from which to eject discs, CDs etc. • Empty the trash by going to the Special menu.	In OS X a few things have changed: • the trash can is located in the Dock; • the Put Away command (and its shortcut keyboard combination) no longer exist; • you now empty the trash via the new Finder menu;	• To be warned of the Mac's intentions to empty the trash, go to Finder preferences > Advanced and not Get Info; and • although media can still be dragged to the trash can for ejecting, the trash can icon changes its appearance when this occurs.
Undo		In OS 9, the Undo command (Edit menu) undoes your last occurring editing action.	In OS X, the Undo command's editing action abilities extend to a variety of desktop actions.	These include dragging an icon into a different folder or to the Trash, renaming a folder, etc.
Users		User accounts are optional in OS 9 and the login screen is quite sophisticated – a user name can be selected from an existing list and your voice can be used instead of a password.	Mac OS X makes some aspects of using a Mac a bit more complicated due to improved security measures. Each user has to set up at least one user account. In short, a name and password must be recorded for at least one user of the computer.	

	OS 9		OS X	
Utilities		Utilities for fonts, printers, preparing, fixing and compressing discs are all available in OS 9.	The utilities in OS X have undergone changes: • Drive Setup, Disk First Aid, Disc Burner (Utilities in OS 9) have been merged into Disk Utility;	• The Print Center utility has taken over the Chooser in OS 9. It manages anything and everything to do with printing.
View menu > View Options		OS 9 provides numerous options to view windows and columns, such as date, folder sizes, origins, labels, icon size and arrangement.	All options in OS 9 are available in OS X. It is now easier to manipulate icon size and arrangement, and you have you the	choice to make global view changes to your window and to adjust your window's background color.
Window ... or multi Windows?	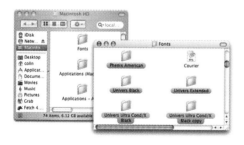	The Mac pioneered a graphic user interface with folders and windows: • double-clicking a folder in OS 9 causes another window to open automatically; • if a file is brought forward in OS 9, any other files relating to the source application follow, hiding all other applications;	Mac OS X extends the usefulness of the graphical environment: • it is not necessary to open another window when you double click on a folder OS X. You can either set a preference to disallow this or work in Column view; and • with new Exposé, you can have immediate	access to any open window with one keystroke. The choices are endless–display your open windows as thumbnails, view only windows of the current application you are working in or hide them all when need to locate a file on your desktop quickly.
Word processing		SimpleText, the free and simple word processing application in Classic, is now called TextEdit in Mac OS X and is very much more sophisticated.	TextEdit creates standard Rich Text Format files which you can open in other programs. It opens text, RTF and documents	created with other applications, find, replaces and formats text, checks spelling and can have pictures added to it.

OSX innovations
Cool new things

About this Mac		To see the amount on your system, as you have always done, select 'About this Mac'. OS X no longer displays the way memory is utilized, but gives information on your processor, system profile, software updates and current version of system software. (Note: if you hold down the Control key and click on the version number, the OS X build number appears.)
AppleScript enhanced		AppleScript in Mac OS X delivers more power, more features and more speed while retaining its ease of use and flexibility.
CD burning		In OS X, everything you need to burn a CD is built-in to the system. You can prepare a disc for burning via Disk Utility and go to the Finder menu to burn it. It's that simple. (Note: you can also use applications such as iPhoto or iTunes to burn your CDs.)
Desktop		The desktop is quite different in OS X. Disk icons may or may not be visible, date and time, monitor and sound settings are located on the top right of the screen. The Finder menu on the left replaces the Special menu and the Apple menu icon is now translucent aqua. The new Dock may or may not be visible, and if so, could be located to the left, bottom or right of the screen – depending on your preferences.
Digital Hub	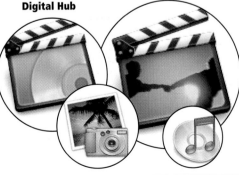	With Mac OS X and applications like iMovie, iDVD, iTunes and iPhoto, Apple has pioneered the 'iLife' concept, making the digital lifestyle possible. In short: • iPhoto helps you save, organize, share and enjoy digital images; • iDVD takes advantage of the power and stability of Mac OS X to make DVD creation faster and easier; • iTunes music software converts music from audio CDs, lets you search and browse your entire music collection, and download songs to MP3 players; • iMovie 2 lets you edit movies, adding professional-quality effects; • GarageBand helps mix your voice or instrument with backing loops, mix, and exporting the result to iMovie, iDVD or iTunes.

Dock

The Dock contains a unique strip of icons of frequently used applications, files, utilities and preferences. You can magnify items on it, add to/remove from it, set preferences, resize it, reposition it, make it disappear and reappear, and immediately notice existing items that are active.

Eject icon

The Trash icon transforms to an Eject icon when File > Eject (Command+E) is selected, or removable media is dragged towards the trash.

Fast user switching

Fast user switching is activated from System Preferences>Accounts. Exclusive to Mac OS X10.3 Panther. It lets you switch between users on a single Mac without quitting applications and logging out. There is no compromise on security either – when a user accesses an account, other accounts remain active in the background. While an account is 'switched out', all data and applications remain absolutely secure.

Finder

In OS X the term Finder refers to a few things: the Desktop; the Finder window that appears when you have selected Finder on the Dock; Mac OS X's new-look windows; and the all new Finder menu, complete with preferences. It has undergone a complete redesign, resulting in a composite of technologies from the original Finder and from the NeXTSTEP file viewer.

Finder menu

This new menu has taken a few items such as 'About the Finder', 'Hide others' and 'Move to Trash' from other menus in OS 9 and tidied them up into the Finder menu. It has a cool option called Services that lets you mix and match spelling checkers, drawing tools and calculation methods between Cocoa applications, as well as the ability to set up your Finder using the Finder preferences menu.

OSX **innovations**
Cool new things

Finder views

Finder view was added to Mac OS X 10.2. The innovative Column view makes file navigation a breeze and previews pictures and movies.

Finder preferences let you view discs, media and servers on your desktop, Home or Computer details and file extensions.

Finder windows

Windows in OS X are dissimilar to anything that have ever been seen before. They:
- don't flicker and flash when dragged/resized;
- have alpha channel support and smooth edges thanks to Quartz;
- have curved interface elements, courtesy of Aqua;

- contain the assembly of 'drawer and parent' which can be added to applications using Cocoa;
- have believable shadows (which individual programs written for OS X now have too);
- feature transparency on windows and pull-down menus;

- can be brought forward without all windows relating to that application following suit;
- contain Sheets;
- have spring-loaded folders in Finder views;
- include customizable tool bars; and
- come equipped with both a back and forward button.

Font Book

Font Book

The Quartz rendering engine in OS X displays and prints beautifully rendered and anti-aliased fonts with auto ligatures and kerning

controls. With FontBook you can:
- preview different typefaces and characters;
- search for fonts by

family, typeface name;
- enable and disable fonts, individually or in groups;
- create and select Collections.

Free Applications

Mac OS X comes with a bunch of free software to use immediately. Some of these include: • the system wide Address Book; • Clock: an alternative to the time display in your menu bar; • Sherlock: locates hard-to-find information, delivers the latest news, up-to-the-minute flight

status details, stock prices, addresses, maps and driving directions; • TextEdit: OS X's word processing application; • iChat: the instant messenger for chatting with your AOL and Mac.com buddies; • Image Capture: transfers images from your digital camera to

your computer; • Internet Explorer (IE): Microsoft's Web browser for the Mac; • Safari: is built for OSX to display webpages quickly and easily; • Internet Connect: dials your ISP or connects to AirPort or Ethernet; • Chess: computerized chess; • Mail: Mac OS X's standards-based e-mail

program; • Inkwell: built on Apple's Recognition Engine, Inkwell's handwriting recognition turns text written on a graphics tablet into typed text; • Preview: for viewing/converting several types of image files (including PDF) and previewing files before printing.

Go menu

Go	Window	Help
Back		
Forward		

It's all systems go, with new Go menu, which:
- provides an alternative to the Window toolbar – go to various locations (such as Home, Favorites, Back, Forward, Enclosing Folder) instead of physically finding the icon in a window, or toggling;
- helps users to the access shared files across the network; and
- provides a list of recently used folders.

Internet

- Mac OS X's BSD (Berkley Standard Distribution) networking stack makes it easier for developers to publish UNIX-style network programs on Macintosh. It provides built-in support for various ways of connecting to the Internet, including dial-up modem (PPP), cable modem, DSL (including PPPoE), built-in Ethernet and AirPort. It allows for the use of standard Internet services as well as Apache, the open source web server technology that runs more than 50 percent of the Web sites on the Internet. BSD also enables the Perl, Telnet and FTP command-line utilities.
- Use the Internet Connect application to connect to the Internet, dial your ISP establish a PPP connection over Ethernet, connect to an Airport network, etc.
- Additional applications in OS X that relate to the internet include: Safari; AirPort Assistant; Mail; Microsoft Internet Explorer for Mac OS X with Java 2; iChat; and Address Book;
- Sherlock can be used in place of a Web browser, providing information such as flight details, access to Web search engines, stock art libraries, and Apple's technical support library.
- Go to System Preferences>Network to change configuration settings.

iTools online collection

This tightly integrated internet service collection is exclusively accessible to .Mac users. It consists of: • iDisk: comprises 20MB of personal storage space on Apple's Internet servers as well as an FTP site for file sharing with other users;
- iCards: electronic postcards that can be customized;
- Email; and
- Homepage: a customizable Web site for Macintosh users only.

Library

Mac OS X Library folders:
- hold information the Mac needs to run each user's environment, fonts and applications;
- contain folders for Favorites, Internet Search Sites, Web browser plug- ins, cached Web pages, keyboard layouts, and sound files etc; and
- are personalized individually. There are three of them on the system and not all can be accessed by everyone.

OSX innovations
Cool new things

Networking & Communications

Mac OS X offers a solid foundation for networking and communications including:

- BSD (Berkeley Standard Distribution) makes it easier for developers to publish UNIX-style network programs on Macintosh. It supports DHCP, BootP and manual network configurations, making it easy for users to integrate Mac OS X computers into existing local area networks;
- consolidation of: AppleTalk, Modem, Remote Access, and TCP/IP settings into the Network pane in System Preferences. It is here that you can connect your Mac to the Internet, your corporate network, or even the old PC Network. (This panel also helps your Mac to automatically use whichever connection methods are available at any time: Ethernet, modem, Airport, or Bluetooth modem.);
- Rendezvous, the networking technology that uses the industry-standard IP networking protocol. It allows for automatic creation of a network of computers, printers and other peripheral devices over Ethernet, AirPort, Bluetooth, USB or FireWire – without manually configuring drivers or settings;
- a number of technologies that make it simple to integrate the Mac into cross-platform networks; and
- automatic switch over to the Ethernet network if you connect to Ethernet using AirPort.

New Applications

Mac OS X has inspired the application developer community to embrace its new graphic interface. technology. Leading developers have demonstrated their support and numerous native products are currently available, or in the process of being made available, to run on Apple's new UNIX-based operating system.

New Folder shortcut		All Mac users take note: making a new folder is slightly different in OS X. The shortcut keyboard command is no longer Command+N.	Instead, it is now Command+Option+N. Although it takes a bit of getting used to at first, users who use the File menu will be relieved to	discover that this remains File > New Folder. (Note: Apple N is now the shortcut for File > New Finder Window.)
Online software updates		Mac OS X has the ability to download software updates automatically, including the latest security updates (automatically installed	through the Software Update mechanism) via System Preferences > Software Update, or via 'About this Mac'.	
PDF: a common file format for Mac OS X		Thanks to Quartz, PDF is a common file format for Mac OS X. Any PDF file saved in Mac OS X can be opened, viewed, and	printed using PDF-compatible tools including Adobe Acrobat Reader 6.5 – on all supported platforms.	Note: Preview is a superb application for viewing and searching PDF files.
Preemptive multi-tasking		Thanks to Darwin, preemptive multitasking: memory for each application is automatically	adjusted and the system remains responsive, so you can turn your attention to other things while processing	the task in the background. (No more quitting an application so that others can run.)
Printing		Printing from Mac OS X is a simple process. Any printer purchased from a major manufacturer will probably have software built into	Mac OS X. This can be turned on in Utilities > Print Center and hey presto! your printer is ready to begin its tasks. To monitor progress,	determine errors etc., go to the Print & Fax System Preference. It will provide you with all the information you need.
Public and Shared Folders		Public Folder: other users can view your files here; Drop Box folder: other users can leave files for you here.	Shared folder: 'free for all'. Other users can copy to it, but only the originator can move, trash or change it.	

OSX **innovations**

Cool new things

Stability (crash-resistant computing)

If an application attempts an illegal operation in OS X (for example, taking up too much memory), the operating system simply shuts it down. This has no affect on the rest of the system.
If the application you are working on in OS X stops responding, you can Force Quit the application without harming other applications, so there is no need to restart your computer.

Symmetric multi-processor support

Image courtesy of **Apple**

Much of Mac OS X is multi-threaded, so applications that use system services such as sound, graphics, and networking accrue the benefits of dual-processors. Symmetric multiprocessing takes advantage of dual-processor systems.

System Preferences

Mac OS X has a whole range of new System Preferences (formerly known as Control Panels, and found in the System Folder in OS 9). These are divided into the following categories for ease of reference:
• Personal: Appearance; Desktop & Screen Saver; Dock; Exposé; International; Security;
Hardware: CDs & DVDs; Displays; Energy Saver; Keyboard & Mouse; Print & Fax; Sound
• Internet & Network: .Mac; Network; QuickTime; Sharing; and
• System: Accounts (with new Fast user switching); Classic; Date & Time; Software Update; Speech; Startup Disk; Universal Access.
Many of these have been greatly improved in the transition from OS 9's Control Panels. These are: International; Displays; Date & Time; Energy Saver; Keyboard & Mouse; Sound; Network and Sharing.
The following preferences are new to OS X:
• Desktop & Screen Saver: to creatively customize your desktop and screen saver
• Dock: to set size, position and visibility of your Dock;
• Classic: helps users run both Mac OS 9 and Mac OS X.
• Exposé: provides immediate access to any open window with one keystroke.
• Universal Access: greatly modified since the first version of OS X. Provides more user friendly speech, sight, hearing, keyboard and mouse facilities.
• Security (incorporating FileVault): this preference gives you the choice of keeping your documents safe with powerful AES-128 encryption.
• .Mac: to gain .Mac membership and subsequent. access to iDisk (up to 1GB of personal storage space on Apple's internet servers.)

Toggling between Classic and OS X

• Choose whether to start up from OS X, Classic or another CD via System Preferences > Startup Disk; • Choose System Preferences > Classic when you need to adjust settings for Classic, such as getting Classic to start automatically when a Classic application is launched.

Undo

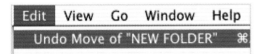

Edit > Undo can undo your last desktop action such as dragging an icon into a different folder or to the Trash, renaming a folder, etc.

UNIX

Mac OS X is made up of a unique combination of technical elements, these include:

• **Aqua:** thanks to Aqua, the Mac user interface has had a facelift. Transparent, shiny and droplet-shaped elements, drop shadows and sheets all contribute towards OS X's new look;

• **Classic:** most Mac OS 9 compatible applications will run side-by-side with Mac OS X applications thanks to Classic;

• **Carbon:** system elements that work in both Classic and OS X;

• **Quartz:** this unique system in Mac OS X uses PDF as the basis of its imaging model. It delivers crisp graphics, anti-aliased fonts, and blends 2D, 3D and QuickTime content with transparency and drop shadows;

• **Darwin:** the industrial-strength, UNIX-based foundation lies beneath Mac OS X's interface. It features a protected memory architecture and gives priority to a primary application, but still lets the user work on other jobs in the background (preemptive multitasking).

• **Open GL:** specifically designed for any application that requires a sturdy framework for visualizing shapes in 2D and 3D;

• **Java:** the Java application environment exists to develop and carry out Java programs on Mac OS X, including Pure Java applications and applets; and

• **Cocoa:** this application, descended from NeXTSTEP, is designed specifically for Mac OS X-only native applications.

Users concept

Mac OS X has secure file access with built-in support for multiple users. Every user on the system has a secure login account and a Home directory for storing personal files, preferences, and system settings. When users log into their personal accounts on a Mac OS X computer, they can access the Macintosh, with their customized desktop, Finder, Dock, and applications, as well as all their personal files.

OSX **innovations**

Cool new things

Utilities

There is an entirely new range of utilities available in OS X. Those most commonly used include:

Disk Utility

Combines the functions of Drive Setup, Disk First Aid, Disc Burner (utilities in OS 9).

Grab

A handy little application for taking screen snapshots that you will use again and again.

Bluetooth: (File Exchange, Serial Utility, Setup Assistant)

All of these help setup and use Bluetooth for file transfer between one or more Bluetooth-enabled devices.

ColorSync Utility:

Works together with ColorSync preferences to specify color profiles for devices.

Print Center:

An alternative to OS 9's Chooser, the Printer Setup Utility manages everything and anything to do with printing.

Windows compatibility and Windows-style filename suffixes

Compatibility:
Point-and-click Windows file sharing simplifies connection to Windows servers and PCs. OS X comes with a PPTP-based virtual private network (VPN) client that allows Mac users to connect remotely to Windows corporate networks.

Filename suffixes:
Mac OS X uses Windows-style (three-letter) filename suffixes to identify the application needed to launch a document. (A preference is available to hide these suffixes if so desired.)

Window control

Exposé provides instant access to any open window with just one keystroke, snapping 'window chaos' into instant order:
• Press F9 and see all open windows in various application. (Clicking on a window makes it become active and places it at the top of the stack.)
• Press F10 and all open windows of your working application will be tiled, while others fade to gray.
• Press F11 and all open windows disappear, giving you access to your desktop in no time at all.

Press F11 and all open windows disappear, giving you access to your desktop in no time at all.

Installing Mac OS X

If you are installing Mac OS X, there are a number of issues you should consider. You may need to update your computer's firmware. The updates may be on the installation CD. Your computer should have at least Mac OS 9.1 and 128Mb of RAM. There should be internal monitor support, or an Apple supplied IXMicro, ATI or nVidia video card installed, as well as at least 2.0 GB of disk space (or 3.5GB if you install Developer Tools).

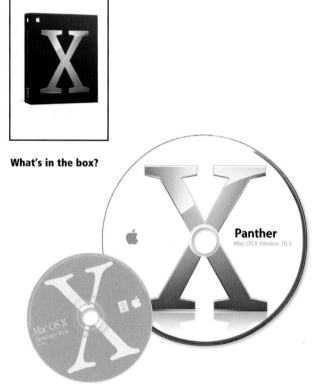

What's in the box?

Panther
Mac OS X Version 10.3

Developer Tools
This CD contains software and documentation for developing applications on Mac OS X. Only install this if you intend to develop applications.

The System
The latest version of the Mac OS X system is delivered on a single disc. Follow the prompts, choose where to install and the system is installed automatically.

Mac OS X 10.2

Mac OS X 10.2.1-
10.2.2

Mac OS X 10.3

Mac OS X 10.3 -
10.3.3

Mac OS X 10.3

Mac OS X 10.3 -
10.3.3

The Mac OS X system can be updated from both software purchases on CD and Software Update online. Any major application updates are available on CD. However, security, networking and other firmware updates can easily be downloaded.

License and destination

You will be prompted to:

(a) Read the License Agreement: This covers the rights and restrictions pertaining to the use of the software.

(b) Select a destination: A destination for the Mac OS X system can be the same place as Mac OS 9 if you choose. Alternatively, you may choose to install Mac OS X on a separate, dedicated partition on your hard drive. Click the 'Install' button and after a short while, your installation will be complete.

Third party hardware software compatibility

Panther includes out-of-the box functionality for many hardware devices. Mac OS X automatically configures itself to support most Canon, HP and Epson USB inkjet printers. Mac OS X ImageCapture will work with USB digital still cameras that support mass storage, PTP and Digital plus a variety of cameras from Canon, Kodak and Nikon. As some devices may need additional driver support, it would be wise to check with the manufacturer of your product to see if Mac OS 10.3-compatible drivers are available.

Authenticate

When you install Mac OS X, you need to create a user account. This must be done by an administrator. As the administrator, user accounts can be added, you can change certain system settings, set up for multiple users and have greater access to the system settings.

Updating Mac OS X

Unless you have the CD updates to hand, the Internet-based Software Update will allow online updating to your system. A new Apple installer, which opens and distributes to the appropriate directories, is neatly settled in the Applications > Utilities folder sporting a '.pkg' extension. This installer assists in the updating of Mac OS X via the Apple menu ('Software Update', 'About this Mac') and settings can be customised in System Preferences.

Software updates
Apple periodically releases free updates to your computer's software. These are listed in Software Update, which can be set to automatically check for updates on a regular basis. Note: Because an internet connection is used to check for updates, you will have to be online at the time.

Customized update
To customize the operation of the Software Update, open the System Preferences panel and find the Software Update icon from the 'System' category (along the bottom of the window). Once launched, Software Update will display options for collecting updates.

Authenticate
To run a Mac OS X update, or most applications for that matter, you need to authenticate with your login and password.

License and destination
You will be prompted to:
(a) Read the License Agreement: This covers the rights and restrictions pertaining to the use of the software.
(b) Select a destination: A destination for the Mac OS X system is limited to locations where you have installed Mac OS X previously. Be aware that some updates will require a recent Mac OS X system such as Mac OS X 10.2.2

Update your software while getting info
Panther lets you update your software while you are checking out the details about your system. The place? 'About this Mac' (found in the Apple menu). As well as discovering information about the amount of memory available on your system, processor information, looking at the system profile, and finding the serial and build numbers, you can select 'Software Update' here too.

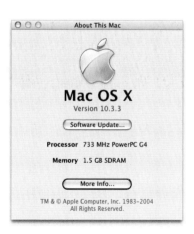

Installing applications

There are two basic strategies by which applications are installed. There is the drag-and-drop method where the disk image is simply dragged to the required location. The second way is using the Apple Installer. You could install it in your Home directory, but no one else can use the application once it is installed there. To allow all users to be able to access and use the application, install it in the Applications directory. To do this, you must be logged in as an Administrator.

Authenticate
Enter your name and password to authenticate your use of the computer. You can do most things as a User, but need to be logged in an as Administrator to install the software. The installation process will begin automatically once your identity has been authenticated.

License and destination
You will be prompted to:
(a) Read the License Agreement: This agreement covers the legal and copyright points pertaining to the application as it arrives on your computer.
(b) Select a destination: Applications can be installed in any location if you are logged in as an administrator. As a user, it is best to install them in the 'Applications' folder, so everyone can see and use them. The Apple Installer will take you through similar panels as the Mac OS X installation and install it painlessly.

Classic applications

When installing applications to be used only under the Classic environment, you may want to install them in the 'Applications (Mac OS 9)' folder. If you find there are problems installing the application to the desired location, log in as Administrator (if possible). This will allow you to install the application anywhere you like. If you find there are other problems installing Classic software while using Mac OS X, boot up your computer using Mac OS 9 (Systems Preferences > Startup Disk) and then install the software.

Alternate installation method

Under the Admin log-in, applications can be installed in one of two ways. You can use the installer application as shown, or you can drag the disk image straight to the Applications folder on the drive.

Root user installation

On rare occasions, some high-end applications may only be installed by going through to the 'root user' level. Administrator level command line moves such as this are best done by an experienced user with a steady hand.

Installation successful

If all goes well, this is the dialog that appears.

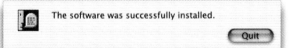

The software was successfully installed.

Quit

SAVING UPDATES TO A NETWORK
You can save updates to install on a network of computers. This way you won't have to access the Internet each time you need an update.

HOT TIP

The keyboard

If you work on one of the latest Mac models, you will find its Apple Pro Keyboard a delight to walk your fingers through. For those of you who need a crash course on what key goes where, this page is for you ...

Keyboard

Fkeys
Function keys are used in a variety of System Preferences, such as Universal Access, Exposé and Displays. They also provide shortcuts for launching applications or scripts in Classic.

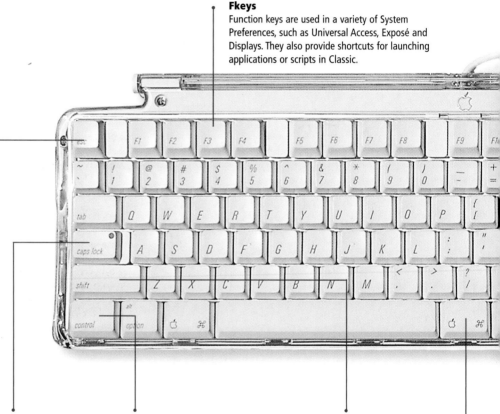

Escape key
This key is used for a quick escape when applications 'misbehave'. It is also used in conjunction with Command and Option to force quit an application without restarting your Macintosh.

Fn key
(Powerbooks only)
Powerbook keyboards contain an 'Fn' key, positioned to the left of the Ctrl key. Pressing this key affects • the function keys F1 - F12; • the embedded numeric keypad; and • certain modifier keys.

Caps Lock
When the Caps Lock key is held down, everything you type is in capital letters. However, note that certain keyboard shortcuts will not work with the Caps Lock key down.

Ctrl key
Holding down the Ctrl key while clicking on an item on the screen will bring up a pop-up (or contextual) menu, showing only those commands that can be performed on the item you clicked on. The Ctrl key is also commonly used for keyboard shortcuts. (Note that it is located on both sides of the keyboard.)

Shift
This key (located on both sides of the keyboard) provides a useful combination with other essential keys for keyboard shortcuts. It also creates capital letters temporarily.

Get connected
USB (Universal Serial Bus) devices can be connected to the slots on the right or left of the keyboard – mice, digital cameras and drawing tablets are a good example of this. What's handy about them is that they can be 'hot plugged' without shutting down the computer.

Volume Control
From left: less volume, more volume and mute buttons.

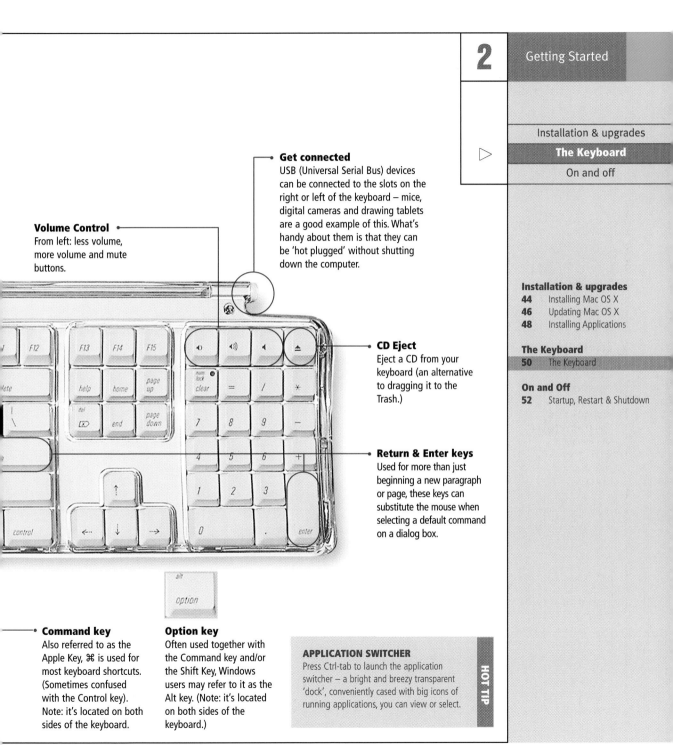

CD Eject
Eject a CD from your keyboard (an alternative to dragging it to the Trash.)

Return & Enter keys
Used for more than just beginning a new paragraph or page, these keys can substitute the mouse when selecting a default command on a dialog box.

Command key
Also referred to as the Apple Key, ⌘ is used for most keyboard shortcuts. (Sometimes confused with the Control key). Note: it's located on both sides of the keyboard.

Option key
Often used together with the Command key and/or the Shift Key, Windows users may refer to it as the Alt key. (Note: it's located on both sides of the keyboard.)

APPLICATION SWITCHER
Press Ctrl-tab to launch the application switcher – a bright and breezy transparent 'dock', conveniently cased with big icons of running applications, you can view or select.

HOT TIP

Start up, restart and shut down

You don't need to be a rocket scientist to learn how to start or restart your Mac. However, there are a few pointers that you just may find handy in Mac OS X such as: a new and easier way to use Force Quit; security and your Mac; keyboard shortcuts when you need to take emergency measures. So, pay attention ... although Mac OS X is very stable, you need to be prepared.

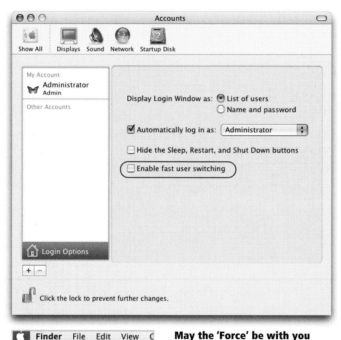

Security and more

The Accounts panel (System Preferences) in Mac OS X 10.3 Panther greatly assists users in managing security levels of multiple accounts. Fast User Switching is one method in particular which is very effective. It allows for switching between users, without having to quit applications or log out, and there is no compromise on security. In addition, users have the choice to hide the Restart and Shut Down buttons ... just one more step to ensure complete peace of mind.

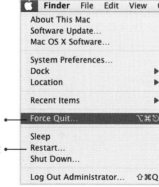

May the 'Force' be with you

If something goes wrong but you can still use the mouse and make the Finder active, choose either:

(1) Force Quit from the Apple Menu. (Mac 'oldies' will recall that this command could previously be accessed only by shortcut key combinations).

(2) Restart to shut down and start up your computer in one quick move.

(3) If you are unable to use your mouse press the Reset button or turn off the power. Note: you can also choose Force Quit from the Dock.

3

Images courtesy of **Apple**

Start all over again
If your Mac won't boot from a hard disk, or you have forgotten a password, you may need to start up the system from a Mac OS X CD-ROM. Here's how it's done:

• Insert CD-ROM;
• Restart, pressing and holding the C key;
• Click the Installer icon;
• Select Reset Password (if you have forgotten your old one) or Disk Utility (to undertake repairs).

KEYBOARD TO THE RESCUE
If your Mac freezes, press Cmd-Ctrl and the Power button (or in some cases, Cmd-Opt-Shift and the Power button) to force a restart. If the Finder freezes in OS X, chances are the underlying OS is still running. Try force quitting the Finder first.

HOT TIP

Administration privileges

When you first used Mac OS X, your Mac created an admin account in your name. This account has administration privileges, which means it can do anything from installing new software, to creating and deleting accounts for non-admin users, to passing oneself off as the all-powerful root user.

Name, rank and serial number
Whenever you attempt to modify you system — by installing software, for example, or creating a new user account — you will be prompted to authenticate (ie, give the username and password of a user account with admin privileges).

Authenticate

Type an administrator's name and password to make changes to Installer.

Name: apple

Password:

Details

Cancel OK

Moving target
Turn admin privileges on or off for each account in the Security panel of the Accounts system preference. (Or in the Users panel before Mac OS X 10.2.)

Who goes there?
Select the account that you want to gain admin privileges by selecting it from this list. Only give admin rights to those who really need them.

Accounts

Show All Displays Sound Network Startup Disk

My Account
apple
Admin

Other Accounts
Ferd Birfle
Admin

Password Picture Security Limitations

FileVault
FileVault secures your entire Home folder by encrypting its contents. It automatically encrypts and decrypts your files on-the-fly, so you won't even know it is happening.

WARNING: Your files will be encrypted using your login password. If you forget your login password and the master password is not available, your data will be lost forever.

A master password is **set** for this computer.

Change...

FileVault protection is **on** for this account.

Turn Off FileVault...

Login Options

+ −

☑ Allow user to administer this computer

Click the lock to prevent further changes.

Unlock the door
If this padlock is closed, you'll need to click on it and authenticate yourself.

The magic box
This is where you add or delete a user account's admin privileges.

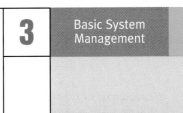
```
000            Terminal — bash — 70x10
Apples-PowerBoook-17:~ apple$ ls /private/var/root
ls: root: Permission denied
Apples-RowerBoook-17:~ apple$ sudo ls /private/var/root
Password:
.CFUserTextEncoding      .nsmbrc
.bash_history            Library
.forward
Apples-PowerBoook-17:~ apple$
```

Skeleton key

The user account 'apple' has admin privileges, so it can use the sudo ('superuser do') command to perform any other action as if it was the root user. Just place 'sudo' before any command that requires root user privileges and provide your admin password

(you don't even need the root user's password) when prompted. In this case, we used sudo to list the contents of /private/var/root. The directory contained five files or subdirectories. sudo remembers your password for a period, so don't walk away without finishing that terminal session.

Access denied

In short, this transcript shows that the /private/var/root directory belongs to the all-powerful root user, and no other user is permitted to view this directory's contents.

Avoiding Problems

To reduce the risk that you'll accidentally damage your system, you should create a non-admin account for your day-to-day work, and only use your admin username and password when necessary.

TECH TIP

System accounts

You might think you own one Mac, but actually you own a thousand. Each of these 'Macs' is actually a different account on your Macintosh, and each of these accounts can have its own secure area to store its owner's documents (the place you go when you click the Home button), its own e-mail address, its own desktop picture — even its own language.

1. Initial account
When you first run Mac OS X, its set-up program will ask you for your name and address, and create a default account to match.

2. What's in a name?
In Mac OS X 10.2 and 10.3, you create, edit and delete accounts in the Accounts panel of System Preferences. Before Mac OS X 10.2, you would do this in the Users panel of Mac OS X's System Preferences. Same concept, different name.

Edit the user
Click this button to change an account's name or password. Note: Mac OS X and earlier only pay attention to the first eight characters of the password. Click 'Security' to grant or revoke an account's Admin privileges (via the 'Allow user to administer this computer' checkbox). Click 'Picture' to change the small picture that represents the account in the login screen.

Out of harm's way
Notice that the user account called 'The Kids' does not have admin privileges. If this is the only account that your children can access, they will not be able to install software, delete your Internet password or make other potentially catastrophic changes.

Accounts aren't just for people
If you do serious web development, you might want to create a secure account for that program alone. That way, if a hacker seizes control of the account that drives your Internet database, they don't have automatic access to the rest of your Mac. Apache, the program behind Personal Web Sharing

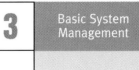

Set the rules

You, as an admin user, can control how a non-admin account's ability can and cannot use your Mac. Just select the account in the Account system preference and then Limitations to come to this window. If you click on Simple Finder, the non-admin account will employ a child-like version of the Mac OS X interface. To create a My Applications folder for this user that only contains the applications you want this account to use, check the box next to the permitted applications in this list.

Avoid the hassle

Click Login Options and put a tick in this checkbox if you don't want to have to select your default account and enter your password every time you fire up your Mac. You can still make your way to the login screen by choosing Log Out from the Finder's Apple menu. To change the user account that automatically opens when you start-up your Mac, select a new account from the popup menu and then give the new account's password when prompted.

Bluetooth

Sometimes we don't need fast networks and fancy features. Sometimes we just want to connect two nearby devices so they can exchange small quantities of data. Bluetooth is the answer, especially if you have a Bluetooth-enabled mobile phone or handheld computer that you can connect to your Mac. Here, we show how to beam a file from one Bluetooth-enabled Mac to another.

Bluetooth

Arrivals desk
Tell the Bluetooth software where it should save incoming files, whether it should ask you before receiving them, and whether it should open the files when they hit your hard disk.

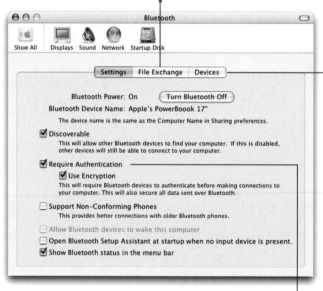

Instant Bluetooth
With Mac OS X 10.2 and 10.3, you need only plug the D-Link DWB-120M USB Bluetooth Adapter into a spare USB port on your Mac and this Bluetooth panel will appear in System Preferences.
(Quit and relaunch System Preferences if necessary.)
To access this panel with earlier versions of Mac OS X, you should upgrade to Mac OS X 10.1.5 via Software Update and then download Apple's Bluetooth software from Apple support (www.apple.com/support).

BSD subsystem install
Note: If you did not install the BSD subsystem (it's installed by default when you install Mac OS X), you will have to install it before you can use Apple's Bluetooth software.

Joined at the hip
If you select this option, the two devices will be 'paired' before the first transfer, and each will store the chosen 'passkey' for future sessions. (Very early versions of the Mac OS X Bluetooth software required manual pairing prior to an attempt to transfer data. Bluetooth is a radio-based technology, so encryption reduces the risk of eavesdropping.

Bonus software
This tab is designed to help you synchronize your Mac with a handheld computer. You don't need to use it to send a file to another Mac via Bluetooth.

Bluetooth Serial Utility
Apple's Bluetooth software directly supports connections to other Macs, phones, Palms, mice and keyboards. Some devices, eg GPS receivers, may require you to set up additional ports using the Bluetooth Serial Utility. Follow the vendor's instructions carefully.

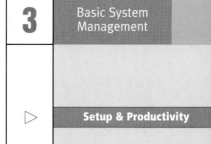

Departure lounge
Drag any file onto the
Bluetooth File Exchange
icon (Applications >
Utilities) to open this
window, which allows
you to send the file to
another Bluetooth-
enabled Macintosh.

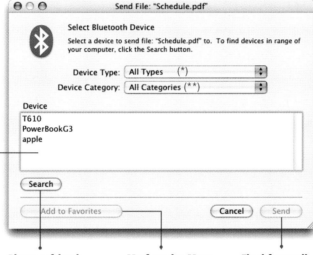

Destination
Macintosh
This window will show
every discoverable
Bluetooth device within
range, and every device
in your Bluetooth
Favorites list. Restrict
the scope by changing
the Device Type (*) or
Device Category (**)
selections.

Phone a friend
Click Search to find all
discoverable Bluetooth
devices within range.

My favorite Macs
When you find a
Bluetooth device that
you want to connect to
regularly, click it once
and then click Add to
Favorites to have it
automatically appear
in this window without
searching.

Final farewell
Choose a device
and then click Send
to send it the file.

HOT TIP

If you want to print a item from
your phone or Palm but you don't
have a Bluetooth printer, try Bluetooth
Print Bridge, a shareware program
from www.scriptsoftware.com. It
sends photos, notes and other items
received via Bluetooth to a regular
Mac printer.

Bluetooth

With the Bluetooth feature turned on, your Mac and a Bluetooth-enabled mobile phone can make 'sweet music' together. Setting up a link between them is simple and only a few moments work –thanks to the Bluetooth Setup Assistant.

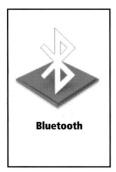

Bluetooth

Bluetooth link setup
We really do want to set up a Bluetooth link, so click Continue and we're on our way.

Mobile phone setup
Any phones in range will show up in this list. It's a good idea to give your phone a distinctive Bluetooth name before you begin.

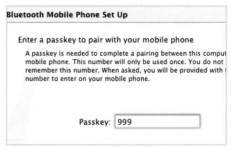

Mobile phone link
Let's link to a phone. (Choose 'Other Device' to connect to another Mac or a PDA.)

Passkey for pairing
Normally, you'll pick a passkey at random and enter the same number on the Mac and the phone. Some devices have a preset passkey, so read the manufacturer's instructions.

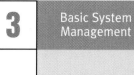

Bluetooth FIle Exchange

Bluetooth File Exchange makes it a snap to transfer a document from a Mac to another Bluetooth-enabled device. Here, we show a transfer between two Macs.

1. Select the destination device.

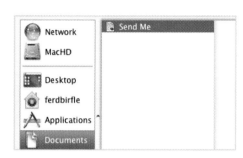

2. Select the file to transfer.

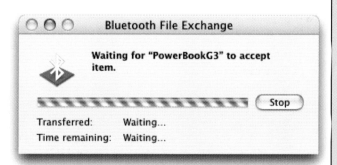

We have lift off

The link is now established, and all that remains is to tell the Mac what you will be doing with it. If you'll be using the phone for dial-up Internet access, you'll need your account name, password and the phone number, just as if you were setting up a regular modem.

3. Wait for the other device to accept the file.

iSync

iSync is a powerful tool that lets you synchronise the information stored on your Macintosh and various other devices such as mobile phones, keeping your office and home computers aligned. Not only this, it's also there for you to use with .Mac services available if you have a .Mac account.

iSync

iSync syncronization
iSync synchronizes your contacts and calendars with your phone or PDA. (.Mac subscribers can perform more extensive synchronisation between two Macs.) Click on the device icon, choose what types of data should be synchronised, and Sync Now.

Bluetooth makes magic
There's more to Bluetooth than file transfer and data synchronisation.
Sailing Clicker is a shareware application that turns a supported Sony Ericsson mobile phone or Palm device into a remote control for a Mac. In addition to out-of-the-box control of applications including DVD Player, iTunes, Keynote and PowerPoint, it can be customised to drive practically any AppleScriptable program. If that's not enough, it's even able to pause and resume your music or video while you make a phone call, display speaker notes on your phone or Palm as you roam the stage, or simply lock your Mac when you walk away.
Apple's not standing still, either. The very day this section was written, Bluetooth Software 1.5 was released, featuring support for Bluetooth headsets and Bluetooth printing.

Palm OS devices

Before you can use iSync
with a Palm OS device,
you'll need to download
and install the Palm
Desktop software and
iSync Palm Conduit from
www.palmone.com. If
you're already using
Palm Desktop, note that
complete synchronisation
between that software
and the Palm device will
not be possible after
installing iSync Palm
Conduit, as iSync
assumes you are using
Address Book and iCal.
You'll need to run
HotSync Manager,
choose Conduit Settings
from the HotSync menu,
select iSync Conduit,
click Conduit Settings
and check Enable iSync
for this Palm device.
Search the Support
Knowledge Library at
www.palmone.com for
solution ID 2132. This
document contains step-
by-step instructions for
setting up Bluetooth
HotSync.

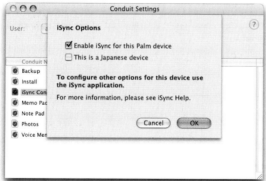

With the software available at the time
of writing, synchronisation between a
Palm device and a Mac had to be
initiated from the Palm's HotSync
feature, not from iSync.

HOT TIP

Getting help

Whenever you need assistance with your system or applications, the Help menu will come to your rescue. Quick to locate (it's one of the Finder menus) and simple to use, this service is also extended to other applications, theoretically giving you help from just about anywhere you will be working on your Macintosh. Apple has done it again!

Help Viewer

Support and more
A selection from the Help menu will launch the Help Viewer, an application used to display information from various Help files on your hard drive.

Back to basics
Lost your way and want to return to a screen you wanted at least three screens before? Simply select the back button until you find what you are looking for. The forward button takes you in the opposite direction. The Home button takes you to the Mac Help window (see below). Additional buttons are available: select 'Customize Toolbar' in the Help Viewer's View menu and make your changes from the drop-down sheet.

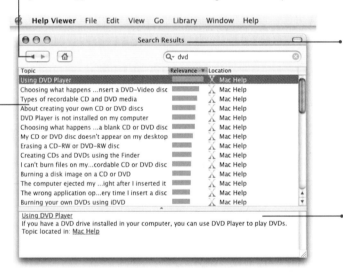

Information nucleus
You can access help for applications other than the one you are currently using — just use the Library menu to select whichever program you need help with.

Life saver
Once you have posed your question or made an enquiry, a list of relevant topics will appear for quick and easy selection.
The degree of relevance and source of help is documented alongside the topic and the lower panel of the Help Viewer window will display a summary and link of selected topic.

How do you do?
By default, the MacHelp window will appear, providing information to new users, featuring OS X improvements, news and support details.

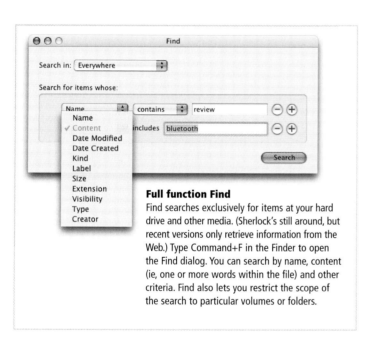

Full function Find

Find searches exclusively for items at your hard
drive and other media. (Sherlock's still around, but
recent versions only retrieve information from the
Web.) Type Command+F in the Finder to open
the Find dialog. You can search by name, content
(ie, one or more words within the file) and other
criteria. Find also lets you restrict the scope of
the search to particular volumes or folders.

Fast Find

Type part of a file name into this box, and
the Finder will immediately locate matching
files. Click on the magnifying glass icon to
control the scope of the search.

About This Mac

Lost? Need to know what the computer you are working on is all about? Go to the Apple Menu and choose 'About This Mac'. It will help you: • to check which version of the operating system you are using; • see how much RAM (random access memory) you have available; and • see the kind of processor you are running.

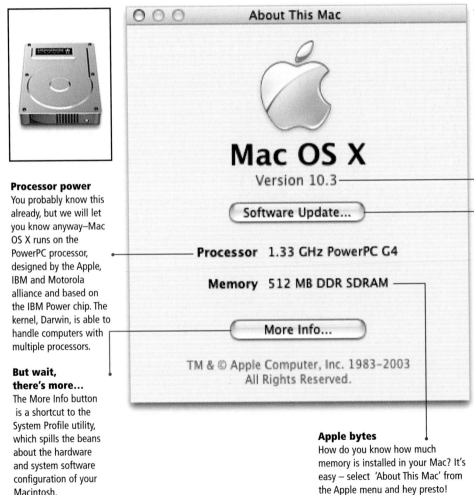

Version in view
All applications these days have a version number which coincides with the date of its release—Mac OS X is no exception. But what does it all mean, and how does the sequence of numbers affect us? The formula is something like this:
• the leap to an entirely new number often means a complete program revision;
• a one decimal modification (for example 10.3 means improved functionality and new features); and
• a two decimal modification, such as 10.3.2 indicates very minor fixes which usually do not require interface changes.

This button takes you to the Software Update system preference where you can check for the latest updates.

Processor power
You probably know this already, but we will let you know anyway—Mac OS X runs on the PowerPC processor, designed by the Apple, IBM and Motorola alliance and based on the IBM Power chip. The kernel, Darwin, is able to handle computers with multiple processors.

But wait, there's more...
The More Info button is a shortcut to the System Profile utility, which spills the beans about the hardware and system software configuration of your Macintosh.

Apple bytes
How do you know how much memory is installed in your Mac? It's easy – select 'About This Mac' from the Apple menu and hey presto! your answer magically appears!

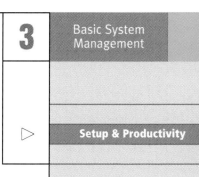

Apple menu
Of all the menus on the menu bar, this is the only one which remains constant regardless of the application you are using or where you are on your computer – meaning that you can depend on everything in this menu to be exactly as you left it. It also means you can use it any time. The only thing that changes is the name of the current user.

EMBEDDED INFORMATION...
Click on 'About this Mac's version number and the OS X build number appears.

TECH TIP

Mac OS X – a new filing concept

Filing systems have always been part of our daily working life and not surprisingly, are a part of our digital world too. The quick and clever filing concept of folders and icons that the Macintosh operating system is famous for, has been redeveloped in OS X and has advanced to an improved, streamlined and very clever system indeed.

iMac   Network

Cyber storage
Everything on your Mac is represented by an icon – whether it's a document, program, folder and disk. These colorful images can be moved, copied or double-clicked to open. Folders, too, are easily identifiable. Some have special icons to match their special functions., others belong to an actual application and have designs with visual clues of what they do. But they all have one thing in common – they're there to make your entire Macintosh experience easier.

Connection Barometer
The Computer window (Go > Computer) has also changed in a big way. It houses the icons for all the disks connected to your machine, as well as the Network icon, which shows up even if you aren't actually on a network. It can also be accessed by clicking the Computer icon on the Finder toolbar.

Why bother?
Opening your hard drive icon (upper right of the screen) reveals a few folders that you can't do anything with. So, why are they there? Mac OS X 10.3 Panther has more security than ever before and many folders that are out of bounds to regular users, are the ones that keep the system running properly. They should not be fiddled with unless you know what you are doing, and have risen to the ranks of root user or administrator.

Mac manoeuvres

- Dragging a file or folder from one folder to another on the same disk, moves it.
- Dragging a file or folder to another drive (or other media) automatically copies it.
- Holding down the Option key while dragging a file anywhere on the same disk copies it.

OS X organizer

Mac OS X makes it easy to find your way around its main folder. In short: • the Library folder contains fonts, Internet plug-ins and other items available to all users of your computer; • the Applications folder contains applications (of course you knew that!); • the System folder contains the Mac OS X system and cannot be changed; and • the Users folder contains the names of all the people using your computer.

Alias Antics

An alias is a 'signpost' to a document or application. And, because it's really only a ghost image, it occupies very little space on your hard drive. Of course, if you are a Mac patriarch, you know this already. If you're not, notice how easy it is to create an alias. Go to File > Make Alias, or press Command+Option and drag the original icon to the spot you'd like the alias to lay claim.
Note: Notice new OS X 10.3 Panther technology at work: selected icons now have a blue background and gray square area.

Finding your way around Mac OSX

Icons, windows, menus, folders and sub-folders are all part
of the extraordinary Macintosh environment that is so simple
to familiarize yourself with. On this page we introduce you to
the items that you are likely to bump into first ...

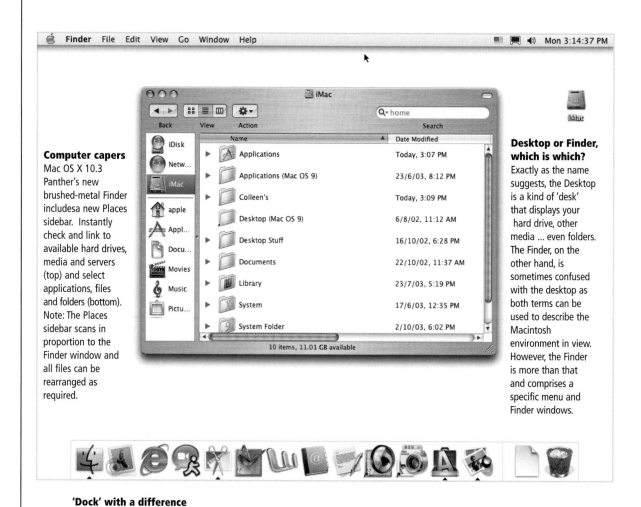

Computer capers
Mac OS X 10.3
Panther's new
brushed-metal Finder
includesa new Places
sidebar. Instantly
check and link to
available hard drives,
media and servers
(top) and select
applications, files
and folders (bottom).
Note: The Places
sidebar scans in
proportion to the
Finder window and
all files can be
rearranged as
required.

**Desktop or Finder,
which is which?**
Exactly as the name
suggests, the Desktop
is a kind of 'desk'
that displays your
hard drive, other
media ... even folders.
The Finder, on the
other hand, is
sometimes confused
with the desktop as
both terms can be
used to describe the
Macintosh
environment in view.
However, the Finder
is more than that
and comprises a
specific menu and
Finder windows.

'Dock' with a difference
A wonderful navigation shortcut tool, the Dock is
explained in full detail later in this chapter. Frequently
used icons are immediately available – a much
needed asset to Mac OS X.

No place like Home

The button with the house icon will take you to your very own Home folder (in this case 'apple'), complete with features vital to your creative wellbeing. It's appropriately iconed too, as it is the place to go back to if you're lost. Another cool feature is that every user who shares a Macintosh will own a tailor-made Home folder – for their own viewing purposes only. (No-one can change your Home unless they login with your user name and password or are granted access privileges to folders in your Home.) Your Home also contains a Public folder, which other users can access if you turn on File Sharing.

Easy Applications

Mac OSX provides you with applications for learning and enjoyment – specially stored in this Applications folder, and more information on these can be found on the pages to follow.

YUP, THE FINDER HAS CHANGED!

It's cool — you can use a single window in the Finder instead of multiple windows. (If you really miss those precious multiple windows, hold down the Command key when you double-click a folder and *voilá*, a separate window appears.)

HOT TIP

Anatomy of the window

Windows opened in Mac OS X 10.3 Panther provide a pleasing brushed metallic view with Aqua enhanced graphics and subtle aids to make navigation, choice of presentation and file finding as quick as a blink. On your OS X journey you will come across Finder windows (via folders or disks), Document windows (via applications) and even a 'Customize Toolbar' window to personalize functionality.

3 colored buttons
Red closes the window; yellow minimizes the window and moves it to the Dock (with the assistance of the Shift key you can slow it down) and green zooms in and out to the last manually-dragged size.

Panther goes metal
See the difference in Mac OSX 10.3 Panther's Finder interface? From its metallic look and feel to the all new Places sidebar - display case for media, servers, hard drives, files, folders and applications - it's all sooo smooth.

Past and future
These handy little transparent buttons bear the symbol of both a back arrow and front arrow to help you toggle back and forward via your current window.

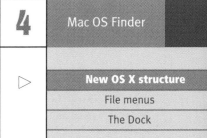
Three different views
Take your pick: (from left) Icon view, List view, and the 'all new' Column view, which displays folders in multiple levels.

Title bar
This handy bar provides the name of the item you are currently viewing and also allows you to move the window around when it's dragged.

Hide and seek
This attractive and transparent window accessory is also known as the Show /Hide button. It does exactly what its name suggests – shows or hides the Places sidebar or toolbar, depending on what's visible at the time.

Finding files easily
Search is built directly into the Finder window toolbar making locating files as easy as pie – simply type in what you're looking for and press Return. The results are directly placed into the Finder window. (Note: you can make your search as narrow or as broad as required.)

Different ways of viewing

Mac OS X developers have thought of everything – not only does the system still cater for those that prefer viewing their files in List or Icon mode, but Column mode too. It is neat, handy and very efficiently set out. Finding, managing and moving files has never been this easy!

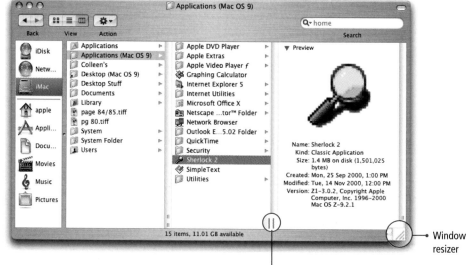

One thing leads to another
Selecting one column in Column view will display its contents. That in turn, will allow you to view its particular offerings and so on and so on ...
Eventually you will know that you have reached the 'end of the road' when the last column displays an icon of its contents. And you can trace it all back by way of the highlighted trail. Drag the scroll bars to navigate easily through each column.

Columns galore
To display a window in Column view, click this button (the Column view) or go to the 'View' menu bar in the Finder and select 'as Columns'.

Just one click
You can have as many columns in your screen as your heart desires. The sizer in the bottom right corner extends your window horizontally, while this will resize the columns proportionally. (Note: holding down Option and dragging the column resizer will rescale the respective column.)

Window resizer

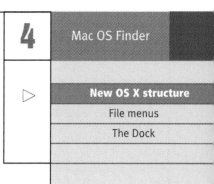

Lists and more
The popular List view can be accessed here, or from the Finder's menu bar (choose View > as List).

Disclosure triangles
These nifty little objects allow you to view the contents of a folder without opening any other windows. Copying, deleting and moving files is much easier here too, as it eliminates the need for window-opening actions. (No more wear and tear on the wrists!)

Expanding triangles
View contents in List view from top to bottom or bottom to top, depending which way the expanding triangle points.

Icon view
All Mac users love the icons view, although its not exactly practical. Fortunately Mac OS X caters for everyone, so icon evangelists can choose and change their preferred viewing options to suit. (Binoculars were never like this!) Access Icon view as illustrated above, or go to the Finder Menu > View > as Icon.

Significant folders

Your Mac OS X disk is cleverly and comprehensively organized. Certain folders are there for entertainment value and ease of use, while others must be fully understood to be properly utilized. On these pages we introduce you to the Users folder (it contains the home folders of all the people using your computer) and the Library folder, responsible for storing folders that hold information the Mac needs to run your 'Home'.

Users

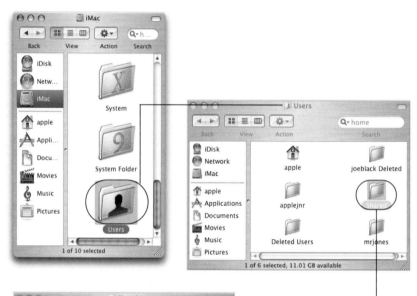

Mac of many faces

It's important to understand the convenience of the User concept. If you are the only person who ever uses the computer you are still considered one of the 'users' and you have a password (it's the one you choose when you excitedly turned on your Mac for the first time). If you are in a position where you share your computer – regardless of the frequency, you will note that each person who logs in to the system has a Home folder individually named inside the Users folder. In this case it's a good idea to familiarize yourself with as much of this multi-user environment as possible.

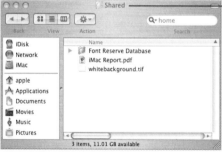

Discover how you can have unique access to certain folders, files and documents and customize your computer without anyone else being able to change your individual settings. The more you experiment, the more streamlined your system

Information overload

There are three Library folders that form part of the Mac OS X system. These include:
(1) The main Library folder (Hard Drive > Library) contains folders that hold information the Mac needs to run your Home, such as fonts and applications. (Note: anything you add to this folder can be manipulated at anytime.)
(2) Of all the items in the System folder, the second Library folder (Hard Drive > System Folder > Library) is the only one

that can be manipulated by the administrator alone. Although it contains folders for Favorites, Internet Search Sites, Web browser plug-ins, cached Web pages,

keyboard layouts, and sound files etc, what you see is not strictly what you will get as the administrator has entirely different view to that of a normal account holder.

(3) The third Library folder (Hard Drive > Users > [Log-in name] > Library) is personalized individually and no-one can open what's inside anyone else's User folder.

77

System Utilities

The Utilities folder is easy to find – it's one of the folders that live in your Applications folder (located on your main hard drive window). Each utility that lives there performs a specific (and vital) function. And because there are so many of these friendly little beasts, here's a synopsis of each.

Activity Monitor
Access system information in graphical representation of items such as CPU, memory, disk activity, disk usage and network usage.

Airport
Use these utilities to set up your computer to join an Airport Base Station

Audio MIDI Setup
Controls audio input and output devices used with your Mac.

Bluetooth
All these utilities help setup and use Bluetooth for file transfer between one or more Bluetooth-enabled devices.

ColorSync Utility
Works together with ColorSync preferences to specify color profiles for devices.

Utilities

Action

- Activity Monitor
- AirPort Admin Utility
- AirPort Setup Assistant
- Asia Text Extras
- Audio MIDI Setup
- Bluetooth File Exchange
- Bluetooth Serial Utility
- Bluetooth Setup Assistant
- ColorSync Utility
- Console
- DigitalColor Meter
- Directory Access
- Disk Utility
- Grab
- Installer
- Java
- Keychain Access
- NetInfo Manager

25 items, 10.93 GB available

- Chinese Text Converter
- IM Plugin Converter
- ▶ Plugin Text Sample

Asia Text Extras
OS X comes with a range of high quality Asian fonts thanks to Unicode support.

Console
A Unix tool, the Console application displays technical messages from system software.

DigitalColor Meter
Provides and translates the percentage values of red, green and blue.

Directory Access
Used to select NetInfo domains or other directories.

Disk Utility
(Administrators only). Tests and repairs the CPU.

Grab
Taking screengrabs has never been easier with with this useful utility.

Installer
Queues multiple installation, completing them in succession.

Keychain Access
Helps keep track of passwords. Also used for secure storage of PINs, etc.

Netinfo Manager
Database to manage Everything that goes on behind the scenes.

OBDC Administrator
Works hand in hand with ColorSync preferences to specify color profiles for devices.

Ports Manager
Allows for installation and management of 3rd party Unix software. (Based on Darwin preferences.)

Printer Setup Utility
Look what's taken over OS 9's Chooser! The Printer Setup Utility manages everything and anything to do with printing.

Network Utility
This is a combination of several network information and troubleshooting tools.

Stuffit Expander
Now this was around before – a quick, easy and very useful expanding application for compressed file formats.

System Profiler
Much more than just an information 'kiosk' for the name, rank and serial number of your Mac, this utility answers just about everything!

Terminal
For more advanced users – the Terminal utility can access the UNIX Command Lines.

Java
1. Applet Launcher allows you to run Java applets without opening a Web browser.
2. Java Plugin Settings application lets you select options for using the Java applet viewer in Internet Explorer.
3. Java Web Start: launches Java applications platform independently via a browser anywhere on the Web.

File access and security

By now you will have realized that Mac OS X is a true multi-user operating system with an exceptionally advanced security system. Although certain folders (such as the System folder) are out of bounds, there are others which can be accessed by the privileged few and others that can be accessed by anyone (such as the Public folder). The trick is to be aware of which folders you are using when filing various items. So pay attention!

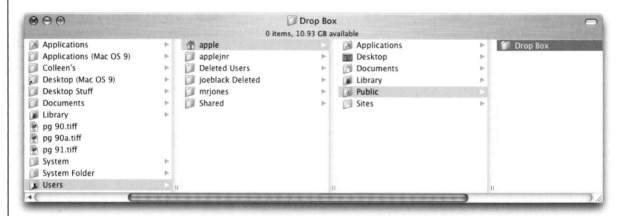

Dirty laundry
Whatever you drop into your Public folder will be accessible to anyone using your computer, unlike many other folders which are out of bounds to those that don't have the privileges to view them. The Public folder can be opened on your computer (Users folder — open folder named for the person) as well as on someone else's computer. It's easy: connect to their computer as a guest (Go Menu > Connect To Server) and mount the appropriate user's hard drive. (Have no fear, nothing can actually be removed from the Public folder – data will only be automatically copied to another user when in transit.)

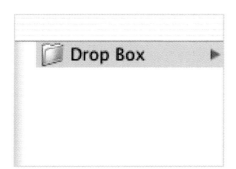

Give and take

Each user's Public folder has a Drop Box, a folder similar to the mail box outside your place of residence. Although anyone can drop anything into anyone's Drop Box, the user can only open his or her own Drop Box to view or copy the contents. Note: if you have something that you need all other users to access, or there is no problem if others see what you are sending to a particular user, utilize the Shared or Public folder.

Which System folder?

Mac OS X does not have the kind of System Folder you were accustomed to in previous systems. Instead, it has a folder named 'System' which is out of of bounds and has a larger number of files than before, all arranged very differently.
(You will also notice that the new operating system no longer contains the System file and Finder file, previously found in Mac OS 9.)
Note: If you are looking for Control Panels to change settings, go to System Preferences in the Apple menu.

The 'Get Info' command

Macintosh 'oldies' are quite familiar with the 'Get Info' command in previous versions of Mac OS. In Mac OS X it changed to Show Info for a brief spell and then reverted back to Get Info in OS X 10.2. Still located in the File menu with the same shortcut keys, it offers impressive new features and greater variety. No doubt it will prove to be a very handy and well-used feature for Mac users – whether they are new to the system or not.

What's this?
The information that you glean from Mac OS X's 'Get Info' command really depends on the item you've selected. In this example, the user has the ability to get information in six different ways.

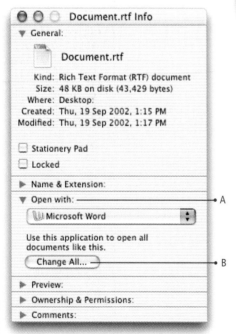

Easy open
It's often infuriating to receive files that have been created in an application that you may not have heard of or don't use enough to actually purchase.

Assigning such a file to an application that you do have is therefore quite a bonus. It's easy – simply click on the file you can't access, select File > Get Info, then choose

'Open with' (A) from the pop-up menu. Assign one application to open all files with the particular file format you have selected and confirm with 'Change All' (B).

Be warned
Once you have done this you will get a warning message ensuring that you are aware of the consequences of these changes.

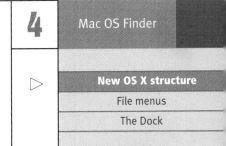
Classic memory

Most Mac 'oldies' love the ease of which you can allocate more memory to applications in Classic. (Provided of course that you have enough RAM to spare.) Mac OS X still allows you to do this in the Classic environment (see (C)), but manages memory very well on its own so there's no need for users to make any memory changes to applications.

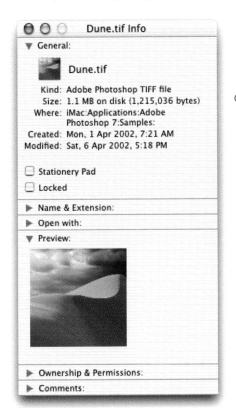

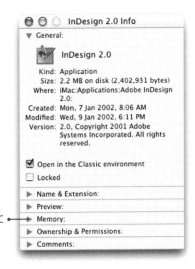

Quick look

Text documents, PDFs, images and movies can be previewed in the Get Info window, and individually depicted.

The 'Get Info' command

Mac OS X will show you the information you need to see depending on: what kind of file format you are looking at; its origins; the kind of file extension it has; and the status of the user's role in viewing and changing files. To find out exactly what we mean, select a variety of different files and go to File > Get Info (Command+I). You're bound to have an array of different dialog boxes at your disposal. This is what some of them are for.

Plain 'n simple
General information is available for any item you choose. This includes details such as the kind of item you are enquiring about, the size of the item, where it can be found as well as when it was created and modified. Additional details which may pop up (depending on what items you have selected), include: • Select New Original (when opening an Alias); • Name & Extension; • Preview; • Ownership & Permissions; and • Comment. (These are all discussed in further detail within this chapter.)

Hide or show?
Would you like to see the filename extension or not? This little box has a big part to play in your viewing abilities. Note: it works in conjunction with the 'Always Show File Extensions' checkbox in Finder preferences.

TECH TIP

QUICK FIND - FILES AND FOLDERS.
To see the hierarchy of your folders while in window view, hold down the Command key and click on the window title.

Classic opening

Carbon applications (those that are able to work in both Mac OS 9 and OS X), can be opened in the Classic environment with a simple click of this button (A).

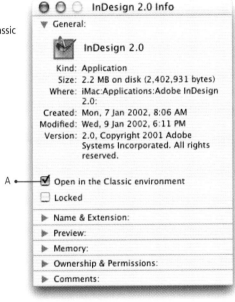

Privileged few

If you would like to find out individual privileges for an item, you can do so with the 'Get Info' command (Command+I). It will tell you who can do what with the item, and if you have the privileges to change the sharing privileges, this can be done here too.

The filename extension

In a bid to encourage Mac and Windows file compatibility, Mac OS X has changed the way it handles filenames. It has embraced an option which has been available to PC Files since DOS first said hello to the world. What is it? The filename extension, of course.

icon.pdf

Filename extensions made simple

'What exactly is a filename extension?', you may ask. In short, it consists of a period (.) followed by three letters which identify the file. What can be particularly confusing to a user is Mac OS X's ability to add its own extension to a file. For example; if you have already saved a document complete with filename extension, Mac OS X will automatically add a filename extension to it resulting in a double extension!

Fortunately, Mac OS X lets you choose whether or not you want to see filename extensions – both globally or individually. You can also preset an extension to a particular application, so OS X knows what to do with it as soon as it sights the extension.

Show and tell

The ' Show all file extensions' option is found in Apple > Finder preferences. If you choose not to select it, file extensions won't appear at all. (Note: this is a global setting and will affect ALL your file names!)

Sense of belonging

With Mac OS X you have the freedom to assign an application to open certain file formats. For example, whenever you receive a file with the .doc extension, you can assign it to a document such as Microsoft Word. This means that whenever a .doc file is visible, it will immediately be transformed into a Microsoft Word document, complete with matching icon. Pressing the 'Change All' button will ensure that every file with that extension will be opened by the application you choose. (Note: the 'Change All' button will only be visible when you have designated a particular application to an extension.)

Now you see it, now you don't

Should you wish to choose different extension options for individual files, select the files one at a time and choose File > Get Info > Name & Extension from the File menu. Then decide whether you want the particular extension to be hidden or not.

Things you get for free

Mac OS X comes with a lot of 'freebies', including a range of software that can be immediately accessed. Stored in the Applications folder, these programs can be reached in a variety of ways, such as by: pressing Command+Option+A; choosing Go from the Finder menu and then selecting Applications; or by clicking the Applications button (on the toolbar in any Finder window). On these pages we whet your appetite.

Address Book
The Address Book works with your Mail application, managing and recording your contact information.

DVD Player
Use to play DVD-Video disks on your Apple supplied DVD-ROM drive.

iChat
Instant messaging application with Rendezvous networking technology. Has built-in compatibility to AOL Instant Messenger.

Internet Connect
Helps you connect to a private network when you're away from the office.

Preview
This option views, open and prints most graphics files, including PDFs.

Sherlock
This nifty search tool is covered further on in the book. Note: it is completely different to what it was before and can no longer be accessed with Command+F.

TextEdit
Apple's rewritten SimpleText, its previous word processing application, and renamed it TextEdit. It's now a native OS X text and RTF (rich text format) editor.

AppleScript
A great invention, use Apple Script third-party scripts or Mac OS X to automate repetitive tasks.

Font Book
Panther's new font management application, complete with a few font collections already set up.

Image Capture
Transfer images from your USB digital camera with Image Capture.

Internet Explorer
Microsoft's Web browser for the Mac, it ships free with Mac OSX. It can also be accessed from the Dock.

iTunes
With this great little digital music player you can encode music CDs into MP3 files, create playlists and burn music CDs.

QuickTime Player
Experience over 200 kinds of digital media with QuickTime.

Utilities
All utilities that live in this folder work with other applications to perform specific functions.

Stickies
Aha, one of Apple's best kept secrets. Or is it? If you aren't using these, you should be. These electronic post-it notes are perfect reminders for almost anything.

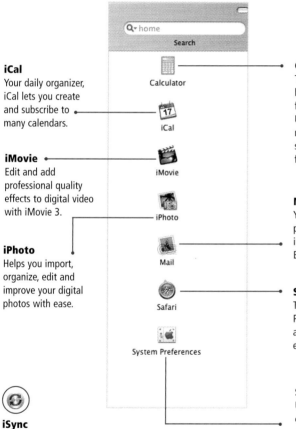

iCal
Your daily organizer, iCal lets you create and subscribe to many calendars.

iMovie
Edit and add professional quality effects to digital video with iMovie 3.

iPhoto
Helps you import, organize, edit and improve your digital photos with ease.

iSync
An addition to Apple's digital hub, iSync allows you to connect and synchronize contact between your Mac and other mobile gizmos.

Calculator
This little desk accessory has been around since Mac first said hello to the world. Use it with the mouse or numeric keypad keys, it's simple to use and handy for almost anything!

Mail
You will get this email program free of charge, in addition to Internet Explorer. Great bargain!

Safari
This Mac OS X 10.3 Panther browser launches and loads pages and briskly executes JavaScript.

System Preferences
Use System Preferences to change the settings of your computer.

Apple menu

The new Apple menu is very different to those included in previous versions of Mac OS. For one, the Apple icon is blue instead of rainbow colored and for another, it's no longer customizable, so what you see is pretty much it. Don't worry, though, the good ol' Dock gives you the freedom that you may think you've lost. (Read all about it further on in this chapter).

Help at hand
When selected, 'About This Mac' shows what version of Mac OS X is running indicates how much memory it has and lets you update your software.

Up with the latest
Software Update can be set to automatically check for regular software updates .

What's your preference?
Clicking here will immediately take you to System Preferences.

Configuration capers
Here's where you can switch your network configurations.

Starting over
Instead of shutting down your Mac and then restarting, this command helps you perform two steps in one.

Enough of this!
This command could only be accessed with shortcut keys in previous Mac OS versions. Now, you can choose this option – it brings up the Force Quit Applications dialog box allowing you to choose the application you want to quit.

Turn off and go home
The tried and trusted way to switch off your Mac.

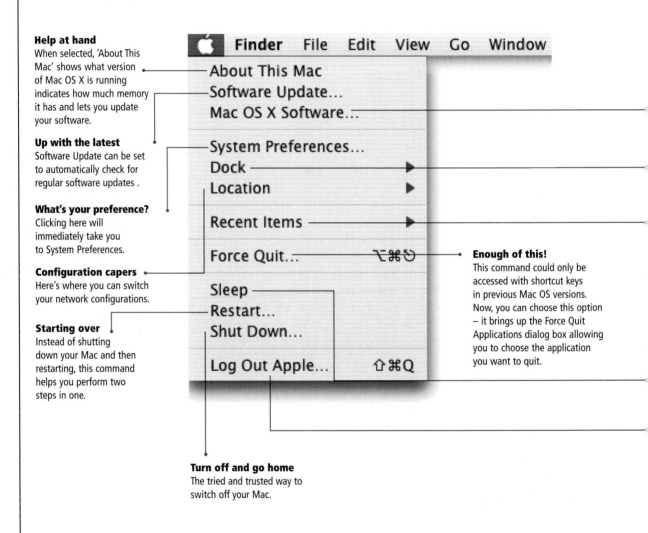

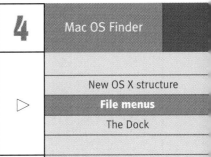

Web connection
Launches Web browser and takes
you to 'Mac OS X Downloads'.

Customizing items
Experiment with the Dock to
your heart's content.

Memory surge
Recently used items can be recalled.
Pick the one you need if it's there.
(Note: these items are customizable.)

Zzzzzzzzzzzzz
Choose this to put your Mac into
its low-powered sleep mode.

How considerate
This command logs out the user
who is currently logged in, after
quitting all running user applications.
This allows users to be switched
without restarting or shutting down.

Finder menu

As the name suggests, the Finder gathers information for you and helps you to do the same. A useful tool, it also allows you to control the way you want your desktop to look and act. The Finder menu controls the way your Finder looks and acts, and as you will see on these pages, it's simple to use.

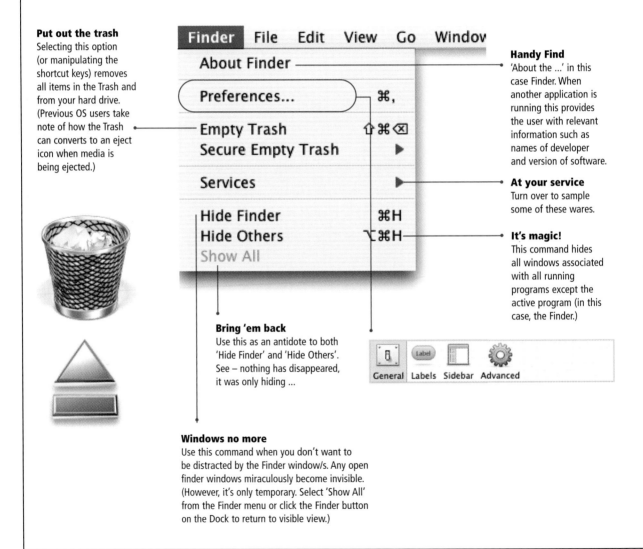

Put out the trash
Selecting this option (or manipulating the shortcut keys) removes all items in the Trash and from your hard drive. (Previous OS users take note of how the Trash can converts to an eject icon when media is being ejected.)

Handy Find
'About the ...' in this case Finder. When another application is running this provides the user with relevant information such as names of developer and version of software.

At your service
Turn over to sample some of these wares.

It's magic!
This command hides all windows associated with all running programs except the active program (in this case, the Finder.)

Bring 'em back
Use this as an antidote to both 'Hide Finder' and 'Hide Others'. See – nothing has disappeared, it was only hiding ...

Windows no more
Use this command when you don't want to be distracted by the Finder window/s. Any open finder windows miraculously become invisible. (However, it's only temporary. Select 'Show All' from the Finder menu or click the Finder button on the Dock to return to visible view.)

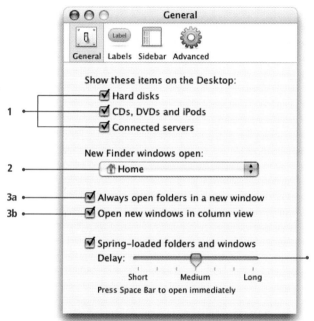

Spring has sprung
Spring-loaded folders is a great feature introduced into all three Finder views. When you hold an item over a folder instead of dropping it in immediately, a window will zoom open beneath your cursor to reveal the contents within and the moment you move out of the window it will disappear. The settings here (left) allow you to choose whether you want this option active and how long you prefer to wait for your folders to open as you drag.

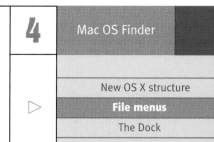

• Do you like to see extensions to identify what kind of file you are dealing with? If so, ensure that 'Show all file extensions' is checked. If not, keep it unchecked and test your general knowledge.

• If you are confident about what you throw out, uncheck 'Show warning before emptying the Trash'. Trash will then be emptied without warning.

Your choice entirely
Get the desktop to look exactly the way you want it to (well, almost) by:
1. Selecting the Disks, Removable media and Connected Servers checkboxes if you require hard drives, CDs, DVDs and other types of disks to appear on the desktop. (If you'd rather have a pristine desktop, don't select these boxes. You can still work with them when they aren't visible. Simply go to the Finder window and click the computer button to see them.)

2. When you click on the Finder icon in the Dock and there are windows currently open, you can specify which one you want to come forward by selecting from the pop-up list attached to it.

3. (a) Users that want the familiarity of previous Mac operating systems will probably prefer to see a new window for each folder opened.
(b) Ensure that each window opened appears in Column view by selecting this option.

Finder Menu

If you have always wished for the kind of operating system that allows you to utilize common features from one application to another, wish no more – every Mac OS X Cocoa program now has 'Services' (Go to Finder and its right beneath 'Secure Empty Trash'). With this command you can mix and match spelling checkers, drawing tools and calculation methods between Cocoa applications. In addition, some third party applications now only exist as Services.

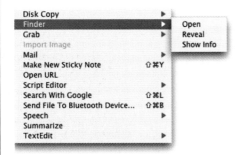

Finder within
Gaining access to the Finder is often a total pain when you have a number of different applications open. Since OS X 10.2, Services included the option for users to go to the Finder from within their current application by merely selecting it from a menu. Beats having to travel back and forth between applications and the Finder, doesn't it?

Grab it quick
For those of you who make images (screen shots) of what is visible on your monitor for training purposes or troubleshooting, Grab is a program for you. With it you can 'snap' the entire screen, a selection of it, or make a timed screen capture and *voilá,* it displays the image in a new window. You can then print it, close it without saving, or save as a TIFF file. [Good news is that Mac 'oldies' can still create screengrabs using Command+Shift+3.] Having Grab in your Services menu means that you can call it up from within the program you are currently working on, instead of toggling around OS X. Note: a great feature of Mac OS X 10.2 was the return of Command+Shift+4 to capture a window. Hit the Space Bar and as you roll over a window it will highlight in blue. Click to capture.

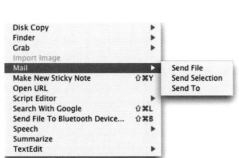

Please Mr Postman
When browsing the Internet, you often come across text you want to pass on to someone else. The good news is that you no longer have to go to the trouble of selecting the text, copying it, launching your e-mail program, pasting the text and sending it. You can now have your selected text pasted into a new outgoing e-mail message in Mac OS X Mail. How? Select the text you want and go to Services > Mail. It's that simple.

Rapid reminders
If you're a fan of Stickies (found in the Applications folder), then you will love this one. It copies selected text from within any application, launches a new Sticky in the Stickies program and pastes in the copied text – automatically.

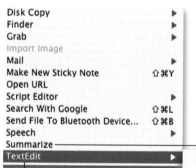

Quick text extraction
After highlighting text in any Cocoa application, select Summarize from the Services menu and see how the Mac extracts the issues of significance from your selection. (It launches a program called Summary Service where a summarized version of your text will greet you.)

Copy and paste? No more!
When used in conjunction with Services, this compact word processor has the ability to:
(a) open a file by name (Note: you need to indicate a full UNIX path to the file to do this);
(b) Select text and images. A shortcut to copy and paste. Simply select text or image from a Cocoa application and choose this option.
The copied item will miraculously appear in TextEdit.

File menu

File management is an essential part of every Mac OS user's workday existence, so it would be advantageous to get to know the File menu inside out – keyboard shortcuts included.

Find the Finder
Have all the Finder windows disappeared? Never fear – you can easily open a new one by selecting this menu option. (Note: this particular shortcut key was used to create a New Folder in previous Mac operating systems). Another way to select the Finder is to go to its icon in the Dock (see more about the Dock later in this chapter).

Putting a lid on it
Closing one window is easy – you can choose this option (or the shortcut keys) or simply select the red button to the left of the window. To close more than one window at a time, hold down the Option key and select the red button to the left of the uppermost window, or press Option+Command+W. Marvellous, isn't it?

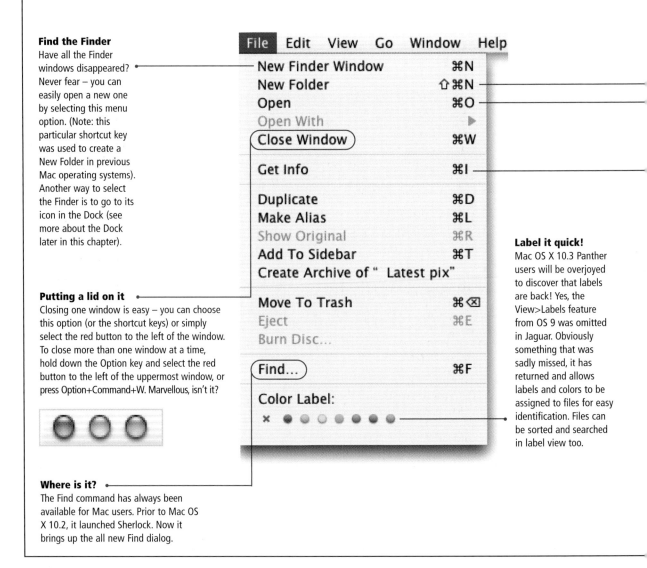

| File | Edit | View | Go | Window | Help |

New Finder Window	⌘N
New Folder	⇧⌘N
Open	⌘O
Open With	▶
Close Window	⌘W
Get Info	⌘I
Duplicate	⌘D
Make Alias	⌘L
Show Original	⌘R
Add To Sidebar	⌘T
Create Archive of " Latest pix"
Move To Trash	⌘⌫
Eject	⌘E
Burn Disc...
Find...	⌘F
Color Label:

Label it quick!
Mac OS X 10.3 Panther users will be overjoyed to discover that labels are back! Yes, the View>Labels feature from OS 9 was omitted in Jaguar. Obviously something that was sadly missed, it has returned and allows labels and colors to be assigned to files for easy identification. Files can be sorted and searched in label view too.

Where is it?
The Find command has always been available for Mac users. Prior to Mac OS X 10.2, it launched Sherlock. Now it brings up the all new Find dialog.

Folder fun

The New Folder command is the same as it has always been, and it does exactly as the name suggests – it makes folders. Only difference is that the shortcut key that we become accustomed to in OS 9, has changed to Command+Shift+N. Take note of this – should you press the wrong keyboard combination out of habit you will get a new window and not a new folder!

Open sesame!

Opening a folder or document is easy. Simply double-click or if preferred, select the icon to be opened and go to File > Open.

(The Open command is also useful if you have more than one icon selected. Try it, and you will see that it opens selected icons almost simultaneously).

Info at a glance

Just about anyone who wants to find out anything about a file or folder will be keen to use this command. It's easy and versatile and you can find out things such as: • What application (and version of it) created the file; • How much space the item takes up (Note: only the item, not the disk drive!); • Location and where it was created; • Where it is found; • Creation and modification details; • Format options (for disks only). You can also choose to lock the folder or file for safety and make any file a stationery pad. (When opened, the file will present itself as new, and the original will remain untouched — much like a template.) Any comments that you would like to add about the file or folder can also be included in this box. Note: information provided in the Info window depends on the kind of item selected. (Word of caution: Classic's Get Info command changed to Show Info in earlier versions of OSX and then reverted back to Get Info in OS X 10. 2. Confused? We are too!)

File menu

Convenience is the key to managing your documents effectively.
Many of the commands under the File menu help make tasks such
as duplication and alias creation as easy as pie. Additionally,
notice new methods of ejecting media and making aliases.

Throw away
The 'Move to Trash'
command was devised
for those who are
reluctant to use a
mouse to click and drag.
If this sounds like you,
you will probably find
it worthwhile to
memorize the shortcut
key.(It's an easier option
than selecting File >
Move to Trash, because
by the time you have
done this you would
have exerted the same
amount of energy doing
a click and drag!)

Power to burn
Use this option to burn
CDs if your computer has
CD recording capabilities.
Simply insert a blank CD-
R or CD-RW disc into
the CD tray. A CD icon
will appear on the
desktop for you to drag
your files and folders
onto. (Be sure of your
choice as no changes
can be made after the
CD is burned.)

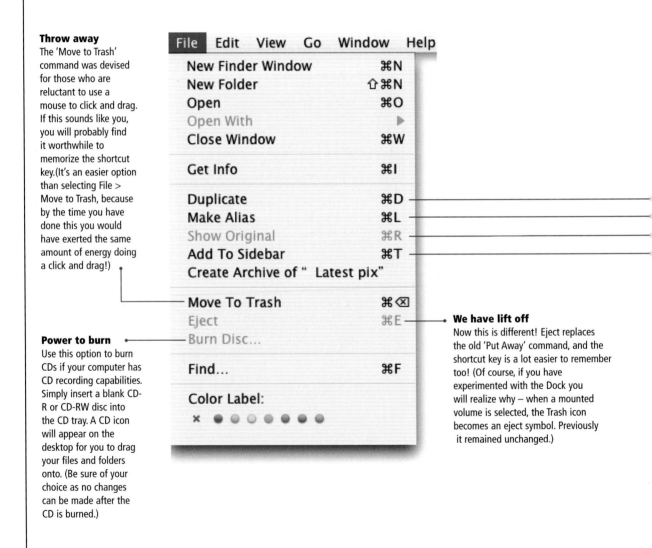

| File | Edit | View | Go | Window | Help |

New Finder Window   ⌘N
New Folder   ⇧⌘N
Open   ⌘O
Open With   ▶
Close Window   ⌘W

Get Info   ⌘I

Duplicate   ⌘D
Make Alias   ⌘L
Show Original   ⌘R
Add To Sidebar   ⌘T
Create Archive of " Latest pix"

Move To Trash   ⌘⌫
Eject   ⌘E
Burn Disc…

Find…   ⌘F

Color Label:

✕ ● ● ○ ○ ○ ○ ○

We have lift off
Now this is different! Eject replaces
the old 'Put Away' command, and the
shortcut key is a lot easier to remember
too! (Of course, if you have
experimented with the Dock you
will realize why – when a mounted
volume is selected, the Trash icon
becomes an eject symbol. Previously
it remained unchanged.)

Double trouble
'Duplicate' is a nifty feature and one that should not be confused with the 'Copy' command (located in the Edit menu). Highlight or choose one or more icon/s and select the 'Duplicate' command. Note: duplicated items are not copied to the clipboard, but rather immediately actioned (this is perfect for the more impatient user).

Where to from here?
An alias is a 'signpost' to a document or folder – in fact, any icon at all. It is simple to make: highlight the icon/s of your choice, select Make Alias, and hey presto! It's done. (Note: if you prefer to use the shortcut key – it's changed from the previous operating system, and no longer Command+M.)

Will the original please stand up?
It's all very well having an alias, but what happens when the original item (from which the alias was made) is corrupted or deleted? Or, what happens if you upgrade an application but forget to upgrade the alias with it? 'Show Original' is a quick way of diagnosing whether there is, in fact, an original.

Easy access
Almost anything can be added to your sidebar by way of this command. It's dead easy – simply select your item and choose 'Add to Sidebar'. The system makes an alias and sends it to the sidebar (located in the Finder window).

A BROKEN ALIAS?
Sometimes the Mac loses track of the original to which the alias points. When clicked on, a 'broken' alias will provide you with the options to delete it, fix it or ignore it.

HOT TIP

Edit menu

If you want to edit or change data, the Mac OS X Edit menu is the place to go. It's reliable and almost as familiar as it used to be, with just a few subtle exceptions. Head this way and we will show you what they are ...

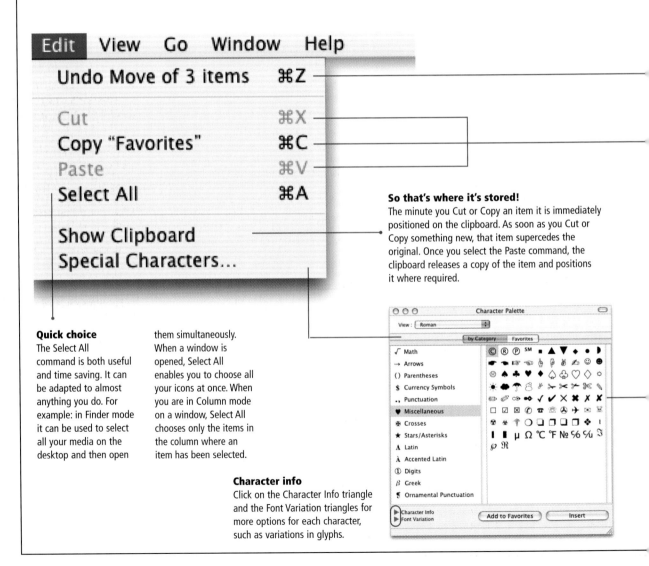

So that's where it's stored!
The minute you Cut or Copy an item it is immediately positioned on the clipboard. As soon as you Cut or Copy something new, that item supercedes the original. Once you select the Paste command, the clipboard releases a copy of the item and positions it where required.

Quick choice
The Select All command is both useful and time saving. It can be adapted to almost anything you do. For example: in Finder mode it can be used to select all your media on the desktop and then open

them simultaneously. When a window is opened, Select All enables you to choose all your icons at once. When you are in Column mode on a window, Select All chooses only the items in the column where an item has been selected.

Character info
Click on the Character Info triangle and the Font Variation triangles for more options for each character, such as variations in glyphs.

Slip, slop, slap
No matter what computer you've used, the 'Cut, Copy and Paste' principle applies. This is how it works: • **Cut** represents exactly what the name suggests. You cut something out either to paste it elsewhere, or get rid of it altogether (notice how the shortcut key X resembles a pair of scissors). It's almost the same electronically, except the item cut gets relocated to the clipboard for onward travel – almost like a 'removal van'. • **Copy,** on the other hand is quite different. The 'removal van' is not required in this case. Instead, the Mac operating system uses a kind of 'camera' to memorize the item to the clipboard, leaving the original one untouched. • **Paste** transports the last item Mac OS X has memorized or removed from the clipboard to the new specified position. (Remember, the item you paste must be your most recent cut or copied item.)

Oops!
The Undo option has always been relied on by Mac users. Now, Mac OS X takes Undo a step further – not only does it undo actions in text mode but it acts on icons too. For example, if you duplicate or move any item to the Trash, you can change your mind and undo it. As always, it only undoes one previous action. If you attempt to repeat an Undo, it will redo the action. (A great help to those who have an aversion to decision-making.)

SCISSORS AND GLUE
In Mac OS X Cut, Copy and Paste does not only apply to text. You can use it on graphics, pictures palettes within applications – even on the desktop itself. Have some fun and do some quick experiments.

Key Caps lives on
If you were a fan of the Key Caps utility (pre-Mac OS X 10.3 Panther), you may have thought it was gone forever. The good news is that it has been revamped and the all new Character Palette can be found under 'Special Characters' or System Preferences > International (Go to the Input Menu button and Check 'keyboard viewer' box in the list of input names).
Now more advanced than ever before, this features lets you check out and select mathematical symbols, letters with accent marks, or arrows and other 'dingbats', Japanese, Traditional Chinese, Simplified Chinese, and Korean characters, as many other characters from various languages. Note: To work out combinations of keys to use for special characters and symbols, turn on the Keyboard Viewer in International preferences, and then choose 'Show Keyboard Viewer' from the Input menu in the menu bar.

View menu

Icon presentation is an all-important facet of the new Macintosh operating system. Apple has gone to great lengths to provide users with as many options as possible to tailor windows to individual requirements. As with most things in Mac OS X, the options you choose are easily altered. (Very important to those who believe that its their prerogative to change their minds – again and again and again ...)

Take your pick
Experienced users will probably find that they gravitate to the View menu for old time's sake. A quicker and more convenient way of changing the way folders are presented on the toolbar, but it's a matter of choice, really.

For the tidy among us ...
As the name suggests, 'Clean Up Selection' tidies up your icons. (You will notice that this option is not available when your files are viewed by List or Column mode). 'Arrange by name' goes hand-in-hand with 'View as icons' and 'Clean Up Selection'. So, apart from having a very tidy looking window, you can view icons in alphabetical order too!

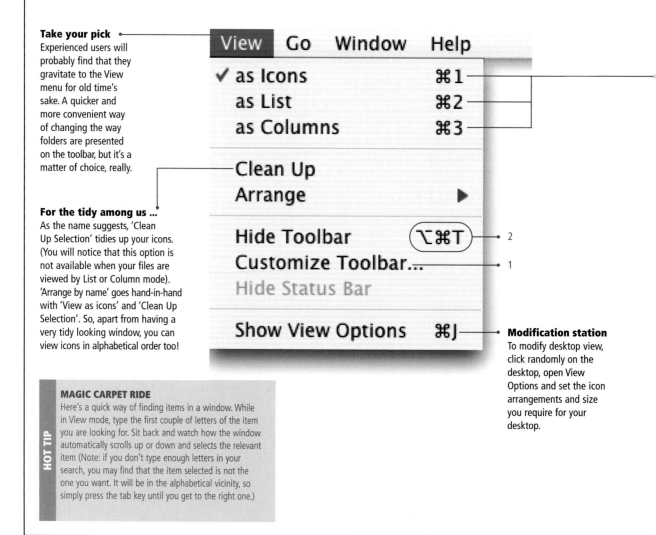

Modification station
To modify desktop view, click randomly on the desktop, open View Options and set the icon arrangements and size you require for your desktop.

HOT TIP

MAGIC CARPET RIDE
Here's a quick way of finding items in a window. While in View mode, type the first couple of letters of the item you are looking for. Sit back and watch how the window automatically scrolls up or down and selects the relevant item (Note: if you don't type enough letters in your search, you may find that the item selected is not the one you want. It will be in the alphabetical vicinity, so simply press the tab key until you get to the right one.)

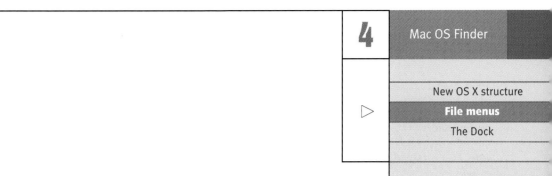

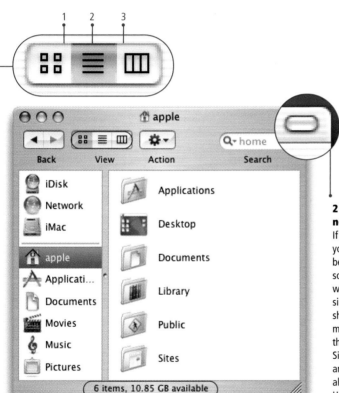

2 Now you see it, now you don't

If the toolbar is something you don't think you will ever become accustomed to, or something that you feel wastes too much space, simply hide it. However, should you change your mind – fear not, it will be there, waiting in the wings. Simply select 'Show Toolbar' and see it return! (Note: an alternative is to click on the Hide/Show toolbar button.)

1 Fact file

The status bar is helpful for a number of reasons – for example, it provides information on how many items are contained within each window and calculates the amount of disk space these items occupy. If you don't need to see this regularly (or at all) select 'Hide Status Bar' and it will vanish ... at least until you show it again.

View menu

Being able to change things to your liking is a great philosophy of Apple's. With new features such as customizing your tool bar and changing your view options, the user's individuality is greatly encouraged. The more control you have over what you want to do and how you want things to look, the better your work (or play) performance. We show you how to optimize this. Read on.

What a view!
View Options exist in Icon (1), List (2) and Column (3) view. In Icon view (1), you can choose to display Icon size, Text Size, Label Position, Snap to grid, item info and/or icon preview in one window or all windows, as specified. A variety of ways to arrange this information and an assortment of background styles are

also available. In List view (2), there's a choice of size of text and icons as well as how you would like them arranged. Size and date of documents, applications and folders can also be displayed. These changes apply to individual windows or globally, as specified. Column view (3) is a little different and as can be seen, provides only text size selection and icon and preview column display choices.

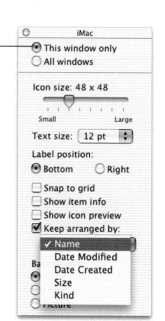

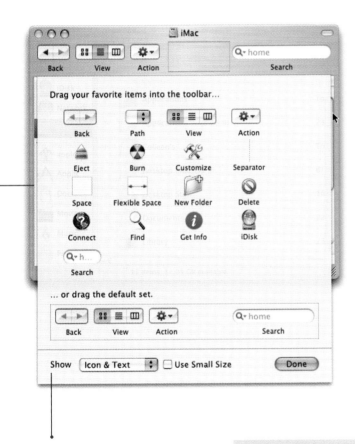

Make it up as you go along
Choosing 'Customize Toolbar', enables you
to get the toolbar to look exactly the way
you would like it to.
Simply choose from the range of icons provided
to create your own Toolbar, or if you prefer to
keep to the OS defaults, select the set provided.

PUFF OF SMOKE?
Deleting icons from your toolbar is similar to
deleting icons from the Dock – with one exception.
When you drag icons from the Dock they turn into a
puff of smoke. When you drag icons from the
toolbar to the desktop they simply .. er .. disappear.

TECH TIP

Go menu

The Finder's Go menu is a novelty to the new Mac operating system and a useful alternative to clicking icons of the same description in your toolbar. As well as this, it offers quick 'flights' to destinations of your choice and the ability to connect to a server without going elsewhere. Take a look.

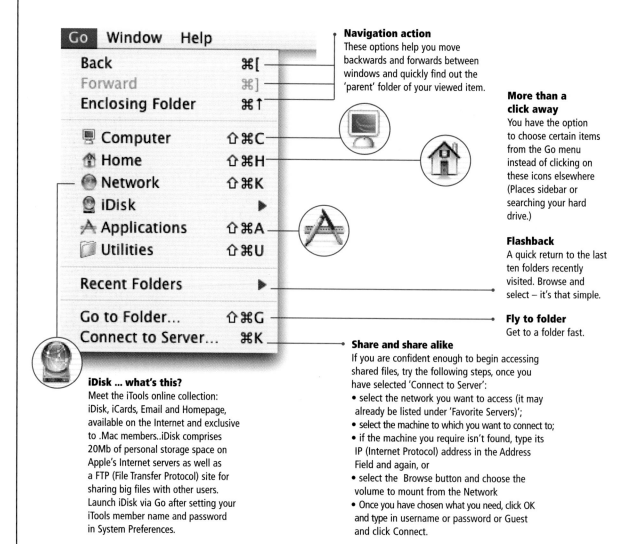

Navigation action
These options help you move backwards and forwards between windows and quickly find out the 'parent' folder of your viewed item.

More than a click away
You have the option to choose certain items from the Go menu instead of clicking on these icons elsewhere (Places sidebar or searching your hard drive.)

Flashback
A quick return to the last ten folders recently visited. Browse and select – it's that simple.

Fly to folder
Get to a folder fast.

Share and share alike
If you are confident enough to begin accessing shared files, try the following steps, once you have selected 'Connect to Server':
• select the network you want to access (it may already be listed under 'Favorite Servers)';
• select the machine to which you want to connect to;
• if the machine you require isn't found, type its IP (Internet Protocol) address in the Address Field and again, or
• select the Browse button and choose the volume to mount from the Network
• Once you have chosen what you need, click OK and type in username or password or Guest and click Connect.

iDisk ... what's this?
Meet the iTools online collection: iDisk, iCards, Email and Homepage, available on the Internet and exclusive to .Mac members..iDisk comprises 20Mb of personal storage space on Apple's Internet servers as well as a FTP (File Transfer Protocol) site for sharing big files with other users. Launch iDisk via Go after setting your iTools member name and password in System Preferences.

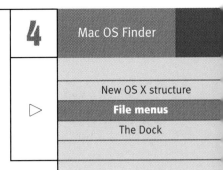

'Do not pass go'

No, we aren't playing Monopoly, we're simply pointing out how easy it is to move around Mac OS X. The 'Go to Folder' command gives you options that you never had in previous versions of the Mac operating system. The pop-up dialog box attached to this command allows you to type the name of the folder you want to go to and then select 'Go' to move on. As an alternative, you can indicate a pathname rather than a folder name. When doing so note that: (a) names are case-sensitive;(b) should begin and end with the slash (/); and (c) can indicate as many levels of the directory as possible. For example: /iMac/Applications/Apple Script/.

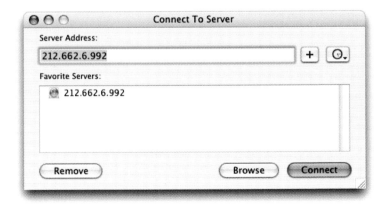

Window menu

The Mac OS X Window menu has been revamped. While some items may be familiar to long-time Macintosh users, others are completely different. And while you are getting to know as much as possible about your windows, there's a whole range of 'magical' effects to make the experience worthwhile.

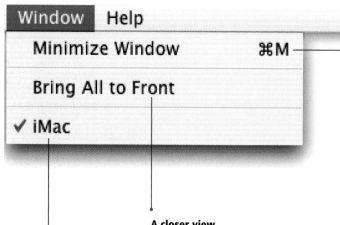

Aladdin's lamp
This option is an alternative to the minimize (amber) button found in any window – it moves the window to the Dock, and if specified, the effect is that of the 'genie' in the bottle. Apart from being a convenient option, it can also provide hours of fun for the young at heart. (See more about the Dock and the Genie effect on the pages to follow.)

A closer view
You may have to play with this option for some time before it finally sinks in. It works most effectively if you have a number of finder windows open which become obstructed when you launch an application. By clicking 'Bring All to Front', you will bring all finder windows in front of your application. We think it's really nifty.

Quick check
For those of you who believe finding windows is intensely painful, this one's for you. All open windows will be listed in this window–simply click to select.

Quick Shrink

Double-click on a window's title bar and watch it minimize (an alternative to both the amber button and the 'Minimize Window' command.) (Note: holding down the Shift key will minimize your window in slow motion.)

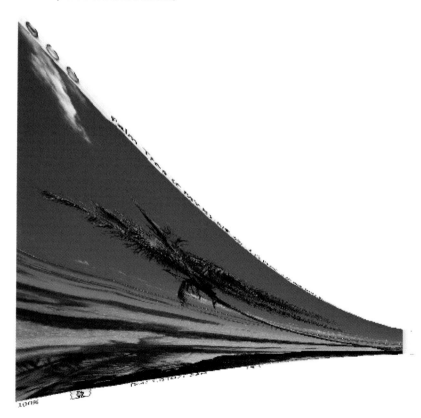

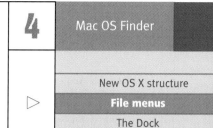

Hello Dock!

Meet the Dock – a unique strip of icons (located at the bottom or side of the desktop), it combines the functions of what Mac 'oldies' were accustomed to in the previous operating system's Application menu, Apple menu, Launcher and Control Strip. At first you may find it difficult to get used to, but after a while you'll take to it as a duck takes to water. And the beauty is that you, the user, can control the way it looks and acts exactly as it suits you.

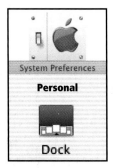

System Preferences

Personal

Dock

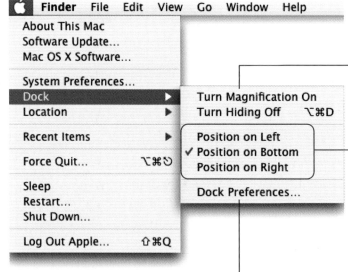

Where to now?
Position your Dock in a different spot or hide it altogether. (To resuscitate it, select 'Turn Hiding Off' from the Dock menu, 'Hide and Show' from the Dock dialog box, or simply choose the shortcut keys.

As you prefer
Dock Preferences can be selected from the Dock pull-down menu (under the Apple menu) or from Applications > System Preferences. Some abilities are duplicated from the Dock menu, but there are others (such as how you'd like to minimize windows) exclusively found in these preferences.

Through the looking glass
A fun effect which makes it easy to see what's available on your Dock as you drag through items with your mouse, it's controlled by:
(a) sliding the magnification bar (Dock > Dock Preferences) to the left or right; and
(b) Selecting Magnification On/Off from the Dock menu.

In the groove

Change the size of your dock with this easy-to-use slider (or click on the Dock and drag its dividing line), found next to 'Dock Size'. If you want your application to do the Dock and Shake, Rattle and Roll while opening, check the box next to 'Animate opening applications.'

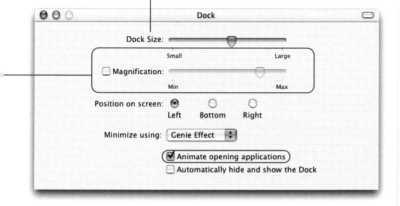

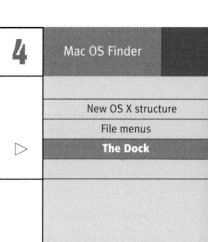

Shrinking Violet

By now you have probably noticed how cool a window slides into the Dock when it's minimized. It will either produce a 'Scale' or 'Genie' effect, depending on what you select in your Dock Preferences dialog box. (And it has different effects depending on where your Dock lies.)

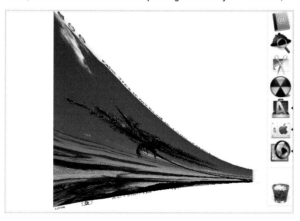

The Dock – a closer look

Oh, what fun it is to work with the Dock. You can move icons of your favorite applications, utilities, documents, folders and disks in and out of it with ease (and animation), find out all the information it has to offer with a mere click of the mouse and immediately see running applications and active documents. Come with us for a closer look ...

Adobe Illustrator 10

1

Easy come ...
Moving icons into the Dock is simple. Click on the icon of your choice, drag it to the dock and watch how the other objects scuttle away, making room for it. (Note: the icon you have in your Dock is only an alias of the real thing and therefore can come to no harm.) There's a neat filing system too – applications and utilities go left, documents, folders and disks go right of the white divider line (1).

... easy go
Removing icons from the Dock is great entertainment value. Select it, drag it away and ... poof .. it vanishes into a puff of smoke.

What's on?
See those tiny black triangles beneath certain icons on the dock? Well, they display which applications, documents and utilities are currently running.

Application Switcher
The presence of the application switcher is an added bonus for dock users. To access, hold down Command and press the tab key. Then, hold down the tab key to activate a cursor to run through active application icons, to quickly choose an application and then switch to others. You can also: • Hide an application by holding down Command, tabbing to an active application and pressing the H key; • Quit an application by holding down Command, tabbing to the application icon you wish to quit and pressing the Q key.; • Cycle backwards among open applications pressing Shift and Tab, while still holding down the Command key.

Back to my roots
Need to find the location of a document lodged in your Dock? Click and hold the icon you require and a pop-up menu will appear. Choose 'Show in Finder' and it will reveal all. (Note: the Finder icon contains a pop-up box which specifies the name/s of window/s currently open. In the case where there are more than one, you can bring a window forward by clicking on its name in the pop-up box.)

Applications only
(a) When working with an Application's pop-up menu on the Dock (Control-click or hold down your mouse on icon on the Dock), note that selecting Option and Command gives you the choice to 'Force Quit' that particular application or see all its active documents.
(b) If you have a few documents open from various Applications, hold down Option and click on the Application you want to work on and all others will vanish!

New concept

QuickTime Player

QuickTime, the elder statesman of digital media playback, has been around for over ten years. Evolving from multimedia CD-ROMs to wireless delivery of digital video, QuickTime has added a wide range of codecs to keep it at the forefront of streaming media playback. QuickTime 6 became the basis of the MPEG-4 standard, positioning it well in the current evolution of digital video compression. QuickTime 6.5 also supports 3GPP and 3GPP2 for multimedia delivery across 3G mobile networks.

QuickTime Player
The QuickTime Player is the front-end of Apple's multimedia technology which allows you to watch movies from your hard drive, movies embedded in Web pages such as movie trailers, or even live streaming video over the Web. It provides basic controls for watching movies with Play, Pause, Fast Forward, Rewind, Start and End buttons. Users are also able to drag the timeline slider to a particular point in the movie and adjust the volume as needed.

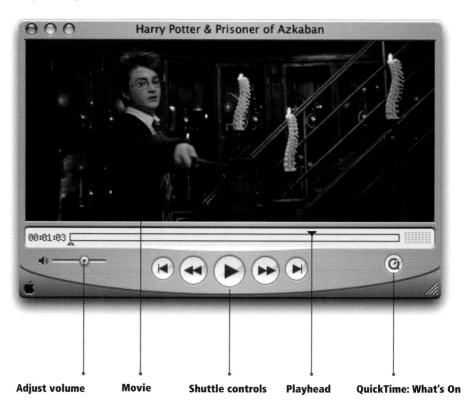

Harry Potter & Prisoner of Azkaban

00:01:03

Adjust volume   **Movie**   **Shuttle controls**   **Playhead**   **QuickTime: What's On**

HOT TIP

QuickTime show
For examples of QuickTime media:
Cubic VR — www.apple.com/quicktime/gallery/cubicvr/ Instant-On Streaming — www.apple.com/quicktime/gallery/instanton.html

Harry Potter and the Chamber of Secrets
Image courtesy of Warner Bros.
Visit: www.harrypotter.com

QuickTime at the movies

One of the more popular uses for QuickTime is to view the latest movie trailers. Apple's QuickTime site (www.apple.com/quicktime/), keeps track of the latest movie trailers from all of the major studios and even some of the smaller ones. Simply click on the movie poster or movie title under each studio to view the trailer. Note: download time will vary according to your Internet connection.

QuickTime at play

Gamers are catered for with the Game Trailers Web page (www.apple.com/games/trailers/) which features a good range of trailers for Mac games.
The QuickTime site will also appeal to music lovers with a wide range of musical genres (www.apple.com/quicktime/whatson/).
Watch music videos, live concerts and interviews with your favorite artists all within the QuickTime Player.

One and the same

When you install QuickTime or upgrade to a new version, you'll be asked for a QuickTime Pro serial number. If you haven't bought Pro, don't panic. Just leave the fields empty and continue. QuickTime and QuickTime Pro are actually one and the same; the difference is that entering a Pro serial number activates some features that aren't otherwise available.

HOT TIP

QuickTime Player

File>Export lets you save QuickTime movies in other formats. Why? Maybe you want to save a version that will download more quickly because the picture is smaller and more heavily compressed, or perhaps you want to apply one of the QuickTime filters such as film noise (which simulates the appearance of old, scratched movie film) to a clip.

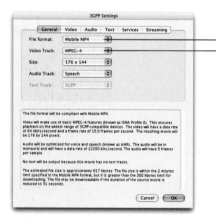

Export Format
Each export format allows fine-tuning to optimize the resulting file for its intended purpose. Settings range from NTSC or PAL for DV output to the file format used for 3GPP.

Full screen
While QuickTime Pro will play movies in full-screen mode, don't expect cinema quality. A 'high quality' movie trailer will typically be enlarged two or three times – depending on the pixel dimensions of your display — and any compression artefacts will be more visible. That said, watching full-screen playback from one or two metres away is generally more satisfactory than watching a small window at normal working distance

Quick sound and sight
On-screen sound and picture controls are accessible with QuickTime Pro. Save the movie once you have the settings right, and you won't need to adjust the controls the next time you play it.

On-line movies

QuickTime Pro makes it easy to save movies that you've watched from a web page. Click the button at the right end of the control bar, and select Save As Source. (Why not Save As QuickTime Movie? Save As Source always retains the original file type, whether it's a QuickTime movie, and MP3 track or whatever.) Pick a suitable folder, click Save, and you can play the movie whenever you wish. This doesn't always work, though: the owners of the material can make it harder to save if they choose (see www.apple.com/quicktime/authoring/qtwebfaq.html).

Why go to QuickTime Pro?

Apple offers QuickTime Pro at US$29.99 which adds media authoring features and extra playback options such as full screen viewing. At the top of the list of features for QuickTime Pro are the import and export options. With the current version you are able to author MPEG-4 content and export as 3GPP, 3GPP2, AIFF,

QuickTime Player	QuickTime Pro	Streaming Server	Broadcaster

AMC, AU, AVI, BMP, DV Stream, FLC, Image Sequence, JPEG/JFIF, JPEG 2000, MacPaint, MIDI, MPEG-4, Photoshop, PICT, PNG, QuickTime Image File, QuickTime Movie, SGI, System 7 Sound, Targa, Text, TIFF and WAV. QuickTime Pro also allows you to cut, copy and paste video and audio giving you basic editing capabilities.

On the playback front, you have the luxury of viewing video in full screen mode. You can also control brightness, color, treble and bass and then save those settings with your movie. Finally, you can prepare movies for streaming with a huge range of presets to compress streaming audio and video for Web delivery.

iLife

With every new Mac you purchase, you receive a library of free software covering all of the major areas you're likely to use with your new 'digital hub'. iPhoto lets you manage your digital photos; iMovie lets you edit digital movies and add effects; iDVD lets you create your own Hollywood-style DVDs; iTunes manages your MP3 collection; iPhoto organises your photographs. Don't despair if you already own a Mac — the latest versions are available on CD-ROM at a modest price.

iTunes

Convert your music CDs to MP3 or AAC, manage your digital music and spoken word collection, listen to Internet radio stations, create playlists, transfer tracks to your iPod and burn CDs.Use your music collection with iPhoto, iMovie or iDVD. See pages 128-129

iPhoto

Transfer images from your digital camera and manage, edit and share your digital photos. Create slideshows with background music from your iTUnes library, or export photos into an iMovie project See pages 122-123

iMovie

Transfer digital video from your DV camera, edit the footage, add still photos from iPhoto, effects, titles, sound effects, and music from iTunes. Save the result back to your camera, in QuickTime format for web and other uses, or export directly into iDVD. See pages 124-125.

iDVD

Take edited digital movies from iMovie, add backgrounds, menus, slideshows from iPhoto, and music from your iTunes collection, then burn a stylish DVD on a SuperDrive-equipped Mac. See pages 126-127.

GarageBand

Combine the sound of your own voice or instrument with backing loops and synthesized instruments, then adjust the mix to get a personal musical creation. Export the result to iMovie, iDVD or iTunes. See pages 132-133.

iPhoto

Thanks to iPhoto, downloading, managing and sharing digital photos is a snap. Maintaining a digital photo library is within the scope of almost every Macintosh user. Many cameras will plug straight into the Mac's USB or FireWire ports, or an inexpensive gadget will read the removable memory cards.

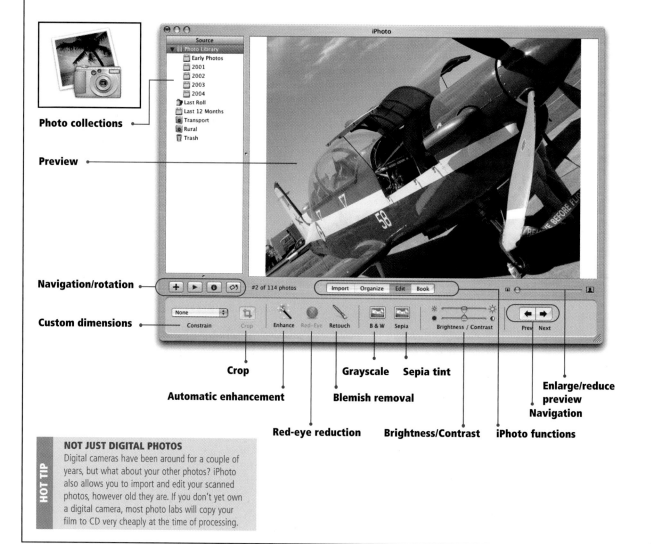

Photo collections

Preview

Navigation/rotation

Custom dimensions

Crop

Automatic enhancement

Red-eye reduction

Grayscale

Blemish removal

Sepia tint

Brightness/Contrast

Enlarge/reduce preview

Navigation

iPhoto functions

HOT TIP

NOT JUST DIGITAL PHOTOS
Digital cameras have been around for a couple of years, but what about your other photos? iPhoto also allows you to import and edit your scanned photos, however old they are. If you don't yet own a digital camera, most photo labs will copy your film to CD very cheaply at the time of processing.

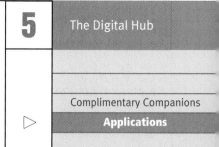
Categorize your photos

iPhoto allows you to create 'smart albums' that display photos according to keywords, titles, file names, ratings and other criteria. Although a few keywords are provided to get you started (eg, Kids, Vacation), you can add your own keywords and apply them to groups of images at once. Once your photos are categorized, you can quickly find them by using a new or existing smart album. Whenever you need to search for images, turn to a smart album.

Image editing

Though you'd never mistake iPhoto for Adobe's Photoshop, you can perform simple image editing with iPhoto. Presets constrain images to formats such as DVD and images can be improved automatically with the Enhance button or you can control the brightness and contrast manually, while red-eye reduction fixes that flash problem. For the vintage look, change the image to black and white or even sepia.

Image sharing

iPhoto offers a wide range of output possibilities: printing on your inkjet printer; creating an onscreen, DVD or Web slideshow; e-mailing your photos via Mail; ordering prints or bound albums (US, Canada, Europe and Japan only); creating a Web gallery; and creating desktop pictures or screensavers.

iMovie

Though iMovie was not the first digital video editing application, it was certainly the first instantly usable solution. In concert with the Apple-developed FireWire interface and the explosion of affordable DV cameras, iMovie was the first to bring video editing to the consumer. In its fourth version, iMovie allows users to capture and edit their digital video through a simple interface which supports titling, effects, transitions and sound effects.

Lights, camera, action!
iMovie is a ridiculously easy way to create polished movies from your digital video footage.

Import/Edit   Shuttle controls   Preview   Movie clips

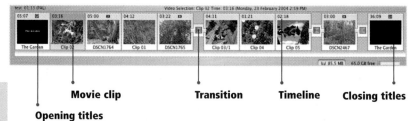

Movie clip   Transition   Timeline   Closing titles

Opening titles

HOT TIP

VIDEO EDITING
Digital video requires lots of storage, so it's a good idea to edit your clips as you capture them to your Mac. That means getting rid of the footage of your feet and the lens cap.

Stills and sounds

Careful use of still photography can enhance your movie, and iMovie provides easy access to your iPhoto library, including your albums and smart albums. The Ken Burns Effect (pan and zoom) can be very effective, but don't overdo it. Choose a photo, then adjust the zoom factor with the slider marked with two different sized photos. If you've zoomed in, drag the preview image so it's centred to your taste. Click the Finish button and repeat the process. Click the Preview button, and if the effect is too fast or too slow adjust the rabbit and tortoise slider. When you're happy, click Apply and iMovie will transform the still into a movie clip. Similarly, the Audio pane gives easy access to your collection of sound effects and your iTunes library.

Transitions

Watch any movie or TV show and you'll see transitions between scenes. iMovie provides transitions to customize with a time slider and direction pen. Preview transitions under the Transitions tab, and when you're done, drag it between the clips to the timeline.

Titles

To create movie credits, select your own fonts and sizes along with speeds and pauses of effects. A wide range of text effects for the opening titles are also available and there's an option to create music video titles.

Effects

iMovie provides a stable of effects to choose from and you can download a few from companies: Gee Three (www.geethree.com); Virtix (www.virtix.com); CSB Digital (www.csb-digital.com); and eZedia (www.ezedia.ca).

iDVD

With DVD players seemingly in every house and office, it makes a lot of sense to turn your iMovie projects into DVDs. Whether they carry short films, home movies, training videos or corporate presentations, DVDs are convenient to store, send and play. Supplied free with SuperDrive (DVD burner) equipped Macintoshes or as part of the iLife package, iDVD helps take your video creations from iMovie and delivers them Hollywood-style DVDs with motion menus, soundtracks and slideshows.

Themes
Apple supplies a selection of iDVD themes including motion menus and soundtracks. You can use your own audio, or still images and video as backgrounds (the Media pane gives easy access to your iTunes and iPhoto libraries, and to your iMovie projects) and third-party themes are available from sites such as: www.idvdthemes.com.

Slideshow
The slideshow is a great feature allowing you to show off your photos with background music and you can include navigation arrows for viewers to skip between photos with their DVD remote.

Preview and burn
While creating your DVD you can turn off motion menus to give your nerves a rest. The Map button lets you check the structure of your project: a worthwhile precaution when using hierarchical menus. Also, rather than risk an imperfect production, be sure to test menus and controls before burning your DVD.

1. Settings

The Settings pane gives you control over: background, motion duration and transition, and audio; the font, color, size, alignment and shadowing of text; and the shape, position and size of buttons. You can also create short movies in iMovie to use as motion buttons.

2. Status

The MPEG-2 encoding required for DVDs takes a reasonable time to process, so the Status pane gives you an idea of how well the background processing is progressing. It also shows how close your project is getting to iDVD's limits.

Digital video camera
Start with a DV camera with iLink (FireWire) connection, and with a single click import your video.

Edit footage with iMovie
Organize and edit clips by dragging them into the timeline, then add transitions and effects.

Make your DVD with iDVD
Create animated menus, buttons, slideshows, choose the audio and encode the video in iDVD.

Burn a DVD for playback
Preview the DVD with the menu control, then burn the DVD for playback on most DVD players.

iTunes

For anybody who has been converting their CDs to MP3 for more than a year, the need to manage an MP3 collection is a constant challenge. iTunes allows you to put your music into a virtual jukebox and provides you with some great playlist features. It can also automatically create playlists based on details such as the year the song was recorded, or even your most frequently played songs. iTunes also supports the AAC format which provides better music quality for a given file size.

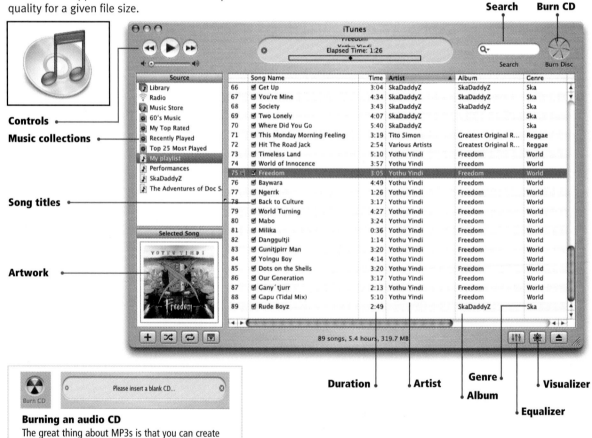

Search

Burn CD

Controls

Music collections

Song titles

Artwork

Duration

Artist

Genre

Album

Visualizer

Equalizer

Burning an audio CD
The great thing about MP3s is that you can create your own 'best of' collections. Collect your favorite songs in an iTunes collection, then click Burn CD and iTunes will convert your MP3s to CD audio format, then burn them as an audio CD. iTunes can also burn an MP3 CD which is playable on other computers and many personal CD players.

HOT TIP

What song is that?
If you have an Internet connection, iTunes will use the Gracenote service to look up track names and other details when you play or import a CD. If you normally work offline, go to iTunes > Preferences > General and uncheck Connect to Internet when needed. When you are online, insert a CD and choose Advanced > Get CD Track Names.

Radio

If you've got a reasonable Internet connection, you can listen to an increasing number of online radio stations categorized by decade, genre or spoken word. The Bit Rate column will give you an indication of the bandwidth requirements and your likely success at an uninterrupted listen.

Equalizer

A welcome addition to iTunes 2.0 was the Equalizer allowing you to choose from a number of presets depending on the type of audio you're listening to. Among the 22 presets are: Acoustic, Rock, Spoken Word, Small Speakers, Electronic, Jazz, Latin, Piano, Hip-Hop, Dance, Classical, Vocal Booster, Pop, Bass Booster, Treble Booster, Bass Reducer, Lounge, Vocal Booster.

Encoding

To 'rip' (encode) a CD, load it into the Mac's drive, wait a few moments for it to appear in iTunes, then click the Import button at the top right corner. 'Ripping' a disc involves compressing the CD quality audio into MP3 or AAC format (at around 1/10th the size). MP3 and AAC audio quality is dependent on the encoding bit rate, which iTunes allows you to specify up to 320Kbps.

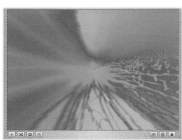

Visualizer

For a more visually pleasing experience, iTunes' Visualizer will create random swirling patterns based on the audio being played. You can choose to play the Visualizer at full screen for a 'Rave party' effect as you jump up and down to your favorite tune.

Sound Check

To have all tracks play at a consistent level, enable iTunes' Sound Check feature (iTunes > Preferences > Effects).

iTunes Music Store

Apple's iTunes music store combines the best of real-life and Internet shopping and avoids the worst of each. It's never sold out, you never have to search for a parking space, and you get immediate delivery. Over 500,000 tracks are available, including the work of many major artists as well as independent bands and labels. You can legally copy the tracks to another computer, your iPod or burn a CD. The bad news (for some) that at the time of writing it's only available to US customers.

Image courtesy of **Apple**

Software jukebox

This amazing software music jukebox, which works on both Macs and Windows-based PCs, helps you find, purchase and download the music you want for just 99c a song (in the USA). iTunes Music Store is not a subscription service. It is also a great legal alternative to file sharing.

And if you are worried about online shopping, don't be—iTunes Music Store is very, very secure. Your transactions are protected with industrial stength encryption software. No more excuses ... quick, get to that 'jukebox'!

Hearty welcome to AOL members

AOL members using iTunes 4.2 can now enjoy all that the iTunes Music Store has to offer. What a service!

Preview any song

Search for the artist, song or album of your choice

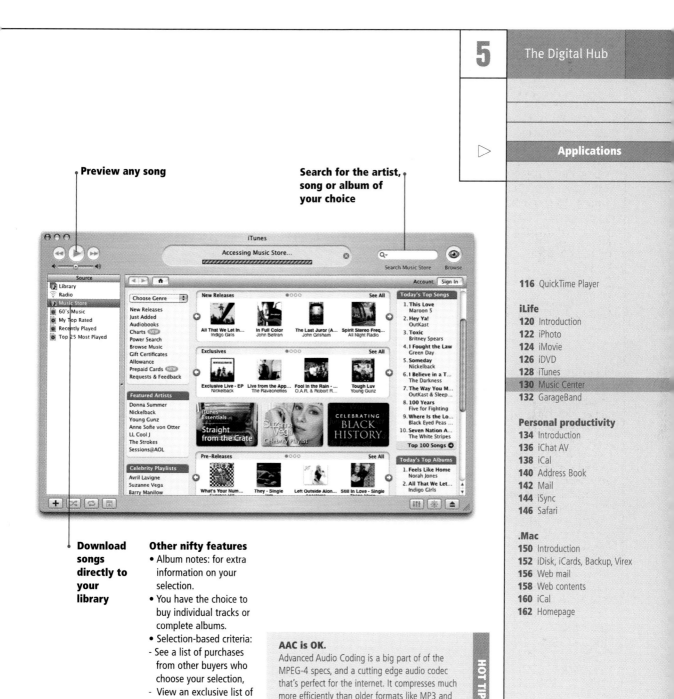

Download songs directly to your library

Other nifty features
• Album notes: for extra information on your selection.
• You have the choice to buy individual tracks or complete albums.
• Selection-based criteria:
  - See a list of purchases from other buyers who choose your selection,
  - View an exclusive list of top downloads based around your selection

AAC is OK.

Advanced Audio Coding is a big part of of the MPEG-4 specs, and a cutting edge audio codec that's perfect for the internet. It compresses much more efficiently than older formats like MP3 and delivers exceptional quality.

HOT TIP

GarageBand

Fed up with other people's music? Create your own tracks with GarageBand, the newest member of the iLife family. Assemble prerecorded loops — drums, bass, horns and more — into a backing track, then optionally record yourself playing a real instrument..

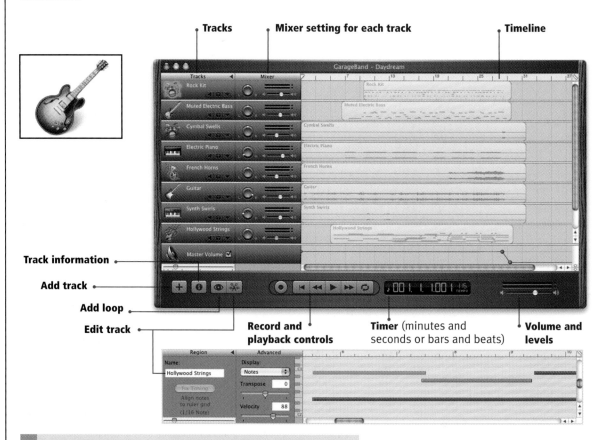

Tracks · Mixer setting for each track · Timeline

Track information

Add track

Add loop

Edit track

Record and playback controls · Timer (minutes and seconds or bars and beats) · Volume and levels

HOT TIP

HARNESSING POWER

GarageBand uses a lot of processing power, and it isn't too hard to make even a late-model Mac stumble under the load as you add more and more tracks. Adjusting the Monitors system preference to 1024 by 768 resolution and thousands of colors may help, and if you're using a iBook or PowerBook, select Highest Performance in the Energy Saver system preference. But the real problem is most likely the number of software instruments you're using. Workarounds are to avoid the use of sound effects, or to 'mix down' a group of tracks once they're exactly right by exporting to iTunes and then reimporting the resulting audio track into a fresh GarageBand project.

Recording

You can record your own tracks using the Mac's built-in microphone, but the quality might suffer thanks to noise from the disk drive and fan — or simply due to the mike's limitations. With some models, you can plug an external mike (or the output from an instrument) into the Mac's microphone socket; the alternative is to use a USB adaptor. Several are qualified for use with GarageBand, including models from Digidesign, Edirol, and M-Audio. Some users report success using PCI audio digitizers, or the audio side of video digitizers.

Effects

Maybe your live recording doesn't sound quite the way you wanted. Choose Tracks > Show Track Info and apply one of GarageBand's preset effects, whether that's Classic Rock guitar, or Male Basic vocals. Click the Details triangle and fine-tune the settings — perhaps a little more reverb and a bit less bass will hide the imperfections.

Want more loops?

If the standard selection of loops isn't enough for you, Apple's GarageBand Jam Pack adds another 2000 to the collection, along with more instruments and guitar amp settings.

Export

The finished piece can be exported as a sound file to iTunes (File > Export to iTunes) with the playlist, composer, and album names specified in GarageBand > Preferences > Export. From there, it can be used in an iMovie project or as a soundtrack for a iPhoto slideshow, or burned to CD. To convert the track to an AAC or MP3 file, pick the required encoder and settings in iTunes > Preferences > Importing, then select the track and choose Advanced > Convert Selection to AAC/MP3.

New	⌘N
Open...	⌘O
Open Recent	▶
Close	⌘W
Save	⌘S
Save As...	⇧⌘S
Revert to Saved	
Export to iTunes	

MIDI IMPORT

To import MIDI files into GarageBand, try Dent du Midi (homepage.mac.com/beryrinaldo).

Personal Productivity

In addition to the iLife suite, all Macs ship with a collection of software aimed at increasing your personal productivity. iCal lets you schedule your time; Address Book keeps track of your contacts; iSync syncs your contacts and schedules with your iPod, Palm PDA, or Bluetooth phone; iChat AV lets you chat with friends; Mail lets you manage email and avoid spam; and Safari lets you navigate the Web in true Mac fashion. All these programs are also included when you buy Mac OS X as an upgrade for an existing computer, and some are available for free download.

iChat AV

Text, voice or video chat over the Internet with other iChat AV users or those of AOL Instant Messenger (AIM) for Windows. Transfer files directly to the person you're chatting with. See pages 136-137.

iCal

Create calendars, share them online with your .Mac account and sync them with iSync to your phone or Palm PDA. Save time by subscribing to published calendars showing (eg) public holidays and sports events. See pages 138-139.

Safari

Mac OS X's own web browser. Fast and standards compliant. Provides protection against uninvited popup ads, and has a very convenient bookmarks manager that integrates with Address Book and .Mac. See pages 146-149.

Mail

A full-featured email client that ties straight into your .Mac account and also lets you manage spam email. Integrates with Address Book so you can keep all contact details in one place. See pages 142-143.

Address Book

Keep track of contacts with fields for phone, address, Web site, email address, and locate them via online maps. Integrates with Mail and applications from other companies. See pages 140-141.

iSync

Sync your Address Book contacts, iCal calendars and To Do lists with your Palm PDA or Bluetooth mobile phone. Also syncs data with other Macs and the .Mac online service. See pages 144-145.

iChat AV

Faster than email, more discrete than a phone call, and cheaper than dialling long-distance, 'instant messaging' has taken the world by storm. With Mac OS X 10.3, having a conversation via keyboard couldn't be easier, thanks to its free, built-in instant-messaging tool, iChat. What's more, iChat AV now handles audio and video as well — but you'll need a broadband connection and a iSight or other FireWire DV camera or Web cam.

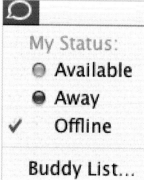

Who are you?
Before you can chat, you'll need a .Mac or AOL/AIM 'screen name', such as your .Mac username (if you've subscribed to Apple's optional .Mac service). If you already have a screen name, enter it and your password into the Accounts panel of iChat's Preferences. If you do not, register with AOL (www.aim.com) or Apple (www.mac.com).

Instant menu
To add this handy menu to your menu bar, put a tick in the 'Show status in menu bar' checkbox in the General panel in iChat's Preferences. From this menu, you can easily logon, logoff, and open your buddies list, from which you can initiate a chat session with any friends or colleagues who are online.

Chat away
To chat with someone on your local network, double-click their name in iChat's Rendezvous window. To chat with someone in your buddies list, double-click their name in the Buddy List window. To add someone to your buddies list, select 'Add a Buddy' from iChat's Buddies menu. If you've already added this person to your Mac OS X Address Book, just click on their name and then the 'Select Buddy' button. To bypass the Mac OS X Address Book, click the 'New Person' button, then enter your buddy's IM service type (.Mac or AIM/AOL) and screen name.

Look and listen

The AV in iChat AV stands for audio and video. Armed with a broadband connection and a suitable camera, you can videoconference with people around the world. If you don't have the camera, you can still have a voice conversation. Instead of double-clicking on a buddy's name to start the session, double-click the green phone or camera icon next to it. The Buddies menu lets you invite them to one-way audio or video chats.

iChat AV is designed to work with routers, but if you do have difficulty in establishing audio or video sessions, the Apple document docs.info.apple.com/articl e.html?artnum=93208 may help you configure the correctly. It also provides advice on firewall configuration, which you'll need to follow if you want to use iChat with Rendezvous.

The other side

Videoconferencing between Mac and Windows is possible with iChat AV 2.1 and AOL Instant Messenger 5.5. So there's no excuse for not chatting with your brother just because he uses Windows!

Webcams and videoconferencing

Ecamm's iChatUSBCam (www.ecamm.com/mac/ichatusbcam/) allows the use of most USB webcams with iChat AV, and also permits videoconferencing on some slower G3-based Macs.

HOT TIP

iCal

The point of the digital hub is seamless integration and improved organization. Your digital video and photos, MP3s and DVDs might be organized, but how about you? iCal allows you to get on top of your schedule by: showing potential time conflicts; setting timely email or audio reminders; using daily, weekly and monthly views; providing a linked To Do list; and adding a Web publishing option for your calendars.

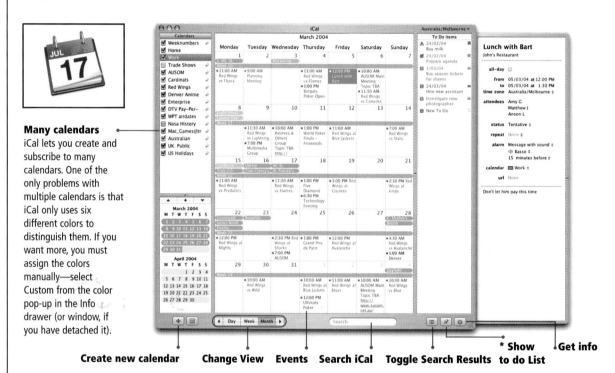

Many calendars
iCal lets you create and subscribe to many calendars. One of the only problems with multiple calendars is that iCal only uses six different colors to distinguish them. If you want more, you must assign the colors manually—select Custom from the color pop-up in the Info drawer (or window, if you have detached it).

Create new calendar   **Change View**   **Events**   **Search iCal**   **Toggle Search Results**   *** Show to do List**   **Get info**

Subscribing to calendars
Apple provides a number of calendars at the iCal web site (www.apple.com/ical) such as public holidays, sporting events, music tours and even Apple Store events. Visit: iCalShare.com

To Do Lists (*)
iCal lets you keep track of tasks with a handy To Do list which can be shown and hidden using the Pin icon in the bottom right corner of the iCal interface. You can also check tasks off as they are completed.

Publish a calendar
Using a .Mac membership, you can publish your iCal calendars online. You can let iCal automatically update your online calendar as you change your local calendar. You can also publish iCal calendars on any WebDAV server.

Festival
location

all-day ☑
from 05/03/04
to 05/03/04
attendees None
status None ⇕
repeat Custom... ⇕

Frequency: Yearly ⇕

Every 1 year(s) in:

Jan	Feb	Mar	Apr
May	Jun	Jul	Aug
Sept	Oct	Nov	Dec

☑ On the:
first ⇕   Saturday ⇕

Cancel   OK

Lunch with Bart
John's Restaurant

all-day ☐
from 05/03/04 at 12:00 PM
to 05/03/04 at 1:30 PM
time zone Australia/Melbourne ⇕
attendees Amy G
Matthew J
Anson L
status Tentative ⇕
repea   None
Message
alarm ✓ Message with sound
Email
Open file
calenda Display a message with a sound (Basso), 15 minutes before
url None

Don't let him pay this time

Name
Jackie Adams
Mischa Dees
Paul O'Brien
Invented Person
Heinrich Schwartz
Charles Shi
Bob Smith
Stephen Smith

116 QuickTime Player

Make it recurring
For an event which recurs such as birthdays, anniversaries or religious holidays, you can select the exact date or the day of the month such as the first Sunday of the month. You can also specify how long you want this event to recur for.

Set some reminders
If you need to be reminded occasionally, iCal has some insurance against forgetting the unforgettable. You can choose to be reminded by an onscreen dialog, an

alert sound or an email. You can also individually specify when you'll be reminded by each alert, so you can give yourself a few timely reminders.

Invite your contacts
Taking advantage of the Address Book, you can invite your contacts to an event by dragging them onto the event from the 'Show the People' window in iCal. When your list of invitees is complete, click on the Attendees label in the Info drawer (or window) and choose Send Invitations.

RECORD AN EVENT

repea   None
Message
alarm ✓ Message with sound
Email
Open file
calenda Display a message with a sound (Bas
url None
Don't let him pay this time

You can use the Info drawer (or window) to enter details of your event. You can enter the title of the event, duration, the calendar it is attached to and event's status such as Tentative, Cancelled or Confirmed.

LAST WORD

○ ○ ○   Event Info

139

Address Book

For most people, the primary use of Address Book is to store email addresses—but there's more to it that that. Address Book is a useful contact manager that works hand in hand with other Mac OS X applications and your other communications devices.

Click on the 'home' or 'work' label, and a menu appears offering to retrieve a map showing that address (in areas served by MapQuest) or to copy the address for pasting into a letter or other document. Click a phone number's label to select Large Type for ease of dialling. If your Mac and phone are both Bluetooth-equipped, select Dial With and Address Book will place the call for you.

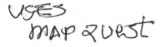

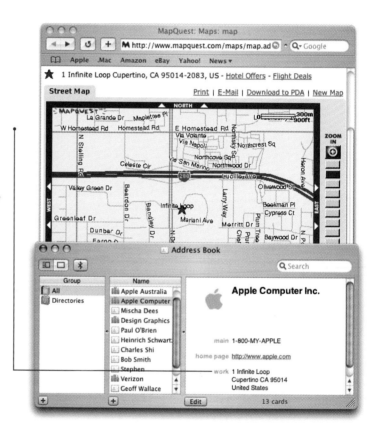

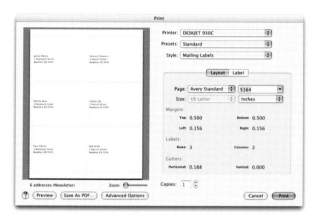

Address labels

Need to print a bunch of mailing labels at holiday time or to send a newsletter? Just select the contacts—that's easier if you have already collected them into a group—and select File > Print. Choose the type of label you're using and click Print.

Fax integration

Address Book also integrates with Mac OS X's fax capability. In almost any application, choose File > Print, then click Fax. Click the button that looks like a head and shoulders silhouette at the top right of the dialog, double-click on the relevant Address Book entries and the fax numbers will be transferred.

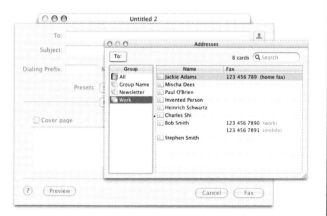

ELECTRONIC SECRETARY
Turn on Speakable Items in the Speech system preference and you can literally tell Address Book to look up phone numbers or send emails

HOT TIP

Mail

Fast, fabulous email–trustworthy, easy and fun. Sending messages via email is still the most popular use of the Internet. To find out what all the fuss is about, fire up Mac OS X's built-in email program, called Mail.

Little black book
We typed 'Inv' and Mail entered the rest of this name and address, because it found 'Invented Person' and her email address in Mac OS X's Address Book, where we had recorded it earlier. If someone sends you an email, you can quickly add them to Address Book by holding down the Control key and clicking on the From: field of the incoming message and selecting 'Add to Address Book' Otherwise, select Address Book from Mail's Window menu to import addresses or add them manually.

Picture perfect
To add a picture to your message, just drag it into your message window. Their own email program will determine whether your pen pals see the picture in the body of the message or as an attachment. To make it easier for other email programs to display your pictures and to make them smaller for emailing), use Preview (in Mac OS X's Applications folder to save them as well-compressed JPEGs.

Miss manners
Always add a meaningful subject line to your email message. This is good etiquette, because it will help your pen pals to find your message after they file it among dozens.

Color and movement
Click the Fonts and Colors buttons to decorate your email message, but be warned: some email programs could have difficulty displaying any message you've decorated in this way. To strip all decoration from your message, select Make Plain Text from Mail's Format menu. To create all future messages as plain text, select Plain Text from the Format pop-up menu in the Composing panel of Mail's Preferences.

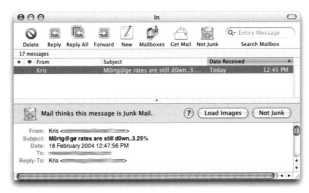

Spam, spam or spam

Junk email–often called 'spam', after a famous Monty Python skit–can take all the fun out of email, until you discover the Junk Mail filter included with Mail 1.2 and later. The filter is in training mode when you start using Mail. Teach it to recognize spam by clicking the Junk button within each piece of spam it misses, and the Not Junk button within every message it falsely accuses. Once Mail has learnt the difference between spam and desirable email, select Preferences from Mail's Mail menu, then select the Junk Mail pane. Click the radio button for 'Move it to the Junk mailbox (Automatic)'. To have mail simply delete all spam, click the Advanced button in the Junk Mail pane, then select Delete Message under Perform the following actions..

Dude, where's my mail?

If you have problems reading all your mail while connected to the Internet and are sometimes warned that your mailbox is full, then your email account may be using a technology called IMAP behind the scenes. (Apple's .Mac email service defaults to using IMAP, for example.)
- Short-term solution: transfer your mail from the IMAP server to your own Mac. To do this, select a mailbox linked to the IMAP account, then select 'Synchronize Account' from Mail's Mailbox menu. Wait while Mail copies the messages, then select 'Go Offline' from the Mailbox menu.
- Long-term solution: force Mail to transfer every message from the server to your Mac immediately. To do this, select the IMAP account in the Accounts panel of Mail's Preferences and then click the Edit button. Tick the 'Remove from server after retrieving a message' checkbox under then Advanced tab, and select 'Right away' from the pop-up menu.

iSync

iSync adds to Apple's digital hub foundation by allowing you to connect and synchronize contact and scheduling data between your Mac and your mobile phone, Palm-compatible PDA, iPod and .Mac account. This means that the information on your iMac will be wirelessly (and effortlessly) synchronized with your choice of many Bluetooth- enabled Sony Ericsson, Nokia, and Siemens phones, and with some Motorola phones by plugging in a USB cable.

What can you sync with iSync?

- Compatible Palm OS devices: Any Palm OS devices capable of syncing with HotSync 3.0 or later and Palm Desktop 4.0 or later for Mac OS X.
- Compatible mobile phones: Sony Ericsson T630 , T610, T616, T68i, P900, P800, T608, Z600; Ericsson R520, T39m, T39c, and T68; Nokia 3650, 3660, 3600, 3620, 6600, 7650, N-Gage Siemens

SX1, S55, S56; Motorola T720, v60i, v60i, v66, v60t, v60t, c350, c331g, c331t, c333g. (Some phones require Mac OS X 10.3.2 or later)

- Other compatible devices: Any Apple

iPod (including iPod Mini) using version 2.0 of iPod software, Pocket PC and many Sony Clie models with additional software from mark/space (www.markspace.com).

.Mac

iSync allows you to synchronize your work and home Macs by storing Address Book and iCal data plus your Safari bookmarks on your .Mac account. By storing the latest information on your .Mac account, you always have access to the most recently updated information regardless of which one of your Macs you may be using.

iPod

With the recent iPod software (version 1.2 or later), you can use iSync to transfer your Mac OS X Address Book contacts and iCal calendar info from your computer to your iPod. iPod software version 2.0 adds the ability to transfer iCal 'to do' items. To synchronize your iPod, choose Add Device in iSync's Devices menu, double-click the iPod in the Add Device window to add it to the devices you want synced.

No Bluetooth?

If you didn't take the Bluetooth option when buying your Mac (or it wasn't available), don't despair. You can easily add a USB Bluetooth adaptor. Apple sells the D-Link DBT-120, which 'just works' with recent Mac OS X Bluetooth software—just plug in the adaptor and you're away. Other manufacturers, including Belkin, also offer Mac OS X-compatible USB Bluetooth adaptors.

Palm OS device

iSync can synchronize your Address Book contacts, iCal calendars and To Do information on your Mac with your Palm's contacts and calendar. Palm synchronization requires the installation of Palm Desktop 4.0 or later and iSync Palm Conduit 1.2 or later plus HotSync 3.0 or later.

Like adding an iPod, you need to choose Add Device in iSync's Devices menu, then double-click the Palm device in the Add Device window to add it to the devices you want synced. Synchronisation must be initiated by running HotSync on the Palm.

Mobile phone

iSync allows you to wirelessly sync a number of Bluetooth-enabled phones such as the Sony Ericsson T68i to your Mac to synchronize events and appointments, names, phone numbers and email addresses. A Bluetooth-equipped Mac can transfer data wirelessly over several feet so you don't have to manually enter details into your phone. Some Motorola phones can be synchronized via a USB cable, but they don't sync 'to do' items.

iCal

iSync multiplies the usefulness of iCal by allowing you to travel with your most up-to-date appointment information. Even more useful is that any details you enter into your mobile phone or PDA while away from your Mac will be synchronized when you return to the office or home.

Address Book

Like iCal, the Address Book becomes indispensable when used in concert with iSync. Now wherever you enter contact information, those details can be synchronized with your mobile phone, PDA and Mac giving you the most up-to-date information without the hassle of typing it in three times.

TOO MUCH?

Apple's iCal is a great tool and you can certainly get carried away subscribing to every available calendar. When using iSync, toggle off some calendars so you don't overload your poor old phone.

HOT TIP

Safari

The days of Apple relying on other companies' web browsers ended with the arrival of Safari. There's nothing stopping you from staying with Internet Explorer or one of the other browsers, but many Mac users say Safari is their browser of choice.

Tabbed browsing
Tabbed browsing is an acquired taste, but a real convenience once you get used to it. When you open links in new tabs, you can quickly switch back and forth between pages. The advantage over opening multiple windows is that a tab never becomes completely obscured. To enable this feature, select Safari > Preferences, click Tabs, then check the Enable Tabbed Browsing box. Experiment with the other two settings to suit the way you work.

HOT TIP

OPENING A NEW TAB
Command-clicking on a link opens it in a new tab, and Command-clicking on a bookmark has the same effect.

Bookmarks manager
Click here for quick access to the bookmarks manager.

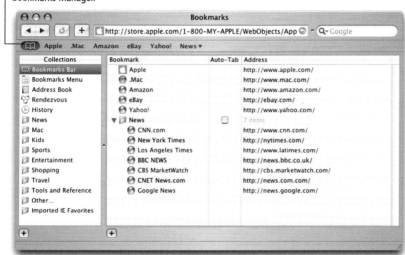

Bookmarks

Safari provides a very convenient system for managing bookmarks. Choose Bookmarks > Show All Bookmarks to reach the bookmarks manager, and double-click on a bookmark to open that page. Create a new bookmark for the current web page by choosing Bookmarks > Add Bookmark. Pick an appropriate folder for the new bookmark, as it pays to be organized from the start! Rearrange bookmarks by dragging them into a different order or into a different collection or subfolder.

Put your most frequently used bookmarks into the Bookmarks Bar, and the not-quite-so-frequently used into the Bookmarks menu. Create new collections or subfolders by clicking the small + buttons at the foot of the Collections or Bookmarks columns. Subfolders within the Bookmarks Bar or Bookmarks menu act as submenus, and this reduces clutter. Delete unwanted bookmarks by dragging them into the Trash (in the Dock) or by selecting them and pressing the Delete key.

Three of the collections are automatically managed. The Address Book collection displays any URLs stored in your Address Book. The Rendezvous collection contains URLs discovered by Rendezvous (most likely for Rendezvous-enabled printers or other devices).
The History collection contains the web pages that you have recently visited.

Safari

It's fair to say that Apple's developers drew inspiration from several different browsers while they were developing Safari. Both Auto-Fill and tabbed windows have appeared elsewhere, but the whole package has proved very agreeable for Mac OS X users. The one fly in the ointment is the tendency for some site builders to develop pages for specific browsers, notably the Windows version of Internet Explorer.

Form Filling,
AutoFill takes the drudgery out of completing web forms with your name and address, etc. It can get the information from your Address Book card, from a list of web user names and passwords, or from forms you've previously completed. Don't use this feature without considering the security and privacy implications, as it might lead to you accidentally disclosing more information to a web site than you intended.

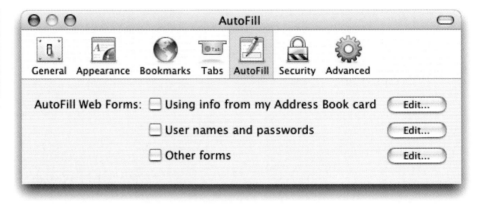

Google me this
Don't bother going to Google's home page, simply type your query directly into the search box at the top right of the window and press the Return key.

HOT TIP

CHOOSING ANOTHER BROWSER
To make a different browser the default on your system, choose Safari > Preferences, click General, and select it in the Default Web Browser menu.

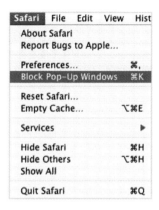

Ad reduction

Choose Safari > Block Pop-Up Windows if you're plagued by pop-up ads. There's a possibility that this feature will also interfere with sites that 'legitimate' new windows, but that's not usually a problem.

Discussion

Apple has worked hard to ensure Safari conforms to formal standards, but there is a chance you'll find a web site that doesn't work. Sometimes the problem is that the site checks for particular browsers other than Safari, more often it's just sloppy coding.

Apple is trying to make Safari more forgiving, so if you find a page that doesn't display properly, choose Safari > Report Bugs to Apple to file a report. But before you do that, make sure you're running the latest version of Safari as Apple keeps making the browser more tolerant.

KEYBOARD CAPERS

In Safari 1.2, you can move between and operate page controls such as links, buttons and lists by using the keyboard if you check 'Turn on full keyboard access' in the Keyboard Shortcuts pane of the Keyboard & Mouse system preference. Use Tab to move between controls, and Return to activate them. Activate lists by pressing the space bar, then use the up and down arrows or press the initial character of the desired item as a shortcut.

HOT TIP

.Mac

.Mac adds to your online experience with a collection of easy to use, convenient and integrated services. Upload files to share with others; synchronise important data between your home and office Macs; backup files in case disaster strikes; make your email, contacts and bookmarks available for web access; publish calendars for family and associates; build a web site in a matter of seconds; or simply send electronic postcards to say 'Our office has relocated' or 'I love you.'

iDisk
Provides online storage that acts just like a local shared disk, only slower. Sits behind many .Mac services. See pages 152-155.

iSync
Sync various data including your Address Book contacts for use online or for transfer to another Mac.

Backup
Backup your important files to iDisk, CD/DVD or a networked volume. See pages 152-155.

Mail
Check and send email via the web using your mac.com address. See pages 156-157.

Address Book
Use your online address book to simplify email addressing. Keep it in step with your Mac's Address Book via iSync. See pages 158-159.

Bookmarks
Use your Safari bookmarks from any computer, and transfer any changes back to your Mac. See pages 158-159.

iCal
Publish your calendars for web access or so other iCal users can subscribe to them. See pages 160-161.

HomePage
Convert your music CDs to MP3, manage your MP3 collection, create playlists, and transfer music to your iPod. See pages 162-163.

iCards
Send electronic postcards featuring stock or personal images to your friends, family or business contacts. See pages 152-155.

iDisk

Imagine a disk drive that was available to you from any Internet-connected Macintosh -- that's iDisk. Use it to store files you need at different locations, or to share digital photos and other content with family, friends or colleagues.

iDisk

An iDisk behaves like any other volume in the Finder, just more slowly. It shows up in the sidebar, or you can open it by choosing Go > iDisk > My iDisk (or Other User's iDisk, if appropriate). It contains a number of predefined folders that tie in with other parts of the .Mac service. Documents is for general storage. Files that other people should be able to download go in Public. Pictures is the obvious place for digital photos and other artwork — it's mandatory if you want to use them in iCards, and the most convenient place for images used on your HomePage web site. Similarly for the Music, Movies and Sites folders. Backup is the destination for files backed up to iDisk, while Library is used by iSync (and potentially other programs).

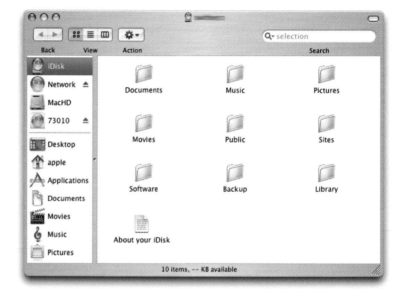

Gimme more

If the standard 100M iDisk isn't capacious enough for your needs, Apple will provide more on payment of the appropriate fee for the space you require. If you want to store hundreds of high-resolution digital photos

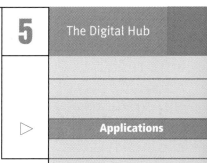

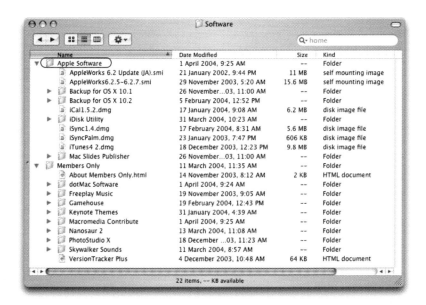

Apple Software folder

The Software folder contains programs from Apple (such as iCal and iTunes updates) plus the various 'members only' software bonuses that .Mac subscribers receive from time to time. Download the files from the iDisk by dragging them onto your desktop or into a local Finder window. The contents of the Software folder are not counted against your quota of iDisk space.

iDisk does Windows

If you need to access an iDisk from Windows XP, Apple's iDisk Utility (a free download from .Mac) makes life easier. Once mounted, the iDisk appears in the Network Drives section of My Computer. The drive name matches the .Mac user name.

153

iCards, Virex, Backup

It's not easy to find stylish electronic greeting cards—unless you're a .Mac subscriber. For that personalized touch, create a card from one of your own photos or artworks. Although Backup can be used with local storage such as a combo drive or SuperDrive, it checks for a valid .Mac account.
Mac OS X viruses are practically unknown, but without protection from software such as Virex, there's risk of spreading infected files received from other computers. For any other problems, .Mac support is available online.

Pick a pic
Pick a picture, add a personal message and select a font. The next page lets you add one or more recipients.

Creating cards
You can create cards from pictures that you've uploaded to your iDisk. For example, you can drag and drop pictures from iPhoto into the Pictures folder in your iDisk.

Backup

Backup is a simple to use backup program. It works with external hard disks (including iPods) and network servers (including iDisk), plus internal and some external CD and DVD burners. Find out more about Backup.

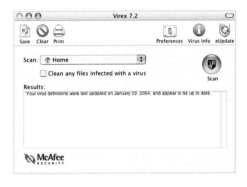

Virex

Virex, a popular antivirus program for Mac OS X, is included with your .Mac membership, so be sure to download and install it. Use Virex to scan downloaded files, email attachments, and CDs or other removable media. If you don't have a permanent Internet connection, it's important to click the eUpdate button at least once a month when you are online.

Support

The .Mac support page lets you quickly check whether all parts of the service are available, and seek help from Apple's online resources or from other .Mac users.

Web Mail

Web mail is a major attraction for some .Mac users. Apart from the ability to send and receive email using your own account on practically any computer with a web browser, it also provides an easy way of deleting unwanted messages without having to download them in their entirety.

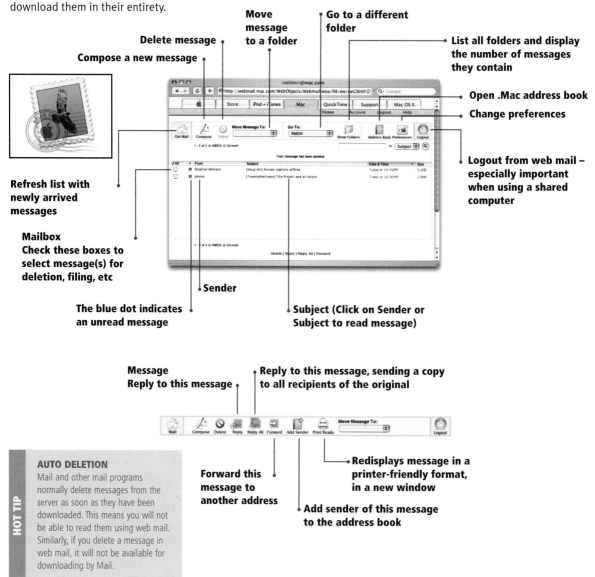

Move message to a folder

Go to a different folder

Delete message

Compose a new message

List all folders and display the number of messages they contain

Open .Mac address book

Change preferences

Refresh list with newly arrived messages

Logout from web mail – especially important when using a shared computer

Mailbox
Check these boxes to select message(s) for deletion, filing, etc

Sender

The blue dot indicates an unread message

Subject (Click on Sender or Subject to read message)

Message
Reply to this message

Reply to this message, sending a copy to all recipients of the original

Forward this message to another address

Redisplays message in a printer-friendly format, in a new window

Add sender of this message to the address book

Including the original text helps the receiver follow the conversation

Bcc stands for Blind carbon cop–use when you don't want multiple receivers to see each others' addresses

Keep copies of your own messages for future reference

Consider carefully whether receivers want your messages cluttered with a picture or lengthy signature block

Moving deleted messages to the Deleted Messages folder gives you a second chance

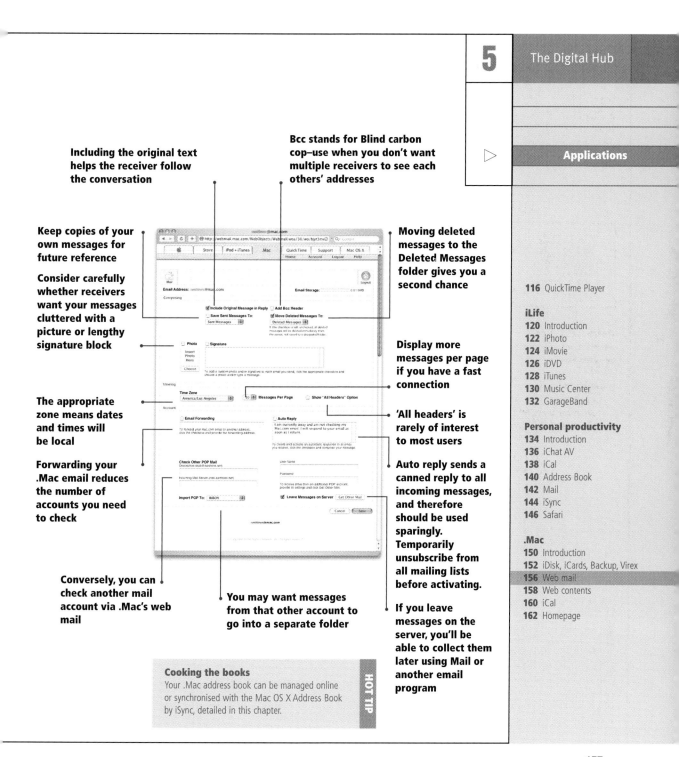

Display more messages per page if you have a fast connection

The appropriate zone means dates and times will be local

'All headers' is rarely of interest to most users

Forwarding your .Mac email reduces the number of accounts you need to check

Auto reply sends a canned reply to all incoming messages, and therefore should be used sparingly. Temporarily unsubscribe from all mailing lists before activating.

Conversely, you can check another mail account via .Mac's web mail

You may want messages from that other account to go into a separate folder

If you leave messages on the server, you'll be able to collect them later using Mail or another email program

Cooking the books
Your .Mac address book can be managed online or synchronised with the Mac OS X Address Book by iSync, detailed in this chapter.

HOT TIP

Web contents

Once you've used iSync to set up the synchronization of your Address Book and .Mac account, follow the Address Book link from the .Mac home page (www.mac.com). [bookmarks sync] After an initial synchronization between the iSync information stored in your iDisk and the .Mac server, you'll be presented with your web-based address book.

• Change preferences

• Log out from .Mac web mail

Create new record • **• Edit existing record** **• Incoming email**

• Delete record **• Compose new email**

Check these boxes to select record(s) for deletion, mail destination, etc •

Click on a record to • display full detail

Address book preferences
Change the presentation of your contacts list, and iSync setting.

Warning!
With every type of synchronization, take care to understand the difference between replace and merge, and when you are replacing be sure to do it in the right direction. Normally, merge is the appropriate choice unless you're sure you want to replace one set of information with another.

Bookmarks (Safari)

Some people consider bookmarks passé, as they find it almost as quick to find the page again using Google. Others keep substantial and well-organized lists of sites they have found useful. If you keep any number of bookmarks, it's handy to have them available wherever you go.

iSync and Bookmarks

Once you've used iSync to set up synchronization of Safari bookmarks with your .Mac account, follow the Bookmarks link from the .Mac home page (www.mac.com). After an initial synchronization between the iSync information stored in your iDisk and the .Mac bookmarks server, you'll be invited to open your bookmarks. They will appear in a separate browser window.

Bookmarks and browsers

You may use your .Mac bookmarks from other browsers such as Internet Explorer on Mac OS X or Windows. Although you can only sync bookmarks with Safari, you may manually add and delete bookmarks regardless of the browser.

To avoid typing errors, drag and drop the URL from the main browser window into the Bookmark URL box in the Bookmarks window.

When using browsers other than Safari, it's best to log into the .Mac web site first. Going directly to bookmarks.mac.com seems reliable only if you have chosen the Save my password option in Bookmarks preferences. That's something you may want to avoid for security reasons.

Talking of security, always remember to logout from Bookmarks rather than simply closing the window when using a shared computer.

iCal

Publishing iCal calendars makes them available for use by other iCal users and by anyone with a web browser. It also provides a mechanism for keeping your calendars synchronized across multiple computers.

Publish

Publish a calendar from iCal by choosing Calendar > Publish. This is simplest if you have a .Mac account, but any other WebDAV server can be used instead. Other iCal users can incorporate your calendar into theirs by subscribing (Calendar > Subscribe). This mechanism is especially useful for events of interest to a particular community, such as a company, club, or church. The publishing process simultaneously makes your calendar available on the web, which is useful if you need to access it while travelling or from a Windows PC.

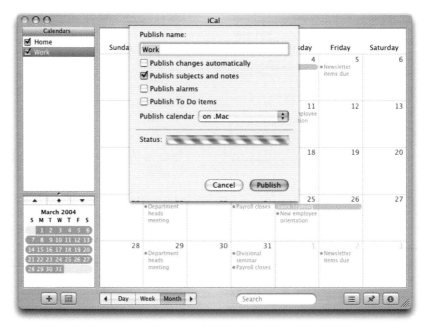

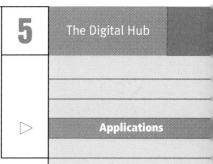

iSync

Configuring iSync to synchronize iCal Calendars and To
Do items will update the information stored on your
iDisk. Synchronizing another Mac — maybe your iBook
or an office computer — with your .Mac account will
keep both calendars in step with each other.

HomePage

Building a web site with .Mac's HomePage is about as simple as it gets. Pre-designed templates take the hard work out of the task, so all you need to do is upload content such as photos, and type in the text. Creating additional pages takes a matter of moments, and it's easy to create multiple sites comprising interlinked pages. You can even password-protect a site to limit access to your chosen few.

Site identity
Start with the purpose of your site. HomePage has templates for photo albums, movie galleries, resumes and more. Then pick the style that provides the best feel for your project.

Picture perfect
We've chosen a photo album, so the next step is to choose from the images already uploaded to our iDisk. Click on the iDisk folder that contains the photos to be displayed (most likely Pictures, but you may want to arrange the collection into subfolders so that different parts of the collection can go on different pages), then click the Choose button.

Personalize please
The resulting page uses placeholder text that you'll want to personalize, so click the Edit icon.

Quick preview
Enter the appropriate text and click Preview to check the appearance of your edited page.

View and visit
Happy with what you see? Then click Publish, and your new page is on the web. .Mac even offers to send an iCard invitation to those you want to visit the page. If you're not satisfied, click Edit or even Themes to make changes.

DIY
Create your own web pages using software such as Freeway (www.softpress.com) or Dreamweaver (www.macromedia.com). Some applications offer HTML output, and at a pinch you can write HTML code in TextEdit. Finished files can be uploaded to your iDisk's Sites folder.

Applications

OS X
anatomy

System Preferences

The level of importance of various Mac OS X preferences is directly proportional to the ease at which they are found. Located in the Apple menu, Dock and Applications folder (usually found in the Places sidebar of your Finder Window), the range covers everything. However, handle with caution and be aware that unless you are an administrator you won't have the authority to change as many preferences as you may like to.

System Preferences

Mac OS X gives users personal control over the system, whether the system is shared with other users or not. Each user has the ability to customize a variety of settings and maintain them separately in one central place—their very own System Preferences.

Edit   View   Window   Help

Show All Preferences   ⌘L

✓ Organize by Categories
Organize Alphabetically

.Mac
Accounts
Adobe Version Cue™
Appearance
CDs & DVDs
Classic
Date & Time
Desktop & Screen Saver
Displays
Dock
Energy Saver
Exposé
International
Keyboard & Mouse
Logitech Control Center
Network
Print & Fax
QuickTime
Security
Sharing
Software Update
Sound
Speech
Startup Disk
Universal Access

Hide Toolbar

Instant spring clean
As with all OSX windows, System Preferences provides you with different viewing choices. To view items by the type of preference, choose View>Organize by Categories.
To view items alphabetically, choose View>Organize Alphabetically

Keep your changes locked
You will discover this icon in most of your System Preferences panels. Clicking on it will prevent further changes to your settings.

Third Party System Preferences
Third party preferences are added with software installed, created by companies other than Apple. If there are any present, they will be itemised in the 'Other' category on your System Preference panel. To remove a third-party preference from System Preferences, press Ctrl and click the preference icon, then choose Remove from the resulting contextual menu.

Mac OSX lifeboat
You will discover this icon in most of your System Preferences panels. Clicking on it will take you to the help menu–providing more information on the topic at hand.

QUICK SELECT
To select a pane in System Preferences using the keyboard, type the first letter of the pane's name, then press the Space Bar to quickly open the selected pane.

HOT TIP

Appearance

Image is all important to you, which is obviously why you own, or work on, a Mac. It is therefore hardly surprising that the very first System Preference we discover under the category, Personal, is Appearance. This is where you can make general color changes to items on your screen, control where scroll arrows appear and ensure that text is displayed exactly the way you like it. Ready to make some changes? Let us begin.

When you launch the Appearance preference (System Preferences> Appearance), you will be given a number of choices regarding the overall look of buttons, menus and windows, text and lists. You can also make changes to scrolling, number of recent items and font smoothing.

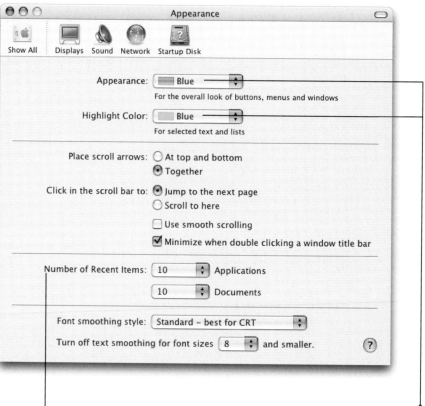

Flashback
Select the number of applications and documents you would like to appear in the Apple menu under Recent Items. (You can choose up to 50 or have none at all.)

Pick a color
Choose a color from the Appearance or Highlight Color pop-up menu to alter the overall look of buttons, menus and windows.

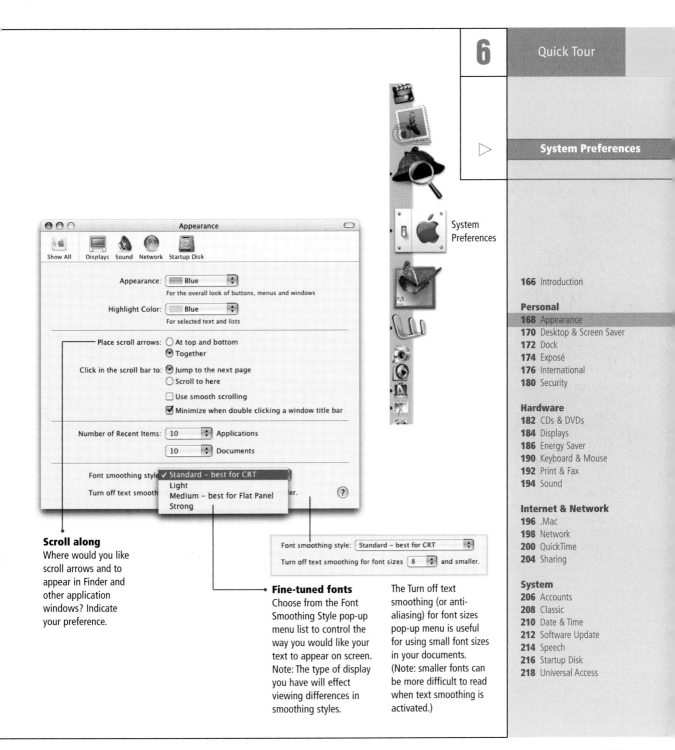

System
Preferences

Scroll along
Where would you like scroll arrows and to appear in Finder and other application windows? Indicate your preference.

Font smoothing style: Standard – best for CRT
Turn off text smoothing for font sizes 8 and smaller.

Fine-tuned fonts
Choose from the Font Smoothing Style pop-up menu list to control the way you would like your text to appear on screen. Note: The type of display you have will effect viewing differences in smoothing styles.

The Turn off text smoothing (or anti-aliasing) for font sizes pop-up menu is useful for using small font sizes in your documents. (Note: smaller fonts can be more difficult to read when text smoothing is activated.)

Desktop & Screen Saver

Mac OS X 10.3 Panther gives you a variety of choices to brighten up a dull desktop and get your Screen Saver into action. From gorgeous backgrounds to abstract patterns and colors to a photograph from any iPhoto Album, it will provide the inspiration you need to get those creative juices flowing and ease your daily stress load.

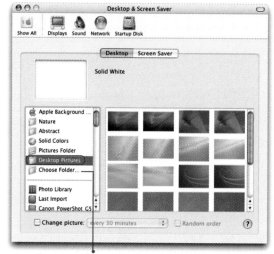

Background blitz
To change the background of your screen to one of the patterns, colors or pictures that come with Mac OS X, choose System Preferences> Desktop & Screen Saver. Select the Desktop panel and make your choice from the list provided (to the left of the panel).

Location, location
To use a picture that is filed in a different location, select Choose Folder from the list provided.

Personal best
Personal pictures can also appear on the desktop (provided that they are in your Home Pictures folder). Simply select Desktop Pictures from the list provided on your Desktop pane.

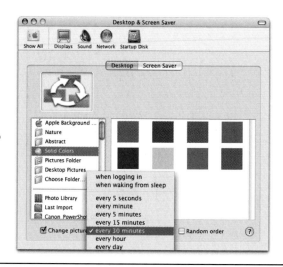

Set the pace
If you want your desktop picture to change regularly or at specific times, select the 'Change picture' checkbox and choose from the accompanying drop-down list.

Screen Saver FX

To change the effects of your Screen Saver, select System Preferences> Desktop & Screen Saver. Select the Screen Saver pane and make your choice from the list provided (to the left of the panel).

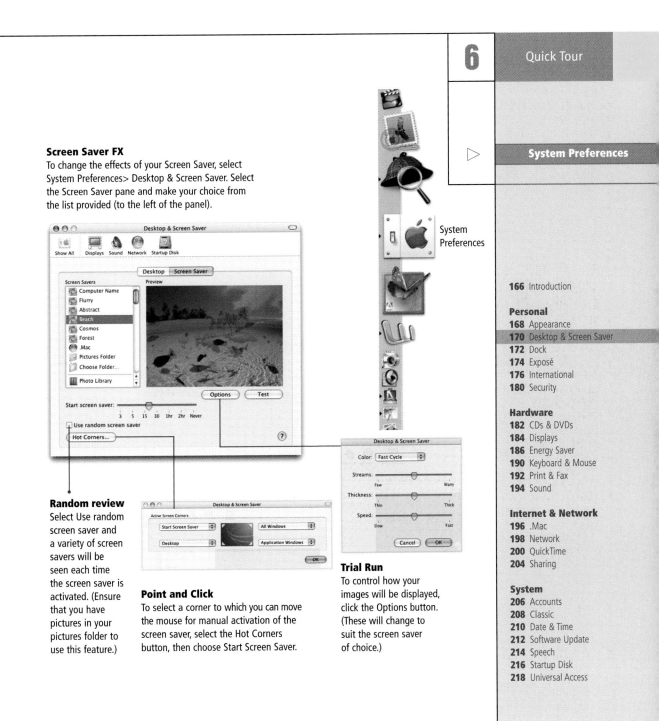

System Preferences

Random review
Select Use random screen saver and a variety of screen savers will be seen each time the screen saver is activated. (Ensure that you have pictures in your pictures folder to use this feature.)

Point and Click
To select a corner to which you can move the mouse for manual activation of the screen saver, select the Hot Corners button, then choose Start Screen Saver.

Trial Run
To control how your images will be displayed, click the Options button. (These will change to suit the screen saver of choice.)

Dock

Change the way your Dock looks and acts by adjusting your preferences. While your Dock can be positioned in various locations on your screen and automatically hidden and then shown again, icons on display can be resized, magnified and minimised using subtle effects. Discover this and more, in the Dock System Preference.

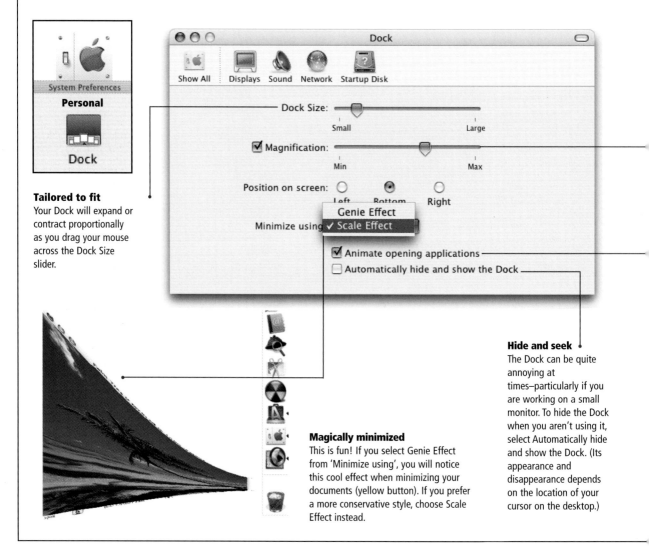

Tailored to fit
Your Dock will expand or contract proportionally as you drag your mouse across the Dock Size slider.

Magically minimized
This is fun! If you select Genie Effect from 'Minimize using', you will notice this cool effect when minimizing your documents (yellow button). If you prefer a more conservative style, choose Scale Effect instead.

Hide and seek
The Dock can be quite annoying at times–particularly if you are working on a small monitor. To hide the Dock when you aren't using it, select Automatically hide and show the Dock. (Its appearance and disappearance depends on the location of your cursor on the desktop.)

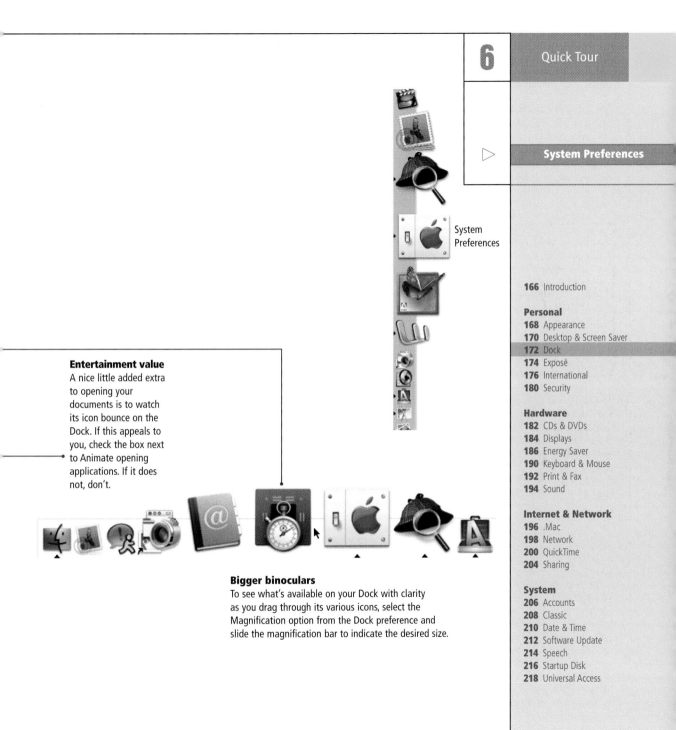

▷

System
Preferences

Entertainment value
A nice little added extra
to opening your
documents is to watch
its icon bounce on the
Dock. If this appeals to
you, check the box next
to Animate opening
applications. If it does
not, don't.

Bigger binoculars
To see what's available on your Dock with clarity
as you drag through its various icons, select the
Magnification option from the Dock preference and
slide the magnification bar to indicate the desired size.

Exposé

Do you spend too much time each day 'walking' through open windows and documents just to uncover the one you need? Are you itching to get all your window chaos into order? Exposé is the answer. Exclusive to Mac OS X 10.3 Panther, it provides you with instant access to any open window, with just one hot key. Preferences to control the way it behaves are as easy as ABC.

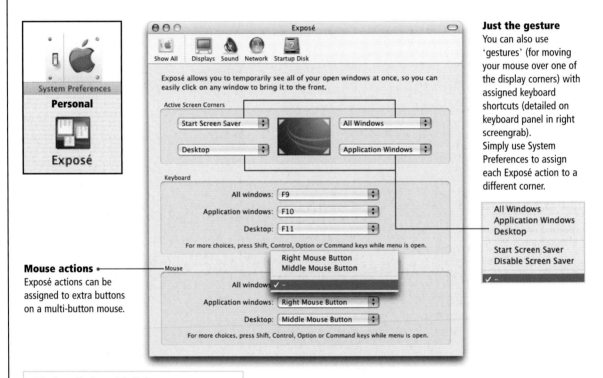

Just the gesture
You can also use 'gestures' (for moving your mouse over one of the display corners) with assigned keyboard shortcuts (detailed on keyboard panel in right screengrab).
Simply use System Preferences to assign each Exposé action to a different corner.

Mouse actions
Exposé actions can be assigned to extra buttons on a multi-button mouse.

Window finder with flair
Exposé is a fabulous feature with its advanced abilities to tile, scale and hide windows.
Keyboard shortcuts can be assigned to (a) enable instant tiling to all open windows; (b) enable tiling to windows of a specific application only and (c) hide all open windows for instant access to your desktop.
The Quartz engine works together with Exposé to neatly scale down and arrange windows, while maintaining visual quality in a reduced size.

Shrink or swim?
The All windows option in the Keyboard panel lets you choose a keyboard combination for window scaling. By default F9 tiles all open windows but this can be changed to suit. (There's a few keyboard combinations to choose from the pop-up menu provided.)

▷

Window wonderland

The keyboard panel in Exposé gives you the choice of nominating shortcut keys to display all open windows as thumbnails, view windows of the current application, or hide all windows to quickly locate a file your desktop.

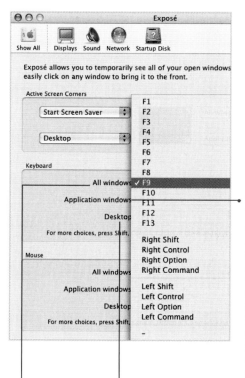

System Preferences

Tile by application

To enable windows of documents of one application to open simultaneously, choose a keyboard combination from the pop-up menu adjacent to Application windows.
By default, F10 tiles all open windows for the current application but this can be changed to suit. (There's a number of keyboard combinations to choose from the pop-up menu provided.)

Hide and seek

To have instant access to your desktop by hiding all open windows, choose a keyboard combination from the pop-up menu provided. (F11 is the default).

International

Mac OS X weaves a coat of many colors with its liberal support for international languages. Controlled through the International window, it can be accessed via System Preferences or by clicking on the flag to the right of the Help menu. (This indicates the international panel.) Not only are the abilities here more innovative than before, but it allows you to shift from language to language without reinstalling software or restarting your computer.

Multi-lingual maze
Dragging your preferred language to the top of the list (left of panel) will ensure that OS X and OS X-compatible software can work in other languages. Every button, menu and dialog box will be language selected.

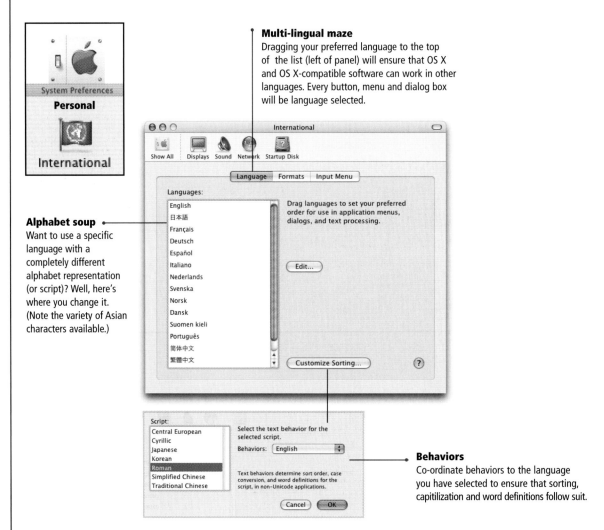

Alphabet soup
Want to use a specific language with a completely different alphabet representation (or script)? Well, here's where you change it. (Note the variety of Asian characters available.)

Behaviors
Co-ordinate behaviors to the language you have selected to ensure that sorting, capitilization and word definitions follow suit.

Pick of the crop
Selecting the Edit button from the International window allows you to choose the ones you prefer to have listed in the Language panel, up to 23 different languages are available.

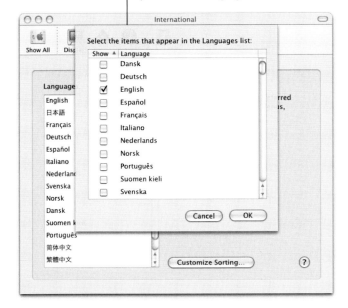

TextEdit speaks Italian ... and more
After you have specified your preferred language from the International window, open a program like Internet Explorer, Stickies, Sherlock or TextEdit (if already open, quit first and relaunch). Then, notice how every menu, button and dialog box follows suit. (The only thing it doesn't do is translate, but then again you wouldn't want to write in an unknown language, now would you?)

OPENTYPE AND UNICODE
OpenType font technology, which takes advantage of Unicode, was introduced with Mac OS X. This, combined with the International and Keyboard preferences built into the Mac, makes your computer truly international.

SYNOPSIS

System Preferences

International

Yesterday the world, today the global village. Mac OS X's International preferences panel caters for wanderlust junkies who require the date, time and/or number formatting of various regions. And, it makes it really simple for each user to customize and maintain these settings separately.

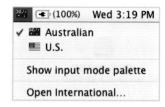

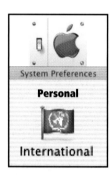

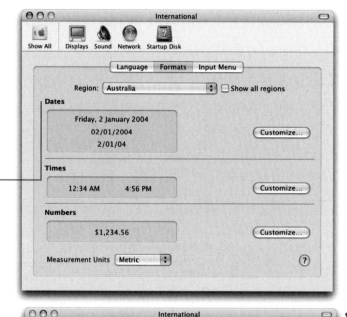

Change of format
The format for displaying date, time and numbers on your computer can be changed to suit the conventions used in a different geographic region. Note: these choices will affect the appearance of dates, times and numbers in Finder windows and numerous other applications. In this example we have nominated Australia to be the required format.

Date with destiny
When the Customize button is selected in any of the sections detailed on the Format panel, a sheet will drop down allowing you to enter the preferred format. In the case of Dates–enter details for Long Date or Short Date.

Time to choose
• Select whether to use a 12 or 24 hour clock here.
• Noon and midnight – how should they be indicated? It's your call.

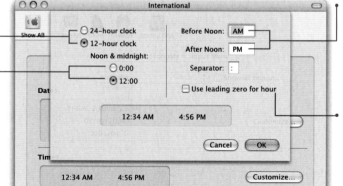

High Noon
Set your time preferences before and after noon (am or pm) and indicate the type of separating punctuation you would like between hour and minute.

Naughts and crosses
Selecting this option (also present in Date section) enables dates prior to the 10th of the month to appear with a zero prefix.

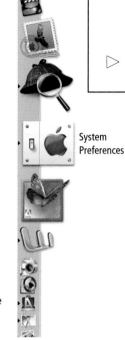

System
Preferences

Numbers galore

When you have chosen Customize from the Numbers section, specify: • Which characters you want to use when decimal numbers are displayed; • Your preference to project decimal thousands with a comma (1,000) or a point (1.000); and • Currency symbol.

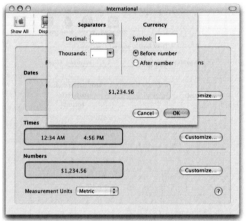

Sneak peek

Results of all changes made in the Date, Time and Numbers tabs are displayed here.

Keyboard menu

When you wish to type in another language, choose the keyboard layout or input method for that language from this menu.

Cryptic 'key' clue

Are our eyes deceiving us, or is that Keyboard Viewer hiding amongst the other Character Palettes? Indeed, we have uncovered what used to be known as Key Caps in pre-Panther versions of OSX. (See also 'Special Characters' under the Edit menu.)

Security

The Security System Preference in Mac OS X 10.3 Panther includes FileVault, to secure your home directory using the Advanced Encryption Standard with 128-bit keys. It also provides the opportunity to set passwords to • unlock FileVault accounts; • control actions such as waking or sleeping your computer and • gain access to system preferences which have been previously secured.

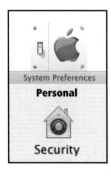

Behind bars

FileVault is perfect if the information on your computer is of a sensitive nature and needs to be kept away from prying eyes. Select the Turn On FileVault ... button to activate it. You will then be prompted to set a master password for the computer that you (or the administrator) can use in case your regular login password is forgotten. See details (right).

Password protection and more

In addition to FileVault, the Security System Preference also provides you with options to set passwords to wake your computer from sleep or the current screen saver, and offers the opportunity to allow all accounts on your Computer to • disable automatic login; • unlock each secure system preference (by means of a password) • log out after a set time of inactivity.

System
Preferences

Master key
Choosing a good password (and keeping a record of it) is just as important as having a reliable security system–the two work hand in hand.
When you launch FileVault, you will be prompted to set a master password to provide a kind of 'safety net' for your accounts.
This is a computer-wide password, set up by an administrator as a safeguard in case the set password is forgotten. (Note: only the master password can override a FileVault user's password.)

Warning: make a record of your master password and store in a safe place. This is imperative! Should you forget both your login password and your master password, you will not be able to log in to your account and your data will be irretrievable.

CDs & DVDs

Turning your attention towards System Preferences' Hardware category, the first icon you will notice is CDs & DVDs. This is the place to go to change how Mac OS X behaves when a CD or DVD is inserted. From blank CDs and DVDs to music and picture CDs and video DVDs, this preference provides you with the option to initiate numerous actions.

Actions for blank CDs and DVDs
Choose an action or instruction to be launched when a blank CD or DVD is inserted, or simply allow the incident to go unannounced. These pop-up menus provide all the options you need.

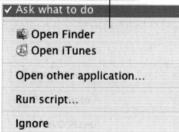

iTunes 4.2
iTunes 4.2 provides you with the perfect tools for burning CDs. It:
• lets you burn as many custom CDs as possible, in less time than it actually takes to play them;
• uses SoundCheck technology to ensure that the volume level on every CD you create is consistent;
• helps you archive your entire music library on DVDs for safekeeping (provided that you have a Mac with a SuperDrive), storing the equivalent of up to 150 CDs on each DVD-R disc;
• will span the collection of Macs and PC CD backup across multiple CDs automatically.

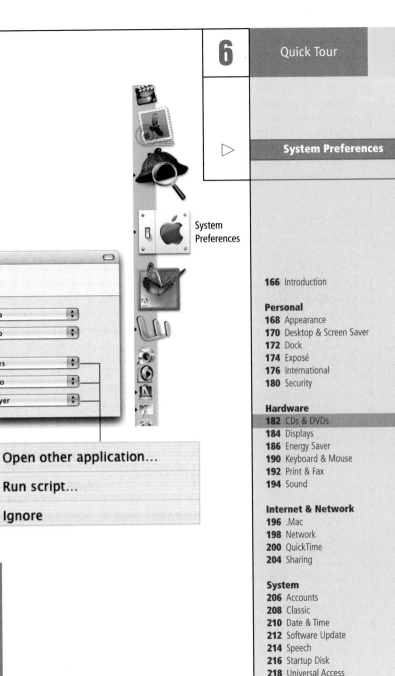

System
Preferences

CDs & DVDs

Show All   Displays   Sound   Network   Startup Disk

When you insert a blank CD: Ask what to do

When you insert a blank DVD: Ask what to do

When you insert a music CD: Open iTunes

When you insert a picture CD: Open iPhoto

When you insert a video DVD: Open DVD Player

Actions for particular CDs and DVDs
Choose an action or instruction to be
launched when a video DVD, music and/or
picture CD is inserted, or simply allow the
incident to go unannounced. (Pop-up menus
provided offer the options you need.)
Note: specific applications are temporarily
assigned to various discs by default.

Open other application...

Run script...

Ignore

Burning a DVD
• with Mac OS X, you can burn DVDs and CDs
directly from the Finder, (but ensure that iDVD
is not running at the time);
• don't use other applications that place heavy
demands on the system while burning a disc;
• before burning a DVD, ensure that you have at
least twice as much free space available on your
hard disk as your project uses. This is to allow for
encoding and burning;
• DVD-R discs cannot be burned again.

HELPFUL HINTS

Displays

Adjust your monitor exactly the way you like it with Mac OS X's display settings, which assist with: • controlling the size of screen picture and resolution; • color depth settings and calibration adjustment; • lighting adjustment; • flicker minimization and • size and positioning changes.

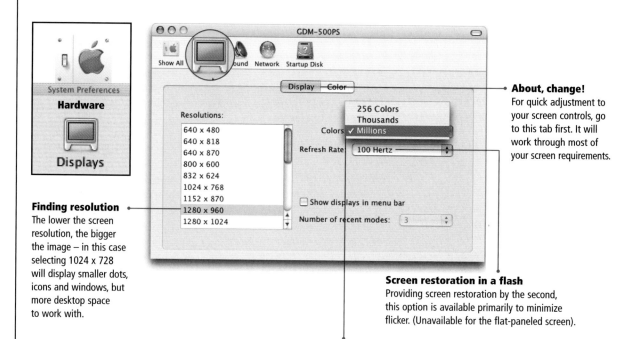

About, change!
For quick adjustment to your screen controls, go to this tab first. It will work through most of your screen requirements.

Finding resolution
The lower the screen resolution, the bigger the image – in this case selecting 1024 x 728 will display smaller dots, icons and windows, but more desktop space to work with.

Screen restoration in a flash
Providing screen restoration by the second, this option is available primarily to minimize flicker. (Unavailable for the flat-paneled screen).

Color Control
Choose from 256, Thousands and Millions of colors, and in Mac OS X there's no compromise on speed for any of them. (Generally, the higher the setting the better the image.)

SYNOPSIS

COLORSYNC AND YOUR MONITOR
ColorSync's monitor calibration system compensates for debilitation in areas such as phosphor set, ambient light and white point, to display images in their intended colors. One of the new ColorSync features in Mac OS X 10.3 Panther provides more control in customizing the color space profile of Apple displays.

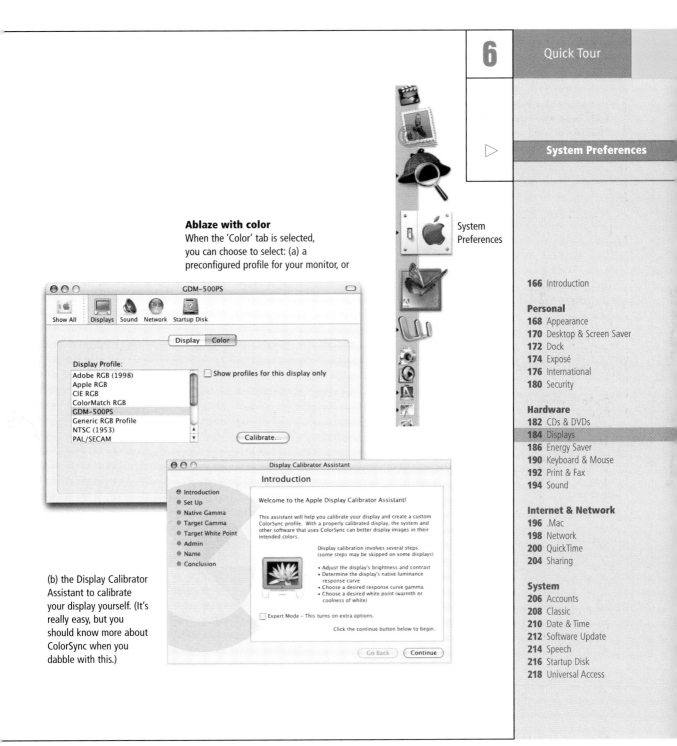

System
Preferences

Ablaze with color
When the 'Color' tab is selected,
you can choose to select: (a) a
preconfigured profile for your monitor, or

Display Profile:
Adobe RGB (1998)
Apple RGB
CIE RGB
ColorMatch RGB
GDM-500PS
Generic RGB Profile
NTSC (1953)
PAL/SECAM

Show profiles for this display only

Calibrate...

Display Calibrator Assistant

Introduction

● Introduction
● Set Up
● Native Gamma
● Target Gamma
● Target White Point
● Admin
● Name
● Conclusion

Welcome to the Apple Display Calibrator Assistant!

This assistant will help you calibrate your display and create a custom
ColorSync profile. With a properly calibrated display, the system and
other software that uses ColorSync can better display images in their
intended colors.

Display calibration involves several steps:
(some steps may be skipped on some displays)

• Adjust the display's brightness and contrast
• Determine the display's native luminance
  response curve
• Choose a desired response curve gamma
• Choose a desired white point (warmth or
  coolness of white)

☐ Expert Mode - This turns on extra options.

Click the continue button below to begin.

Go Back   Continue

(b) the Display Calibrator
Assistant to calibrate
your display yourself. (It's
really easy, but you
should know more about
ColorSync when you
dabble with this.)

185

Energy Saver

Energy Saver provides you with settings to optimize use of power. Using this neat preference, you can schedule startup and shutdown of your system. There are even separate options to put your hard drive and display to sleep. (For example: you may wish to take a break from your computer while burning a CD. The hard drive needs to perform, but the display can go to sleep.)

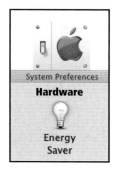

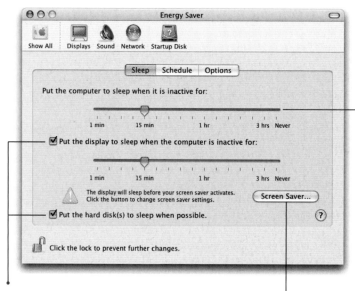

Gentle lullaby
When your computer is 'asleep', it is turned on in a low power mode and takes less time to wake up than it does for the computer to start up after being turned off. Choose Apple>Sleep to put your computer to sleep instantly or choose exactly when to put it to sleep (after a specific time of inactivity). These settings are controlled in System Preferences > Energy Saver, then choose the Sleep panel. (Drag the top slider to see how long the computer should be idle before going to sleep.)

Display takes a nap
Sometimes you only require the display to go to sleep, instead of the hard drive. To set up timing for this, check box alongside 'Put the display to sleep when the computer is inactive for:' and drag bottom slider to the desired time to set when inactive. To ensure that the computer's hard disk goes to sleep during inactivity, check box alongside 'Put the hard disk(s) to sleep when possible'.
Note: iBooks and PowerBooks automatically go to sleep when closed.

Screen Saver activation
As an added extra, you can set a nominated Screen Saver to kick into gear when your computer goes to sleep. Selecting this button will take you to the Desktop & Screen Saver System Preference, where you can set timing and/or choose another image from the list provided.

System Preferences

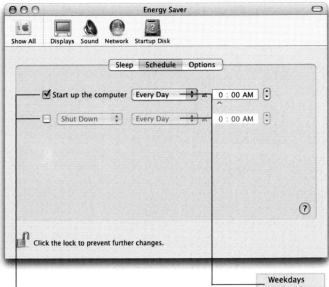

'Sleeping pattern' settings

Not only can you set sleep options over time, but you can also turn your computer on or off, or put it to sleep according to a particular schedule. Choose the Schedule pane in Energy Saver, and:
• to start up the computer during a given period, select the 'Start up the computer checkbox', then click on the pop-up menu to set a day (or set of days) to suit. Enter a specific time of day in the 'at' field.
• to shut down the computer or put it to sleep at a given time, check the bottom box. Choose Shut Down or Sleep, then go to the pop-up menu and choose a day (or set of days) to suit. Type a specific time of day in the 'at' field.

Energy Saver

The Energy Saver System Preference also provides options to specify computer response to modem rings, network administrator access and power interruptions. Also, PowerBook and iBook users can set their processors to highest or lower processor performance to help optimize battery life.

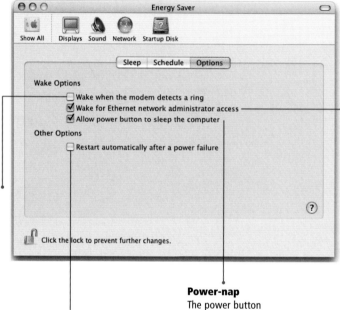

Can you catnap?
Your computer can be set to remain available to requests through the modem, while sleeping. How? By checking the box 'Wake when the modem detects a ring'.

Network accessibility
If you would like your computer to sleep, yet remain available to network administrator access, check the box 'Wake for Ethernet network administrator access'.
Note: if you select this option, you will need a Wake-on-LAN packet (the ability to switch on remote computers through special network packets) to wake the computer. Terminal commands ssh and telnet won't do the trick.

Power, interrupted
The option to 'Restart automatically after a power failure' allows (or disallows) your computer to start up automatically after a power interruption.

Power-nap
The power button on your computer can be used to put your computer to sleep. Simply check the box 'Allow power button to sleep' and when desired, press the power button once. (To wake your computer from sleep, press a key on the keyboard or click the mouse) Note: this option is available only on some computer models.

[Settings for iBooks
and PowerBooks only]

Battery center
Select settings for either:
• battery power–to ensure laptop gets the longest battery life; or
• power-adapter–to ensure the best performance when laptop is plugged into a wall outlet.

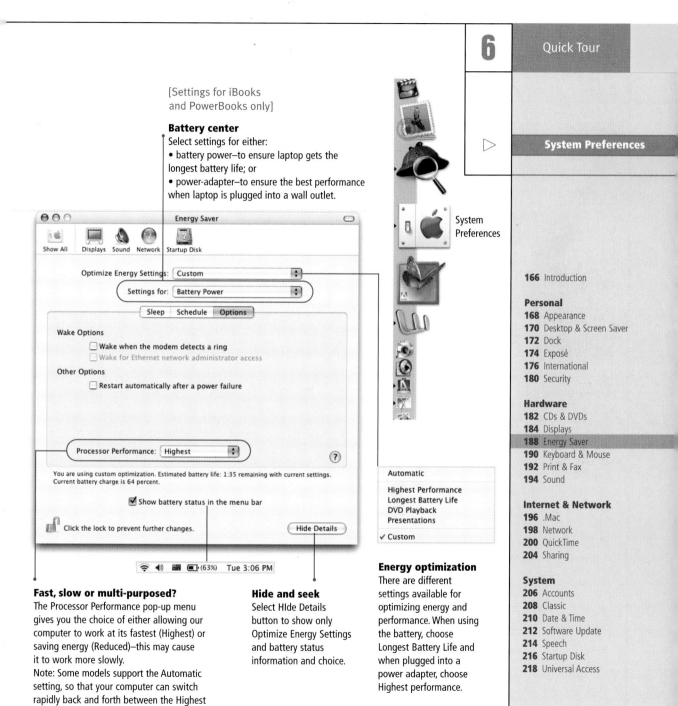

System Preferences

Fast, slow or multi-purposed?
The Processor Performance pop-up menu gives you the choice of either allowing our computer to work at its fastest (Highest) or saving energy (Reduced)–this may cause it to work more slowly.
Note: Some models support the Automatic setting, so that your computer can switch rapidly back and forth between the Highest and Reduced settings to optimize energy use.

Hide and seek
Select HIde Details button to show only Optimize Energy Settings and battery status information and choice.

Energy optimization
There are different settings available for optimizing energy and performance. When using the battery, choose Longest Battery Life and when plugged into a power adapter, choose Highest performance.

Keyboard & Mouse

Preferences for your keyboard and mouse have joined forces in Mac OS X 10.3 Panther and now co-exist in Keyboard & Mouse Systems Preference panels. Keyboard preferences operate menus and commands on Mac OS X without the mouse, while Mouse preferences provide you with options to control speed for tracking and scrolling.

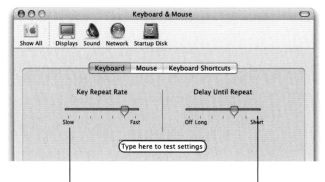

Deja vu?
If you think you've seen these preferences elsewhere in this book, you are definitely paying attention! Keyboard preferences are associated with System Preference's Universal Access and can be accessed via its Mouse and Keyboard panes.

Repeat that, please
A repeating character is a key on the Macintosh keyboard, which when held down, continues to type its corresponding character across the page. This can be controlled by various modes of speed control–dragging the Key Repeat Rate slider from left to right will indicate exactly how slow or fast key repetition occurs.

Try it out
When you have chosen your desired Key Repeat Rate and/or Delay until Repeat rate, check out this field to test your settings.

Delayed reaction?
Delay Until Repeat options control the repeating procedure involved when you hold your finger on a key. It is advisable to indicate Long delay settings if you're heavy on the keyboard. Select Off if this option is not required.

Mouse untrapped
Selecting the Mouse pane will help you change the speed at which your onscreen pointer moves. It will also tell you the speed to use for your computer to recognize a double-click. Dragging the appropriate sliders will set your speed. Again, notice the field available for you to test these settings.

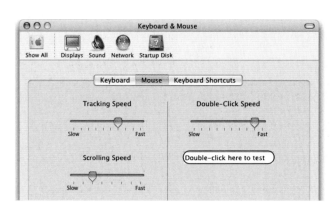

Trackpad settings
If you have a PowerBook or iBook computer, a 'Trackpad' pane will replace the 'Mouse' pane, providing you with settings to change speed of onscreen pointer movement when your finger is moved on the trackpad, and speed to use for double-click recognition. This is where you can also apply settings to use the trackpad to click, double-click or drag.

Easy access
If you prefer using keys instead of the mouse, activate Turn on full keyboard access. It allows you to carry out a number of actions with your keyboard.

Quicken the pace
Keyboard Shortcuts give you the option to assign keys on your keyboard to a certain task, instead of choosing options from a menu. This handy preference lets you disable or change many of the shortcuts that work the same in all applications (globally).

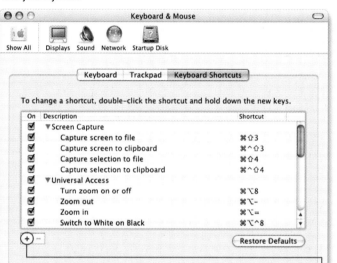

System Preferences

Finger fun
• To change the key combination for your shortcut, select the character in the shortcut list and insert your own key combination shortcut.
• To disable a shortcut, deselect the checkbox next to listed description.
• To return to default OS X shortcuts, click Restore Defaults.

Devising your own shortcuts
To develop your own shortcuts for tasks you plan to execute regularly:
• Scroll to the bottom of visible list until you reach 'All Applicatons' (not demonstrated on this spread);
• Click on the + button;
• Select your Application (or Other);
• Assign keystroke as your shortcut.

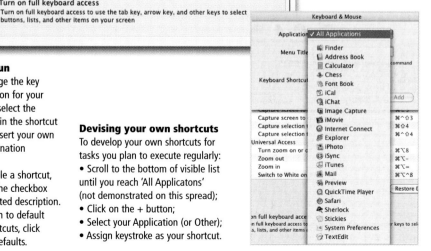

Print & Fax

Mac OS X 10.3 Panther 's printing system gives you instant access to the printing preferences most frequently used, provides you with more printer drivers than ever before and offers built-in faxing. Where do you find all this? Why, the Print & Fax System Preference, of course!

System Preferences
Hardware

Print & Fax

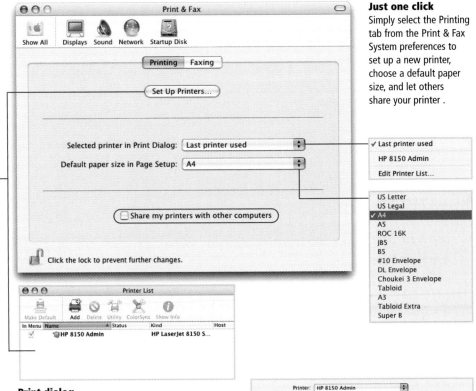

Just one click
Simply select the Printing tab from the Print & Fax System preferences to set up a new printer, choose a default paper size, and let others share your printer .

Printers galore
Mac OS X 10.3 Panther now includes more printer drivers than ever before, supporting hundreds of printers from Brother, Canon, EPSON, hp, Lexmark and Xerox right out of the box. The GIMP-Print (v4.2.5) open source printer driver project also comes bundled, providing you with access to even more printers.
To add a printer to your Printer List, simply click on the Set Up Printers button and click the Add icon (in the Printer List.) A sheet will drop down and take you to a list of installed printers to choose from.

Print dialog
A Print dialog will appear when printing from almost any document, allowing you to print and/or:
• Preview: this feature helps you reduce waste by providing a color-accurate-on-screen rendition of the print job at hand before it is committed to paper.
• Save as PDF
• Fax: lets you send document as a fax using your Mac's built-in modem.

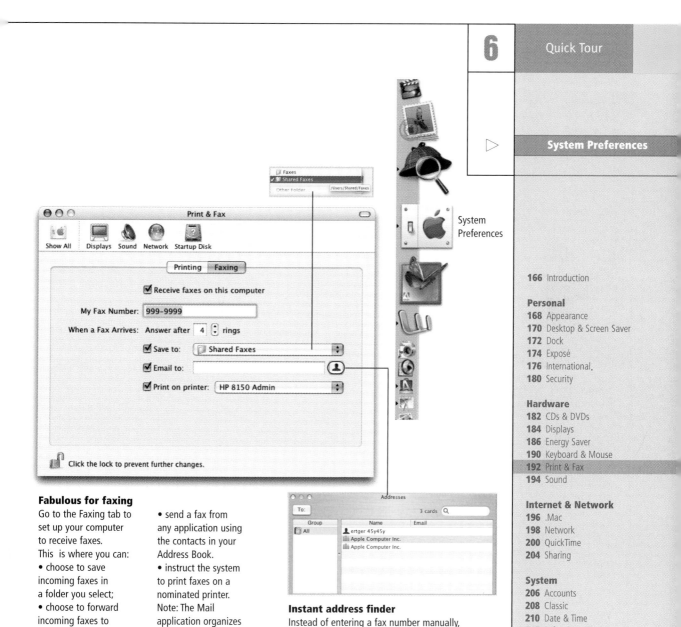

System
Preferences

Fabulous for faxing

Go to the Faxing tab to set up your computer to receive faxes. This is where you can:
• choose to save incoming faxes in a folder you select;
• choose to forward incoming faxes to an email address and or/print them;

• send a fax from any application using the contacts in your Address Book.
• instruct the system to print faxes on a nominated printer. Note: The Mail application organizes faxes received, for viewing in Preview.

Instant address finder

Instead of entering a fax number manually, let your system do the work. The figure icon (alongside the 'Email to:' field) instantly transforms you to your Address Book and uses fax numbers from your Address Book.

Sound

Customize the sound of your Mac with this unique set of
preferences, where you can choose the kind of device to hear
sound played through. You can also set sound effects to
alert you when the computer wants your attention.

Sound icon
If you prefer not to open
this panel each time you
want to change the
volume, drop the sound
volume icon in the menu
bar instead.
(You can also adjust
volume settings from
your Apple Pro Keyboard.)

Alert sounds
Your choice! As you select
each of these, you will hear
its sound. The name
highlighted indicates the
new alert sound. Sounds
can be changed anytime.

Move over Beethoven!
Selecting this box
(apparent in all three
Sound panes) will allow
you to move your Sound
Icon to the far right of the
menu bar for easier access.

Sound of silence
This is where you can mute all sounds
on your Macintosh (even your alert —
so you, along with anyone else, won't
know when you are making a
mistake!) Note: this option is
available in all three Sound panes.

Extra, extra ... hear all about it!

To input sound (voice, music etc.) into your computer via internal microphone or external microphone, select the Input pane. Once you have selected your chosen device, adjust the volumes accordingly.

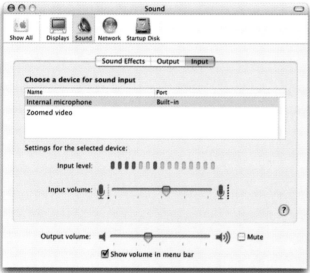

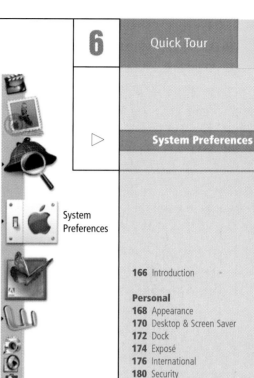

System Preferences

Sound blast

The Output pane is useful to hear sound played through speakers (both internal or external), headphones or stereo equipment connected to your computer.
• To listen through built-in speakers, external Apple Pro speakers, or a connected stereo, select Built in Audio.
• To listen through external USB speakers, select from the list provided.
Adjust the volumes of your selected device accordingly.

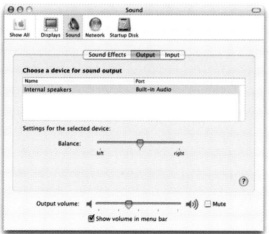

.Mac

The .Mac panel (first of the Internet & Network group of System Preferences) introduces you to the exciting world of Apple's optional .Mac internet service by making it easier to join, manage and use. It also provides you with settings to control how you utilize your own personal space on Apple's internet servers, courtesy of iDisk.

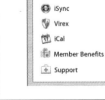

Name, rank and serial number
Once you enter your .Mac name and password, that information is available throughout your system. For example, when you click the Mail tab you'll see that your Mac can use this information to automatically connect you to your .Mac email account — no fiddling required.

.Mac wants you
Apple's .Mac service isn't compulsory, but you could find it really handy. To get in on the action, click this button.

.Mac motivators
.Mac is a suite of Internet essentials that lets you access your email (.Mac Mail), bookmarks (.Mac Bookmarks), names and details of people you want to contact (.Mac Address Book), and documents from any machine; and synchronize your most important data between multiple Macs (iSync).

In addition, your .Mac membership gives you access to iDisk–your very own personal storage space on Apple's Internet servers and includes powerful virus protection (Virex from McAfee) and backup software (.Mac Backup). Then, there's also HomePage, iCal, iCards and .Mac Slides Publisher for further entertainment.

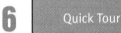

Off-site storage

If you sign up for .Mac, you get a 'virtual hard disk', accessible via the Internet from any Mac. Use the iDisk panel to view available free space on your iDisk, buy more space from Apple, create a local copy of it and control who can access it.

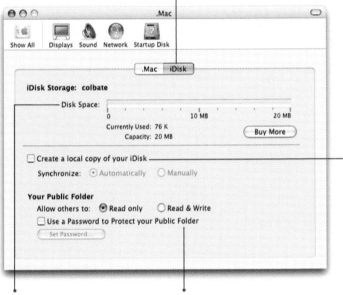

System
Preferences

Store and purchase

Using iDisk Storage, you can:
• monitor your personal storage space (members get 100MB of space and can purchase up to 1GB of total storage, while .Mac trial members get 20MB of storage space);
• purchase more storage space and expand iDisk to suit your needs.

Public access

Here's where you set limits or provide access to your public folder.
• Allow (or disallow) others to read or, read and write, files in your public folder;
• password protect your public folder (Mac version only).

iDisk duplicator

If you want to create a local copy of your iDisk on your computer, this is where you do it. Choose the way you'd like it synchronized at the same time. (Note: Changes you make to the iDisk on your computer are synchronized with your iDisk on .Mac while you're connected to the Internet.)

Network

Whether you want to connect your Mac to the Internet, your corporate network, or even the old PC that you put in the kid's room, the Network panel in System Preferences is where you plug in the required numbers. This panel also helps your Mac to automatically use whichever connection methods are available at any time: Ethernet, modem, Airport, or Bluetooth modem.

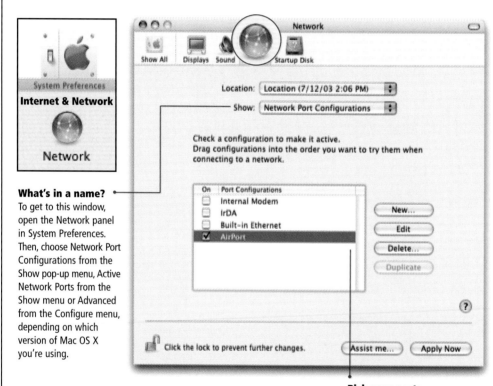

What's in a name?
To get to this window, open the Network panel in System Preferences. Then, choose Network Port Configurations from the Show pop-up menu, Active Network Ports from the Show menu or Advanced from the Configure menu, depending on which version of Mac OS X you're using.

Pick your ports
Because our Mac will not be using a modem, an Ethernet cable or a Bluetooth mobile phone to connect to the Internet, we have only put a tick in the AirPort checkbox. If you use Ethernet to connect to the Internet from your desk at work and a wireless AirPort network to connect from the meeting room, put ticks in both those boxes, sort the best connection method to the top, and configure both options. Then, your Mac will automatically select the best option that's available at any time.

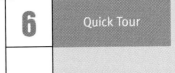

System
Preferences

AirPort options

Because we have selected AirPort in the Show menu, we can configure the TCP/IP and panes with the specific settings we require when we connect via AirPort. Each connection method can have its own settings.

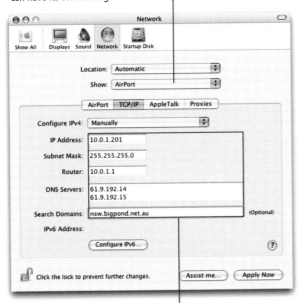

First things first

The option you pick here will affect the boxes that are available below. In fact, most parts of the Network panel are interdependent. If you find you just can't enter the setting you require in one part of the Network panel, it's probably because you've entered a contradictory setting somewhere else.

Endless numbers

The information entered here would come from your ISP or your company's network manager. So would the information under the Proxies tab. However, if you configured your Mac for Internet access when you first used Mac OS this data will be entered already.

OLD-FASHIONED ARCHITECTURES

Only enable AppleTalk if you must communicate with an old printer or Macintosh that does not know how to use contemporary standards like TCP/IP or USB. Using AppleTalk unnecessarily will reduce your network throughput.

TECH TIP

QuickTime

The powerful multimedia architecture of QuickTime lets you view, create, import and export media on your computer. Its free, open source, standards-based QuickTime Streaming Server delivers media either in real-time or on-demand over the Internet (data is displayed on delivery and not stored on your hard drive). This innovative application provides an abundance of media authoring capabilities, as revealed here.

System Preferences
Internet & Network

QuickTime

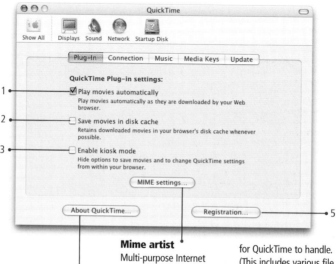

What is QuickTime?

QuickTime is many things: a file format, an environment for media authoring, and a suite of applications. More simply, QuickTime software allows Mac and Windows users to play back audio and video on their computers.

Introducing ... QuickTime 6.5

Released ten years ago, QuickTime continues the revolution with QuickTime 6.5, MPEG-4 file format. Featuring MPEG-2 playback delivery, it now has extensive support for both 3GPP and 3GPP2, and delivers continued support: for Apple Applications, MPEG-4; MPEG-2 playback; playback of .amr and .sdv files, Macromedia Flash 5, DVC Pro PAL, JPEG 2000 for Mac OS X, Applescript (Mac only), and a whole lot more.

Mime artist

Multi-purpose Internet Mail Extensions (MIME) identify various data for appropriate handling by a server or by one's own computer. In this example, the MIME settings pane provides:
• a list of general data type categories available for QuickTime to handle. (This includes various file types included in each general category, as well as each file's possible MIME type.); • the option to customize which file types for QuickTime to handle; and • the option to revert to the original MIME default settings.

Information kiosk

(4) Displays a slide show of QuickTime developers logos and relevant Web site address details.

Officially yours

(5) Register and upgrade your copy of QuickTime online. Simply select this button and enter the necessary information in a separate window.

Multi-mannerisms

QuickTime plug-in settings affect the way QuickTime behaves in your Web browser. In short: **(1)** Movies are played automatically when this option is checked (Mac OS X selects it by default). **(2)** Instant replay of downloaded movies is possible when this setting is selected. (Note: to use this feature, you must have enough space in your browser's cache.) **(3)** To avoid clogging up your hard disk with big files, select 'Enable kiosk mode.' It disables the pop-up menu which usually appears when viewing a movie in a browser, hiding options to save movies (including drag and drop copying of movies).

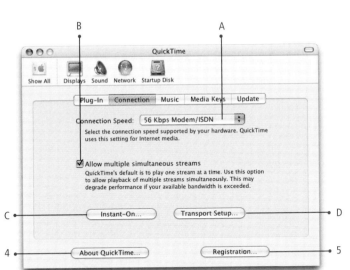

B A

System Preferences

C

D

4

5

Connection chaos?
This pane contains sections which effect the download, speed and quality for QuickTime media playing in a Web browser. These include:
A. Expedient media delivery (taking into account hardware limitations as well as the speed of Internet connection);
B. Multiple simultaneous stream option, but as cautioned, this could be at the expense of performance if bandwidth is exceeded. (In most cases users would be safer to leave this option unchecked.);
C. Instant-On. Selecting it will bring up a sheet which allows streamed media to be played automatically. Once this is enabled, there is a choice of response level, ranging from immediate to short delay. (Note: although streamed media will start playing without delay, it is important to be aware that network congestion may reduce the quality of playback.);
D. The Transport Setup button opens a window allowing QuickTime to select preferred protocol for data transmission.

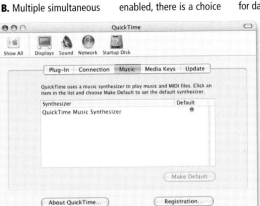

Making music
Musicians will find this option particularly useful. In addition to the QuickTime Music Synthesizer, other newly-installed third party music synthesizers will appear in this list. To select music files handled by your synthesizer (other than the QuickTime one), make appropriate selection and choose 'Make Default'.

QuickTime

Security measures and regular software updates are a vital part of Mac OS X, so it's not surprising that these concerns are addressed in many custom made applications too. Hop across to the QuickTime preference settings to manage viewing restrictions and update QuickTime and QuickTime third party software ... quick as a flash and oh, so easy!

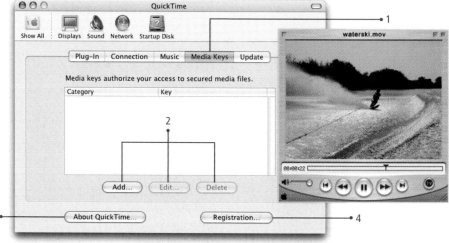

Key to security
(1) Security measures are sometimes employed on certain QuickTime files using passwords or media keys that lock the file. To authorize access and utilize such files, media key and file category information must be entered into the Media Keys pane.

(2) Media key information can be added, deleted and edited as illustrated above.

(3) Info Kiosk
Selecting this button will display a slide show of QuickTime developers logos and relevant Web site address details.

(4) Officially yours
Register and upgrade your copy of QuickTime online. Simply select this button and enter the necessary information in a separate window.

QuickTime Player   QuickTime Pro   Streaming Server   Broadcaster

Introducing ... the QuickTime Suite
• QuickTime Player: for playing back audio and video files; • QuickTime Pro: for flexible multimedia authoring; • Browser plug-ins: for viewing media within a Web page; • PictureViewer: for working with still images; • QuickTime Streaming Server: for delivering streaming media files on the Internet in real-time; • Darwin Streaming Server: for delivering streaming media with Linux, Solaris, and Windows; and • QuickTime Broadcaster: for delivering live events on the Internet.

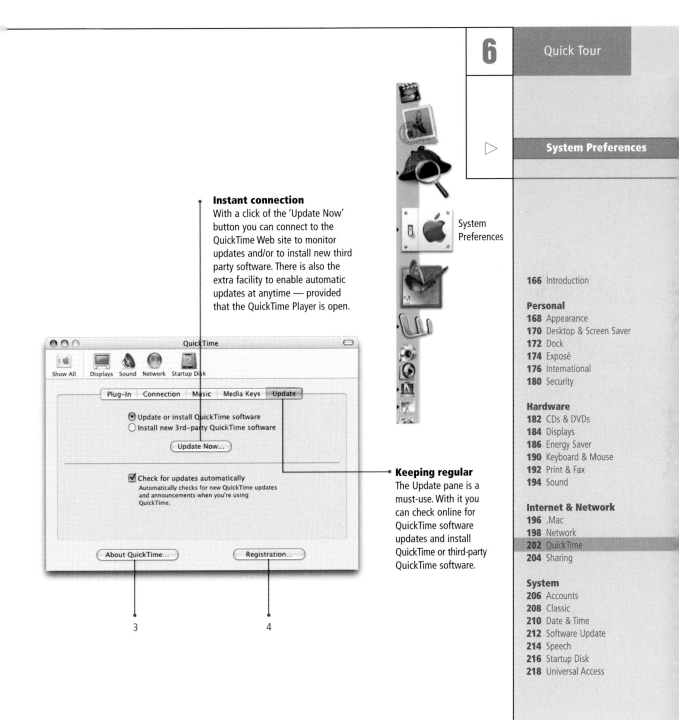

Instant connection

With a click of the 'Update Now' button you can connect to the QuickTime Web site to monitor updates and/or to install new third party software. There is also the extra facility to enable automatic updates at anytime — provided that the QuickTime Player is open.

System Preferences

Keeping regular

The Update pane is a must-use. With it you can check online for QuickTime software updates and install QuickTime or third-party QuickTime software.

Sharing

No Mac is an island. If you want to share your files, your printer, or anything else with your friendly, neighbourhood Mac or Windows users, the Sharing panel in System Preferences is the place to do it. (Likewise if you want to keep it all to yourself.)

IP is everything
The services in the Sharing panel generally use TCP/IP — the networking protocol that underlies the Internet — to do their thing. Hence it's handy to see your TCP/IP address* ('Network Address') in the Sharing panel, together with a direct link ('Edit...')** to the Network panel, where you can change it.

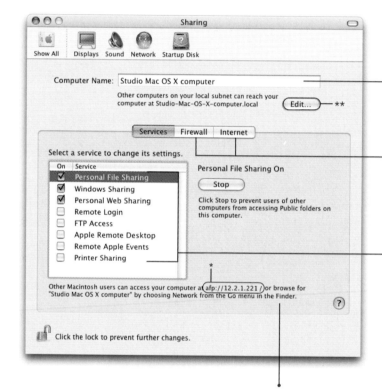

Time for action
Because we've switched on Personal File Sharing, other Mac OS X users on your local network can browse the contents of our Public folder. To do this, they would select 'Connect To Server' from the Go menu and enter the address given here.

Rendezvous
Rendezvous is Apple's name for Zeroconf, a nifty new technology that allows computers, printers and other devices to find each on a local network without any fiddling by the user. Stick two Mac OS X 10.3 systems on the same local network, and — thanks to Rendezvous — they'll be able to instantly yak via iChat. Stick a Zeroconf printer on the same network as a Mac OS X computer, and the Mac will be able to see and use the printer instantly.

System
Preferences

Public image
If you enable Personal File Sharing, then other users will see this name when they search for your computer on their local network.

No extra charge
When Apple released version 10.2 of Mac OS X, it added two nifty new features to the Sharing panel—a firewall, and instant Internet sharing.

Personal File Sharing
Provide other Mac users with access to some of the files on your hard disk.
Windows File Sharing
Give Windows users the same access.
Personal Web Sharing
Host a Web site from your Mac.
Remote Login
Connect to your Mac from another, via the UNIX command line.
FTP Access
Allow friends to download files from your Mac via the Web.

Apple Remote Desktop
Manage a network of Mac computers, distribute software and monitor network activity.
Remote Apple Events
Allow an AppleScript running on another Mac to communicate with yours.
Printer Sharing
Share your Mac's printer with other Macs on your network.

Service checklist
Note: if you opted out of installing the BSD subsystem when you installed Mac OS X, you will not be able to use the FTP Access and Remote Login services.

TECH TIP

Accounts

If you are the appointed Administrator and plan to set up accounts for other people using your Mac, you will be working with the Accounts panel (introduced in Chapter 3) quite frequently. The first item in the group marked System, this is where you will go to create, edit and delete users and assign login pictures and passwords.

What's in a name?
In Mac OS X 10.3 Panther you create, edit and delete accounts in the Accounts pane of System Preferences. Before Mac OS X 10.2 you would do this in the Users panel of Mac OS X's System Preferences. Same concept, different name.

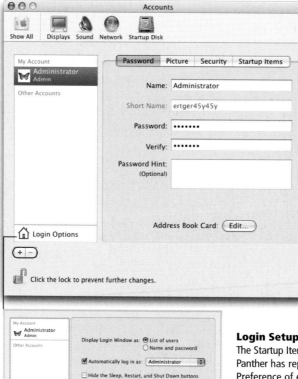

Hatch, match, despatch
As you can see (left) one user is currently registered. To add new users, click on the [+] button. Any user (except the administrator) can be deleted by pressing the [-] button.

At your own risk
Click on Login Options and the Accounts panel will display options for your Login window, log in identity, to show or hide Sleep, Restart and Shut Down buttons and enable/disable fast user switching.

Login Setup
The Startup Items pane in Mac OS X 10.3 Panther has replaced the Login System Preference of earlier versions of OS X and the Startup Items folder of Classic. This is where you select an application to start automatically upon login.

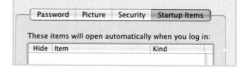

Mac of many faces

When you have setup an account (or accounts) in your Password pane, you may wish to change the picture assigned to you by default. Go to the Picture pane, and either select a picture from the icons on display, or click the Edit button. This will enable you to choose from your own images on the hard disk, a list of recent pictures you may have used or to take a video snapshot.

Note: the selected picture becomes the user's identity 'icon' and will be used when logging in and in the 'My Card' in Address Book. It also becomes the default picture in iChat.

System Preferences

Your very own security vault

The Security pane provides the choice for each user to use FileVault independently of the others. When you select the Turn On FileVault button, you will be prompted for an administration user name and password, as well as the password for the user requiring security.

Classic

Mac OS X's 'Classic' environment is a bit like running the old Mac OS 9 and the new Mac OS X side-by-side on your Mac. Your Mac OS 9 programs won't benefit from Mac OS X's best features when they run in Classic mode, but at least they should run. If you can't update all your programs for Mac OS X, here's how to make the most of Classic.

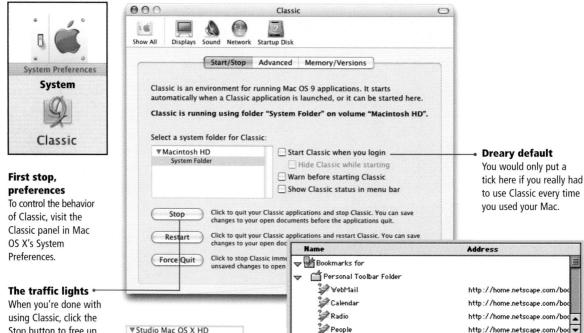

First stop, preferences
To control the behavior of Classic, visit the Classic panel in Mac OS X's System Preferences.

The traffic lights
When you're done with using Classic, click the Stop button to free up system resources. Restarting Classic could solve temporary problems with your Mac OS 9 programs, just like restarting a Mac that's running Mac OS 9. Only force Classic to quit if clicking the Stop button does not work. If Classic was not running, there would be a Start button here, not a Stop button.

Hey, I'm here!
If Classic says it can't find a system to use and all the disks listed in this window are dimmed, switch to the Startup Disk panel in System Preferences, select the Mac OS 9 system you want to use with Classic, and return to the Classic panel to find that the disk holding that system is no longer dimmed. Remember to return to the Startup Disk panel to reselect Mac OS X as your startup system.

Dreary default
You would only put a tick here if you really had to use Classic every time you used your Mac.

Step back in time
This window looks different because it belongs to a Mac OS 9 program running in Mac OS X's Classic mode. When we double-clicked on this program to launch it, our Mac automatically launched Classic first.

Old problems, old fixes

Remember, running Classic is like running Mac OS 9 alongside Mac OS X. So if Classic starts misbehaving, you have to try all those boring troubleshooting tricks that we used to depend on in the days of Mac OS 9, like rebuilding Classic's Mac OS 9 desktop database or restarting Classic with all Mac OS 9 extensions disabled. Find these tricks under the Advanced tab of the Classic panel in Mac OS X's System Preferences. Or, use Mac OS X native software exclusively and farewell all these hassles forever.

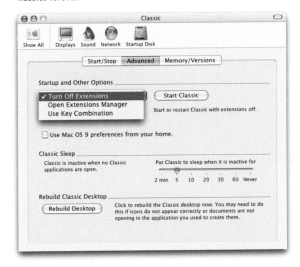

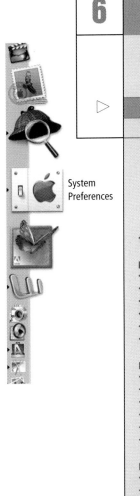

System Preferences

Old faithful

Mac oldies will recognize this one. The Memory /Versions pane is a sleek reconstruction of the previous operating systems' 'About this Computer' window. Use it to check memory and version information on the Classic environment, operating system, support and applications – to name just a few.

Date & Time

Although you may believe that setting the date and time on Mac OS X is more a convenience than a necessity, this is not strictly true. Date & Time preferences are vital to your Mac for allocating time and date to your documents, deciding when to show you alerts and working out software download time limits. There are a whole bunch of other reasons too, so read on to find out more ...

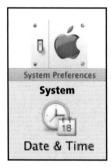

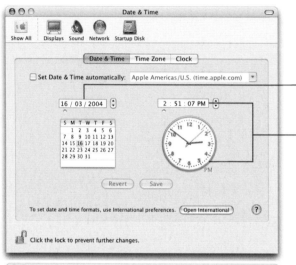

Network connect
Connect to a network time server if you have a full time connection (for example ISDN, DSL, cable, satellite), by checking the 'Set Date & Time automatically' checkbox, then choose the server geographically closest to you.

Virtual traveller
This option is helpful to anyone interested in travel or geography. Educate yourself on various time zones of different countries (simply select the continent of your choice and ensure that the drop-down menu corresponds to the country that your querying).

Time for a change?
Changing the date and time is really simple:
• To change the date, click the month and year arrows (either left or right) and then select a date in the calendar;
• To change the time, select the hour, minutes or seconds, then key in the new number/s or click on the arrow buttons instead. (A cute alternative is to drag the hour and minute hands around the clock and see how the time changes!). Click the Save button to confirm if you are happy with your changes. Note: To set date and time formats, click on the 'Open International' button. This will take you to the International System Preferences, where you can make your changes.

▷

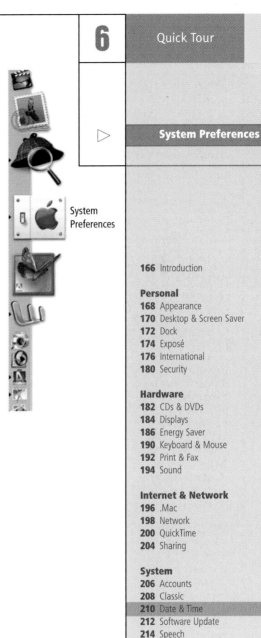

System Preferences

What a view!

The 'Show the date and time' option can be unchecked if you don't require the time to be shown in the menu bar or window. If it is checked, you have a variety of viewing options available for your convenience. Choices, choices and more choices ...

CLEVER OS X

If you are in a time zone that changes to daylight savings, your clever Mac switches over automatically.

HOT TIP

Software Update

Your Mac has the ability to keep itself fit by automatically downloading software updates from the Internet. This feature is called Software Update, and you control it via the Software Update panel in Mac OS X's System Preferences.

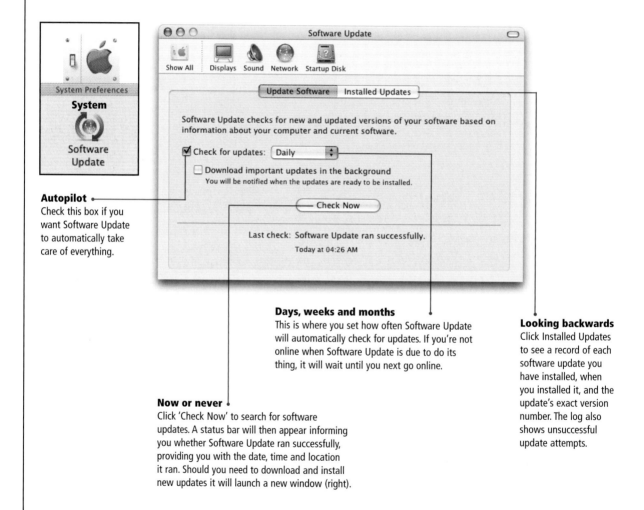

Autopilot
Check this box if you want Software Update to automatically take care of everything.

Days, weeks and months
This is where you set how often Software Update will automatically check for updates. If you're not online when Software Update is due to do its thing, it will wait until you next go online.

Looking backwards
Click Installed Updates to see a record of each software update you have installed, when you installed it, and the update's exact version number. The log also shows unsuccessful update attempts.

Now or never
Click 'Check Now' to search for software updates. A status bar will then appear informing you whether Software Update ran successfully, providing you with the date, time and location it ran. Should you need to download and install new updates it will launch a new window (right).

System
Preferences

Software Update

New software is available for your computer.
If you're not ready to install now, you can use the Software Update
preference to check for updates later.

Install	Name	▲ Version	Size
☑	AirPort Software	3.3.1	812 KB
☑	iSight Update	1.0.2	920 KB

The AirPort 3.3.1 Update improves the reliability of AirPort connections when
changing network locations. The update is recommended for all users with an
AirPort Extreme and AirPort enabled computer or an AirPort Extreme base station.

◯ Restart will be required.   (Quit)   (Install 2 Items)

Time for action
When Software Updates finds an update for you
to install, it presents you with this window. If any
of the shown updates are not needed, select and
choose Make Inactive from the Update menu.
Put a tick in the install box of each update that
you do wish to install, and then click the Install
button. You will need an administrator's password
to complete the process.

THE WHOLE KIT AND CABOODLE
Software Update can update Mac OS X and
the programs that Apple preloaded on your Mac.
However, it can't update the programs that you have
added to your Mac yourself. Some of these programs
will up-to-date themselves automatically. Visit:
www.versiontracker.com/macosx/ to check for
updates for the rest.

HOT TIP

Speech

Imagine being able to talk to your computer and get it to carry out tasks such as launching and quitting applications, opening and closing windows – even checking your email? In Mac OS X it has become a reality using Speech preferences. It's easy and fun to use and won't require too much gray matter to work out. Try it – you're sure to like it.

Open Speech Commands window
Speech Preferences...

Feedback Window

When 'Apple Speakable Items' is activated (see on/off pane) you will notice the appearance of a circular feedback window. Click the arrow at the bottom of the feedback window and choose 'Open Speech Commands' window to get a list of commands.

Speech Recognition

Speech Recognition gives your Mac the ability to recognize and respond to human voices. Provided that you have a microphone (or one already built into your Mac), you can start using Speech Recognition immediately – it won't need to be 'trained' to learn your voice. Note: Speech Recognition can only be used on applications that support it.

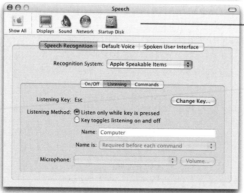

Who's speaking?

1. Activate your Mac's response with the listening key (in this case Escape). Note: Should you need to have the listening switched off at times, you can change your selection. Simply depress the Escape key for approximately a second. This will turn listening on until you hold down the key again.
2. This 'Listening Method' indicates that the Escape key must be depressed for approximately half a second as a sign that you will soon be sending a command to your Mac.

On demand commands

With a program using Apple Speech Recognition, you can ask 'What time is it?' (General Speakable Items command), or open your spreadsheet by saying 'Open the February forecast', (Specific Application command), or use voice command to switch out of the game you are playing and into Adobe Photoshop (Application switching command).

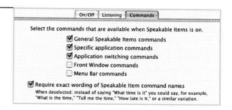

Eloquent alerts

Use the Spoken User Interface pane to select when you would like text to be converted into spoken commands from your Mac. As well as using talking alerts, you can also get your computer to speak to you when:

• an application requires your attention; • text is partially hidden due to the position of your mouse on screen; and • a certain key (your choice) is pressed.
Note: different settings are demonstrated to give you a better idea of sound you are in store for.

System Preferences

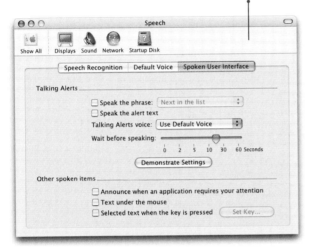

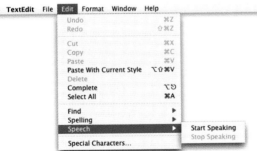

Cellos
Deranged
Fred
Hysterical
Junior
Kathy
Pipe Organ
Princess
Ralph
Trinoids

Just listen!

Once you have chosen a voice (Speech > Default Voice) for the computer to use, you can adjust the speed at which it will talk. Your nominated 'voice' will feature whenever an application is speakable. Open a document in TextEdit, select Edit > Speech > Start Speaking. Sit back and listen.

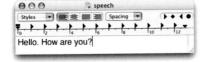

Startup Disk

Startup Disk makes it easy for you to choose the disk you want your computer to start up from (or even which CD you want to boot an operating system from). Choose the system that you want, click on it, press Restart and 'Bob's your uncle' – each time you boot up your computer it will launch the operating system of your choice.

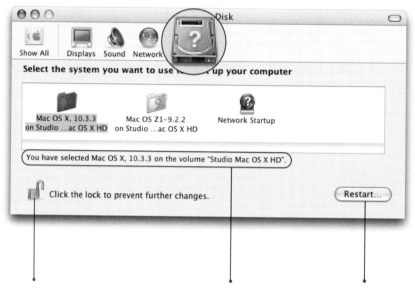

What a choice!
Selecting the Startup Disk System Preference gives you a choice of disks to start up or restart your system with.

Enough of this!
If you're happy enough with the way your operating system runs, you can prevent further changes by selecting the lock.

Which is which?
In case you weren't paying attention, Mac OS X provides a description of your current operating system. (Also highlighted, for ease of reference). By selecting System 9 as your Startup Disk, you are physically changing the operating system (almost like going back in time, without any presence of OS X at all). In order to revert back to Mac OS X you will have to change your Startup Disk in OS 9.

A fresh start
Just as you would restart your system after any software installation, you would select the 'Restart' button once you have changed operating systems.

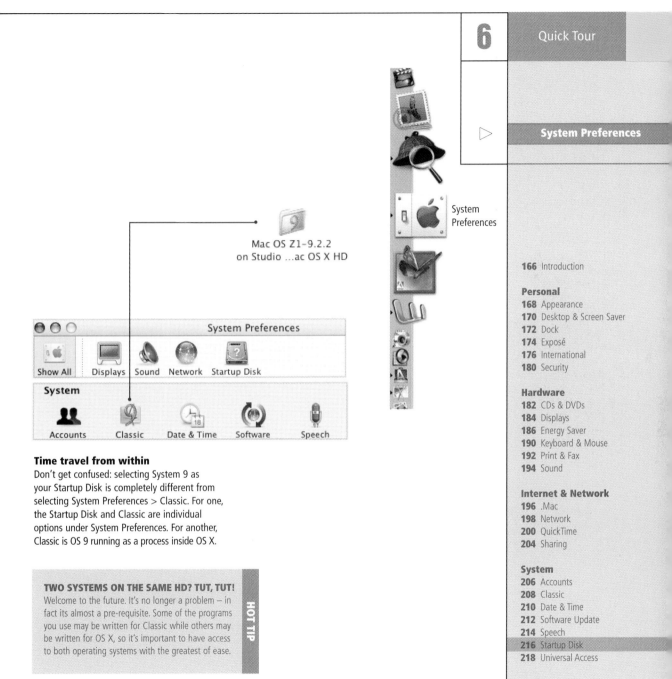

Mac OS Z1-9.2.2
on Studio ...ac OS X HD

System
Preferences

System Preferences

Show All | Displays Sound Network Startup Disk

System

Accounts Classic Date & Time Software Speech

Time travel from within
Don't get confused: selecting System 9 as
your Startup Disk is completely different from
selecting System Preferences > Classic. For one,
the Startup Disk and Classic are individual
options under System Preferences. For another,
Classic is OS 9 running as a process inside OS X.

TWO SYSTEMS ON THE SAME HD? TUT, TUT!
Welcome to the future. It's no longer a problem – in
fact its almost a pre-requisite. Some of the programs
you use may be written for Classic while others may
be written for OS X, so it's important to have access
to both operating systems with the greatest of ease.

HOT TIP

Universal Access

Users with keyboard difficulties aren't the only ones to benefit from Universal Access technology. Users with impaired vision will be impressed with Mac OS X's range of options to magnify what's on screen. Users with hearing difficulties can set up their Macs to flash the screen instead of beeping an alert. Users experiencing difficulty with the mouse can use the numeric keypad to move the cursor around the screen. It's control, convenience and help all the way...

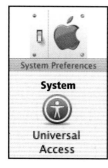

Access control
Universal Access features for Seeing, Hearing, Keyboard and Mouse panes can be turned on or off courtesy of these check boxes (*), present on all three screengrabs featured here. They control assistance devices and text-to-speech.

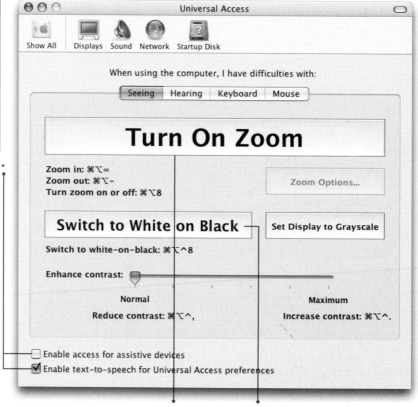

Eye spy
Mac OS X provides a range of options to help those with impaired vision see what's on the screen.

• The 'Zoom' display option uses the Quartz rendering and compositing engine to magnify the screen contents and make graphics and type smooth.

• The 'Switch to White on Black' option gives display higher contrast, allowing text to be read more easily.

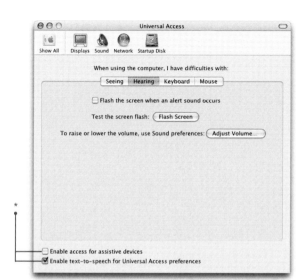

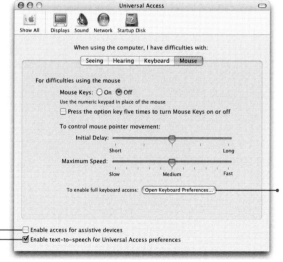

System Preferences

Flash that screen!
Users who have difficulty hearing may not require a beep alert. A flashing screen is an optional alternative for this, and can be tested before final selection has been made. Note: the Adjust Volume button takes you to Sound preferences for those who prefer a beep alert but may require to adjust the volume.

Hide and seek
This option is a great help to those who have trouble using the mouse. It allows for:
• the use of the numeric keypad instead of the mouse. (It's really fun to use – choose 1 to go left and down, 3 to go right and down, 7 to go left and up and 9 to go right and up. 5 makes the selection and opens it when double-clicked);
• speed and reaction of mouse to be fine-tuned;
• full keyboard access to be enabled. Go to keyboard preferences first and adjust settings there.

Universal Access

Universal Access lets you individualize the way you work. Going beyond the requirements of the U.S. Federal Government's Section 508 Accessibility statute, the system provides smooth, elegant features to those with difficulties using computers. The details before you reveal how to allocate one key to do the work of many, navigate integral system controls via the keyboard and prevent unnecessary key repetition.

Access control
Universal access features for Seeing, Hearing, Keyboard and Mouse panes can be turned on or off courtesy of these check boxes. They control assistance devices and text-to-speech.

Catch those Zzzz's ...
If you think there is something wrong with your keys (they may be repeating for apparently no reason at all), select the 'Set Key Repeat' button or Universal Access>Mouse>Open Keyboard Preferences to set your key repeat rate or delay time until next repeat.

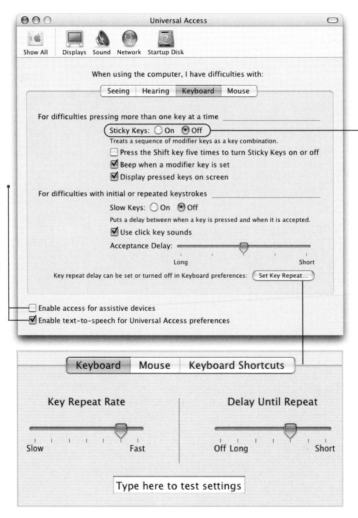

Stick 'em up!
Selecting a series of combination keys can be a problem, which is why many Mac 'oldies' will be delighted to discover that the popular 'Sticky Keys' (from days gone by) has not been discontinued. It works on the 'sound and sight' principle and is a great help for setting the pace of any keyboard combination.
 Activate it by:
(a) pressing 'On' in Sticky Keys (or tap the Shift key five times);
(b) indicating whether or not you would like:
• the system to beep when modifier key is set;
• pressed keys to appear on the screen;
(c) tap a keyboard combination, one at a time and at a comfortable pace.

System
Preferences

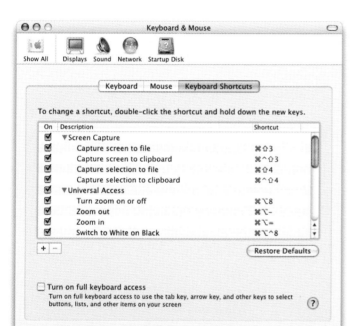

Flick of the wrist
Keyboard shortcuts allow you to carry our tasks on your computer by using keys on your keyboard. A number of global keyboard shortcuts can be disabled or changed by deselecting the checkbox next to its description in the list. To change an existing keyboard combination shortcut, select the character in the Shortcut list, then type a new shortcut by holding down the key combination you want. Note: Activate 'Turn on full keyboard access' to navigate menus, the Dock, windows, toolbars, palettes and other controls via the keyboard instead of the mouse.

Pardon?
Speech recognition can be used to launch applications as well as execute application commands instead of typing or mousing. The system will also speak alerts, selected and partially hidden text.

More technical

Network and Internet settings

If you continually move your Mac between work, school and home, there's no need to manually update your network/Internet settings each time. Instead, Mac OS X allows you to record the settings required for each location, and toggle between them with a single click.

Automatic ease

When you first set up your Mac for Internet or network access, Mac OS X stores your settings in a default location file called Automatic. To edit the network/Internet settings for that location, choose it from the Location pop-up menu, then reconfigure any part of the Network panel of System Preferences. To edit another location's settings, select it instead before you start making changes.

IP what?

IPv6 support is new to Mac OS X 10.3 Panther, but most of the Internet still runs on IPv4. Your friendly network administrator will tell you how and when to use IPv6 — if you don't have one (friendly or otherwise), you can almost certainly ignore this. IPv6 will become important over the next few years as it overcomes the shortage of IPv4 addresses.

Beyond Mac OS X

Mac OS X's Locations feature allows you to automatically change your Internet/network settings when you move your Mac. However, the version of Mac OS X that was current when this book went to press (Mac OS X 10.3.3) could not automatically select a new default printer, time zone or email address for each new location. That's where Location X steps in — it can switch all these settings and more. This program is shareware, meaning you can download a demonstration version to try before you buy from: homepage.mac.com/locationmanager/

Horses for courses
If your Mac is set up to access the Internet at work and you want to use it to connect from home as well, select Edit Locations from the Location pop-up menu to come to this sheet. Give the new name 'Work' to Automatic, duplicate that location, rename the duplicate location 'Home', and start editing Home's settings.

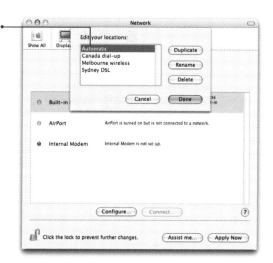

Instant switch
Once you've created a group of network/Internet settings for each location, switching between them is just a matter of selecting the current location from the Apple menu's Location submenu. Mac OS X takes care of the rest.

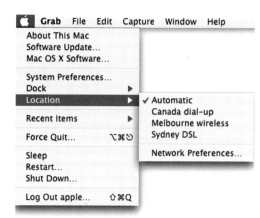

Network and Internet settings

Adjusting PPP settings for dial-up Internet connections is usually as technical as it gets in the Network system preference, but in some cases, a little fine tuning may be necessary. In particular, you will need to activate AppleTalk if you want to share files and printers with computers running old versions of Mac OS.

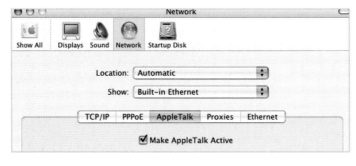

Talk the talk
Old versions of Mac OS can only use Apple's own AppleTalk protocol for sharing files and printers. If you need to connect to a vintage Mac, check the Make AppleTalk Active box in the AppleTalk pane. Otherwise, leave it disabled.
Unless your network administrator tells you otherwise, leave the AppleTalk Zone and Configure menus alone.

Do you PPPoE?
Some broadband services require the use of PPPoE instead of a normal Ethernet connection. Follow your service provider's instructions for setting it up. If the Mac has multiple users, you'll normally check the Save password box so they all have Internet access. Enabling the PPPoE menu lets you quickly make and break connections without opening System Preferences.

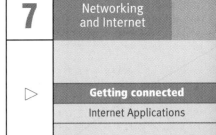

Dialup

Configuring a dialup connection is usually easy — just type in your account name, password and the access number. (If you're mobile, remember to set up the correct numbers for different locations.) If you'd rather be asked for the password each time you connect, just leave the box empty. Many Macs are fitted with an internal modem as standard, and that's the default setting. If you're using an external modem, go to the Modem pane and select your modem from the list. If it isn't there, install the appropriate driver file. If it didn't accompany the modem, ask the vendor.

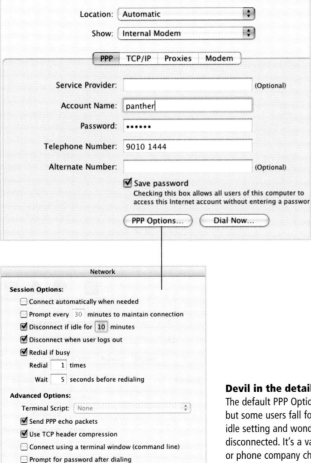

Devil in the detail

The default PPP Options are generally sensible, but some users fall foul of the Disconnect if idle setting and wonder why they keep being disconnected. It's a valuable feature if the ISP or phone company charges by the minute, but otherwise consider disabling it or extending the period. Only change the Advanced Options in accordance with your ISP's instructions.

.Mac

.Mac is Apple's pay-to-play collection of Internet-based services for Macintosh users. A .mac.com email address (accessible via the web as well as normal email programs) and storage space on Apple's servers are top of the list for most subscribers, but there are plenty of other attractions. If you're not convinced, sign up for the two-month free trial and see for yourself.

Identify yourself
If you have a .Mac account, Mac OS X will configure itself to use your iDisk and mac.com email address.
Enter your member name and password as part of the Mac OS X installation process, or later in the .Mac system preference.

iDisk inside
A local copy of your iDisk is useful when working without Internet access. Any changes are stored, and then when you are online again, the two copies can be brought back into synchronization. Auto synchronization is fine if you have a broadband connection, otherwise choose manual and update when it is convenient. Manual synchronization is triggered by clicking the button that appears next to the iDisk icon in the Sidebar.

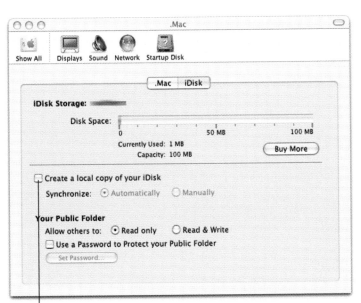

iDisk behavior
An iDisk behaves much like any other network volume, but it is stored on Apple's servers. You can use it as your web site, to store files that you need to access from different locations, or to allow other people to download your files or upload files to you. The .Mac preference shows how much space you have used.

There's more
A .Mac account brings you many features and benefits beyond iDisk and email—antivirus software, file backup, address book, bookmark synchronization and more.

Sherlock

If you want to track an international flight or translate 'dia de los muertos' from Spanish to French, you don't have to open a Web browser in the hope of eventually finding a Web site that can help you. Instead, get Sherlock 3, built into Mac OS X 10.2 and later, to do the legwork for you.

Sherlock

Viewing channels
Click here to view all the channels available through Sherlock 3. (Tip: to alter which channels you view permanently in the toolbar, select 'Customize Toolbar' from Sherlock 3's View menu.)

Finders keepers
Enter a departure city and an arrival city and click the green search button, and this Sherlock 3 channel will find all known flights that match. Note: your search can be restricted to a particular airline or flight number.

Pick your channel
Sherlock 3's built-in channels can provide quick access to Web search engines, stock art libraries, online auctions, a dictionary, an automatic language-translation service, and Apple's technical support library.

Lost and found
Sherlock 3 is a completely different beast to Sherlock 1 and 2. Apple has moved the ability to search for files according to their name or their content (yes—you can search for screenplays containing the work 'rosebud') from Sherlock to the Finder's Find command.

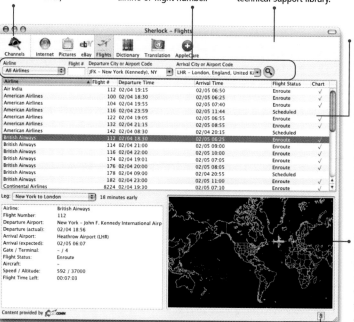

Instant results
Sherlock found 30 flights that matched our criteria. For each flight, Sherlock provides a summary of the available information, such as the airline and flight number. Click a flight once to view all available information about the flight in the two panels below.

Find detail
Our search for New York-to-London flights turned up this aircraft, which was over the middle of the Atlantic at the time of our enquiry.

Narrow the search
Click this unobtrusive button to restrict the search to the airlines and airports of particular continents.

Fast find
Give Sherlock's Internet channel a 'natural language' query (like 'Why is the sky blue?')
and it will scour the Internet for the most useful response.

Sherlock 2 vs Sherlock 3
You may notice that Sherlock 3 does not support Sherlock 2 channels.
Sherlock 3 channels are built using a new technology that communicates
directly with XML servers, which are multiplying at an astonishing pace.
Find more Sherlock 3 channels by clicking the Channels icon and then
selecting the Other Channels folder..

Disk maintenance and repair

Maintaining your disks is a must to maximize performance and prevent problems. Mac OS X system administrators will find Disk Utility (Applications > Utilities) perfect for basic disk maintenance and repair as well as more advanced tasks such as RAID and partition management.

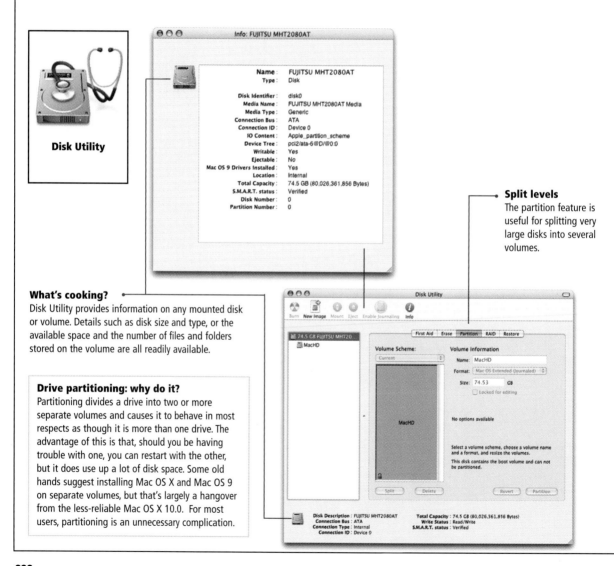

Disk Utility

Split levels
The partition feature is useful for splitting very large disks into several volumes.

What's cooking?
Disk Utility provides information on any mounted disk or volume. Details such as disk size and type, or the available space and the number of files and folders stored on the volume are all readily available.

Drive partitioning: why do it?
Partitioning divides a drive into two or more separate volumes and causes it to behave in most respects as though it is more than one drive. The advantage of this is that, should you be having trouble with one, you can restart with the other, but it does use up a lot of disk space. Some old hands suggest installing Mac OS X and Mac OS 9 on separate volumes, but that's largely a hangover from the less-reliable Mac OS X 10.0. For most users, partitioning is an unnecessary complication.

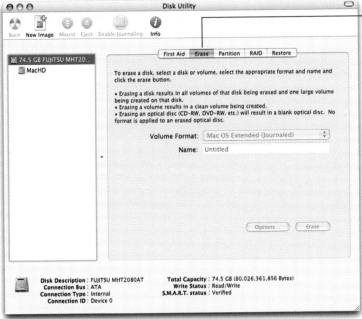

Eraser 'tool'
Erase removable disks and any partitions (apart from the startup disk) with this feature. But handle with care – erasing destroys all the data on the disk. Note: You must erase a CD-RW or DVD-RW disc before you can reuse it.

Image courtesy of **Apple**

Disk maintenance and repair

Disk Utility has several functions, but the one you'll use most often is First Aid. Many software-related problems can be avoided by running Disk Utility and choosing Repair Disk Permissions before and after installing software, and especially before and after using Software Update. Incorrect permissions can prevent programs from running correctly, and can prevent a software installation or update from completing properly.

Disk Utility

Rescue remedy
When things become a bit strange in the OS department, it's a good idea to go to First Aid, which checks, repairs and verifies problems on any mounted disk (apart from the startup disk) and media.

Repair Disk Permissions often cures weird behaviour. Regularly repair permissions before and after installing or upgrading software — especially Mac OS X itself.

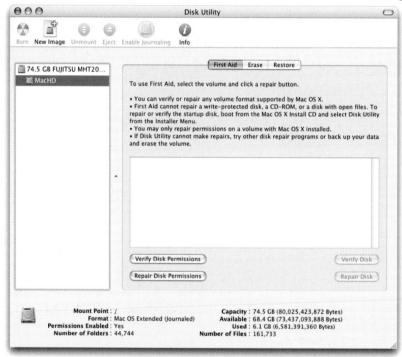

First Aid
You can only run Repair Disk on the hard drive if you boot up from the Mac OS X Install CD. That's no big deal, as the disk is checked and if necessary repaired during startup. Sometimes more extensive repairs are necessary, in which case a third-party program such as DiskWarrior may be used instead.

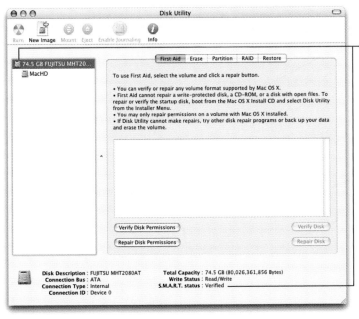

Status Report

Modern hard disks have self-testing capabilities. Mac OS X 10.3 Panther's Disk Utility is able to interrogate and report the status of your drive. Click on the drive name (not the volume name which appears in Finder windows) and look at the S.M.A.R.T. status at the bottom of the window. 'Verified' means the disk is in good order; 'About to fail' means it's time to back up your data and replace the disk. For most users, that means a trip to a qualified technician.

Partitioning

When Mac OS X first appeared, some experts recommended creating separate partitions for Mac OS 9 and X. These days, the vast majority of hard disks are set up with one partition.
If you're sure you need multiple partitions, Disk Utility will set them up for you. In most cases you'll need to start up from the Mac OS X Install CD, because you can't change the partitioning of the boot drive.

REPLACING YOUR DRIVE?

If a replacement drive is necessary, take the opportunity to fit a larger disk. Depending on the size of your old drive, you may be able to get considerably more space for little extra cost.

HOT TIP

235

Disk maintenance and repair

As well as working with real disks and volumes, Disk Utility operates on disk images — files that can behave like disks. Disk images are often used to distribute downloadable software (typically shareware and freeware) as they are a very convenient way of keeping related items together. They can also be used to collect and test a group of files that will eventually be burned to CD or DVD.

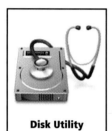

Disk Utility

Image is important
To create a disk image from a volume or folder, choose Images > New. Images created from volumes can be used as a backup mechanism — use the Restore pane to get the data back again.

No longer needed
Unmount lets you unmount one volume of a partitioned drive, leaving its other partitions untouched. If you try to eject the partition from the Finder, other partitions on the same drive will also be unmounted unless they contain open files.
Normally, you'd use Eject to eject removable disks (including CDs) and mounted disk images.

Keep a journal
Journalling reduces the risk of file system corruption in the event of a power failure or crash, and reduces the time taken to restart after such events.
Journalling is enabled by default in Mac OS X 10.3 Panther, and should be left on in most cases.

Create a new disk image by clicking the New Image button in Disk Utility's toolbar. Choose the size appropriate for the purpose: presets cater for common purposes, or set your own using the Custom option. Use encryption if the image will be used to store sensitive information. The default format (read/write disk image) is normally appropriate, but the sparse disk image option will only occupy as much real disk space as needed for the data it contains, regardless of the nominal size of the image.

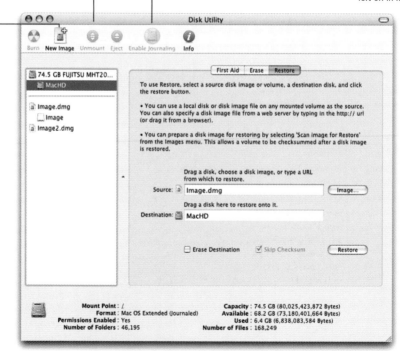

To create a CD or DVD copy of a disk image, select the image file (not the mounted volume) in the Disk Utility window and click Burn.

Storage solution

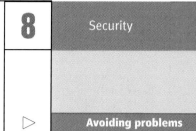

If you don't know what RAID is, you probably won't need to use this feature, but we'll tell you anyway. RAID (redundant array of independent disks) is a multiple disk storage solution that deposits the same data on different drives for reliability, or puts pieces of one file on different drives for speed. The operating system recognises the multiple disks as one hard disk.

System changes alert

Making changes to Mac OS X can be fun and powerful, but it can also foul things up if you're not sure what you're doing. Here are some areas to handle with care—or to avoid altogether.

Alert !!!

Not for ten

Control Panels allow you to make changes to Mac OS 9 in the same way that System Preferences allows you to make changes to Mac OS X. You can open these Mac OS 9 Control Panels in older versions of Mac OS X, but generally speaking you should not. Making changes to Mac OS 9 Control Panels from Mac OS X can confuse your Mac and cause unexpected trouble.

Mac OS X 10.3 Panther protects you from yourself.

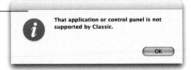

That application or control panel is not supported by Classic.

Classical treasures

Mac OS 9 users can get in the habit of trolling through their System Folder, deleting any files that look out of place, and seeing what happens. Don't do this in Mac OS X. 'Classic', the feature that enables you to run Mac OS 9 alongside Mac OS X, depends on a suite of files that it places in the Mac OS 9 System Folder. If you delete them, you won't be able to use Classic.

Too much power

The Utilities folder in Mac OS X's Applications folder is full of utilities that allow you to view and change almost every aspect of your system. Terminal and NetInfo Manager are the two most powerful utilities in this team, and the two most dangerous if misused. Do not even look at them unless you're sure that you know what you're doing, or if a Mac OS X expert is guiding you through the process.

Invisible UNIX

Mac OS X usually does a grand job of hiding UNIX folders such as 'bin', 'etc', 'sbin', 'usr' and 'var' from you, the user. If these folders do become visible, don't be alarmed—just leave them alone, because fiddling with them could damage your system.

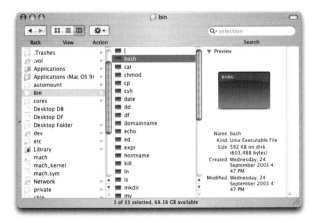

Suddenly revealed

When you restart in Mac OS 9 (assuming your computer can do so), you'll see some files required by Mac OS X's Mach kernel. Leave them alone. You might also be tempted to try to delete a Mac OS X user while you are running Mac OS 9, either by dragging the user folder to the Trash or via the Multiple Users control panel. Again, don't do this. The only place you should try to delete a Mac OS X user is the Accounts panel in Mac OS X's System Preferences.

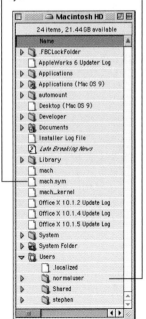

Net Info Manager

In Mac OS X, one user account can do anything: create, change and delete any file; start, stop or alter any program; and connect or disconnect any user. This user is called 'root', and its absolute power can corrupt your system absolutely. Only enable and use the root user if you must, and you know exactly what you're doing. The majority of administration can be achieved without enabling the root user at all.

Net Info Manager

First things first
Before you can use the root user in Mac OS X, you will have to enable it. Do this using NetInfo Manager, which is in Utilities in Mac OS X's Applications folder.

Moving target
Before Mac OS X 10.2, these functions were under the Security submenu of the Domain menu. Now, Security is a menu of its own.

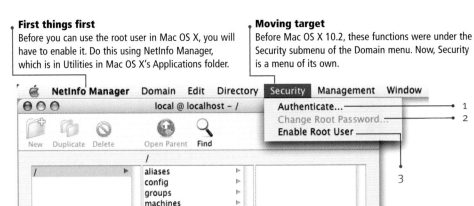

1. Who goes there?
You will have to 'authenticate' (provide your Admin username and password) before you can enable the root user. In fact, you'll probably have to authenticate more than once.

2. Password protect
Your root user password should be different to your ordinary Admin password, and impossible to guess. Note: the system only checks the first eight characters of your password.

3. Shut the gate when you leave
This menu item changes to Disable Root User after you enable root. Disable the root user as soon as you're finished with it.

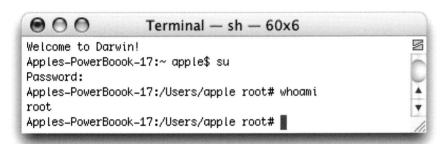

```
000                 Terminal — sh — 60x6
Welcome to Darwin!
Apples-PowerBoook-17:~ apple$ su
Password:
Apples-PowerBoook-17:/Users/apple root# whoami
root
Apples-PowerBoook-17:/Users/apple root#
```

Superuser ahoy

After you've enabled the root user, there are two ways you can login as root. First, you can choose Log Out from the Apple menu and log back in the root. This will require you to type 'root' as your username, so click the Other button if you're presented with a list of users rather than username and password fields. Once you login as root, you will be able to do anything. For example, you can delete corrupt files that otherwise refuse to budge, but you can also drag vital system resources to the Trash, so be careful. If you are comfortable using Mac OS X's command line, you can login as root through the Terminal. Just type 'su', then give the root user's password when prompted. Then type 'whoami' to confirm you're now the root user. You are only the root user within that particular Terminal window, so to end your root user session, close the window.

WARNING
Never create a user account with the name 'root', as conflicts between this account and the real root user can make your computer behave strangely.

System Profiler

System Profiler (Applications > Utilities) can make your
Mac stand up straight, push out its chest, and provide a lot
more information than just its name, rank and serial number.
In fact, using Profiler, almost any question about your Mac can
be answered.

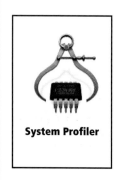

System Profiler

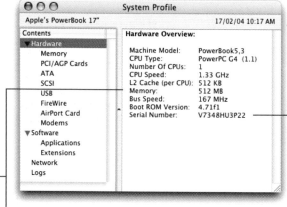

Name, rank, serial number
Remember to jot down your Mac's
serial number before it gets stolen.

Memory is made of this
For everyday bragging, you only need to know that your Mac has 320MB of RAM (memory). However, if you're thinking of buying extra RAM, you must know what kind of RAM your Mac requires and whether you have any vacant slots that could take additional DIMMs (memory chips). If all the slots are full, you'll need to replace one or more DIMMs with higher-capacity parts.

Share your profile
The simplest way to send someone a snippet from your profile is to drag the information from a System Profiler window to the body of a new email message. If you wish to save your entire profile, select New Report from the File menu, customize the report if you wish, and then click the OK button. When the report appears, choose Save As from the File menu. The report is just a text file—to open it, drag it onto Apple System Profiler or any word processor or text editor.

System build
Usually, you only need to know that you're running, say Mac OS X version 10.3. However, sometimes a technician might ask you for your operating system's exact build number: in this case, 7B85.

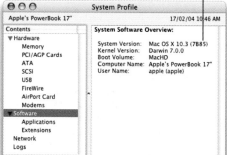

Where on earth ...?
Your Macintosh can connect to almost any network using Ethernet. Every single computer that has an Ethernet port also has its own, unique MAC address —that's short for 'media access control', not Macintosh. Find your MAC address here, if your network manager asks you to provide it.

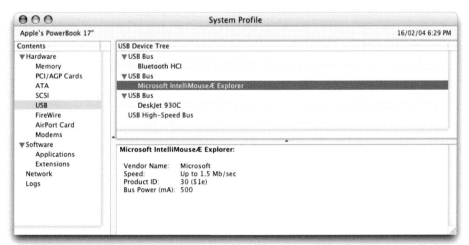

Hard word on hardware
Any hardware that's connected to your Mac via USB should appear in this window. If your mouse stops working, look for it here. If System Profiler doesn't know that your mouse exists, you could have a damaged wire that's failing to connect. But if Profiler does know that your mouse exists, your Mac can 'see' it, so the problem is elsewhere. You can do the equivalent check on FireWire and other devices.

A rose by any other name....
Prior to Mac OS X 10.3, System Profiler was known as Apple System Profiler. The version accompanying 10.2 did a better job of grouping related information

HOT TIP

Firewall

There's a flipside to connecting your Mac to the Internet. While it allows you to access a world of information, it can also give hackers the opportunity to break into your Mac. Luckily, Mac OS X includes a firewall—the traditional tool for guarding against intruders—and Mac OS X 10.3 Panther makes it much easier to use.

Firewall

Relax
The firewall is on, so you're protected. You can click Stop to turn it off and Start to switch it on again.

Selective access
This firewall is configured to allow other computers to access the Mac's web pages and shared files. At present, it does not allow Windows file sharing, remote login, or FTP access. In Mac OS X 10.3 Panther, activating an item in the Services panel automatically opens the corresponding firewall port.

At your service
Mac OS X provides a range of networking 'services', such as the ability to share files with Mac users ('Personal File Sharing'), PC users ('Windows File Sharing'), and as Web pages ('Personal Web Sharing'). To allow or block access to these services from other computers, go to the Services panel, select the service in question, and click Start or Stop. Mac OS X will take care of updating the firewall's settings.

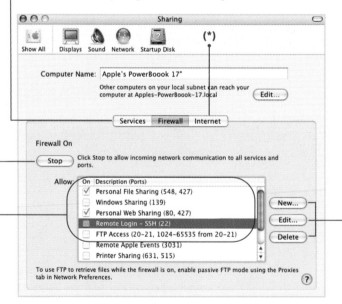

Finding port numbers
You can find the usual port number for most services in the Internet Assigned Numbers Authority's list (www.iana.org/assignments/port-numbers) or in the software's documentation. For example, to allow MP3 Sushi (streaming audio) traffic when the firewall is enabled, you would enter Other, '8810, 8888', and 'MP3 Sushi'. A Mac-specific list of port numbers is available in the Apple Knowledge Base (kbase.info.apple.com).

(*) Share you protection
With Mac OS X providing a secure connection to the Internet, the obvious next step is to share that connection with the other computers in your home or business. Interested? Jump to the Internet panel.

Provide a passport
If the firewall is on, it blocks all incoming network traffic that it has not been told to allow. To allow a new form of incoming network traffic, click the New button. If the service you wish to permit is listed in the Port Name pop-up menu, select it then click OK. Otherwise, select Other from the pop-up menu. Enter a name and port number for the service.

```
●○○                 Terminal — less — 80x24
IPFW(8)             BSD System Manager's Manual              IPFW(8)

NAME
     ipfw - IP firewall and traffic shaper control program

SYNOPSIS
     ipfw [-q] [-p preproc [-D macro[=value]] [-U macro]] pathname
     ipfw [-f | -q] flush
     ipfw [-q] {zero | resetlog | delete} [number ...]
     ipfw [-s [field]] [-aftN] {list | show} [number ...]
     ipfw [-q] add [number] rule-body

DESCRIPTION
     ipfw is the user interface for controlling the ipfirewall(4)

     Each incoming or outgoing packet is passed through the ipfw rules.  If
     the host is acting as a gateway, packets forwarded by the gateway are
     processed by ipfw twice.  When the host is acting as a bridge, packets
     forwarded by the bridge are processed by ipfw once.

     A firewall configuration is made of a list of numbered rules, which is
     scanned for each packet until a match is found and the relevant action is
     performed.  Depending on the action and certain system settings, packets
:
```

Firewall and a half

While the Firewall pane in the Sharing panel in System
Preferences is easy to use, it lacks many features found
in commercial products, such as the ability to be
remain silent during intrusion attempts (rather than
sending back 'access denied' messages). One means of
increasing your control of Mac OS X's firewall is to
open Terminal (Applications > Utilities folder), type
'man ipfw', and follow the instructions. Another is to
use a commercial firewall, like the one included with
Norton Internet Security.

FileVault

Mac OS X's Unix underpinnings offer a degree of security, but that's not enough for everyone. If you're concerned to keep prying eyes out of your files, FileVault (new in Mac OS X 10.3 Panther) will automatically encrypt and decrypt your files as you use them. You don't need to be a spook to be concerned about security and privacy.

FileVault

Using FileVault

Each user can choose to use FileVault independently of the others. Select the Security pane in the Accounts system preference and click Turn On FileVault. You'll be prompted for an admin user name and password, as well as the user's password, so it's easier if the administrator enables FileVault while creating the account.

Last chance hotel

Access to FileVault-encrypted files is usually restricted to the account owner. Admin users can set a master password that will allow recovery of data if an individual user forgets his or her password. Mac OS X will not allow the use of FileGuard until a master password has been created.

Secure encryption

FileVault works by moving the contents of the Home folder into a securely-encrypted disk image file. (Shareware and freeware are often distributed as disk image files, but they are not encrypted.) The trick with FileVault is that the mounted image is automatically inserted into the directory structure where the Home folder would normally be. This makes it transparent to most applications.

Is FileVault for you?

FileVault is useful for iBooks and PowerBooks that contain sensitive material. If the physical security of a desktop Mac is adequate, you probably don't need FileVault.

You normally wouldn't want to encrypt very large files such as digital video projects, especially as the associated applications tend to be processor-hungry. Either leave FileVault off, or store the files outside your Home folder.

Mac OS X is generally very stable, but if your system is prone to crashing, get that fixed before activating FileVault to reduce the risk of losing data.

Shred that data

Whether or not you use FileVault, Secure Empty Trash is another tool to help keep your secrets secret. Found in the Finder menu, Secure Empty Trash overwrites trashed files before deleting them, making it practically impossible to resurrect them. (The normal Empty Trash command leaves the data on the disk and makes the space available for reuse.) Tools such as Norton Utilities can scavenge this data and reconstruct deleted files.

Breaking and entering

How hard it is to break into FileVault depends on the strength of the password.

A good password is long and contains many different characters—but that can also make it harder for you to remember!

Automatic decryption

If you care enough to use FileVault, disable the auto-login feature, otherwise your Home directory will be automatically decrypted without the user having to enter a password!

HOT TIP

The Terminal

All you know about Mac OS X's Terminal application is that it's located in the Utilities folder. You may have heard that this is a gateway to UNIX, and thus the keyboard is the only tool you will need to utilize its command line interface. At this stage, you are terrified and don't know where to begin. Which is where we come in, and show you that it's really not as bad as it looks. Ready?

Terminal

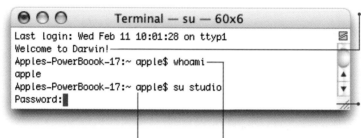

What a welcome
When you launch Terminal you'll notice a simple window containing this friendly little greeting.

Made to measure
Terminal windows are no different to other Mac OS X windows and can be resized with ease. The title bar displays the width and height of the window separated by an X.

Reaching Darwin
Darwin is the name given by Apple to the version of the Unix operating system that underpins Mac OS X. When the Mac OS X system boots up, the first thing it does is load Apple's Darwin operating system which runs silently in the background, and can only be reached on the command line via the Terminal program.

Quick crossover
When using the Terminal program you are logged in as the same specific user indicated in the Mac OS X GUI. But there's one essential difference that's prominent when using UNIX commands – you can change user identity for part of your Terminal session by typing in 'su' (switch user).

Mistaken identity?
If you are a little forgetful, the command line prompt will cleverly remind you who you are and the name of the Mac you're using. In addition, you can type the 'whoami' command and the shell discloses your identity.

Identity access
Typically, you cannot access other identities in Terminal until you create other accounts or enable root login in NetInfo Manager.

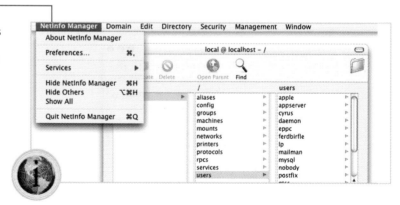

LOGIN WITHOUT LOGOUT
Using Terminal to execute a few commands as another user means that there is no need to toggle between Login and Logout. Simply switch user (su) on the command line, execute required commands and terminate the shell session.

HOT TIP

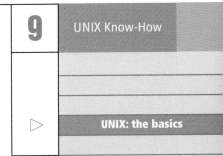

Warning
Mac OS X 10.3 defaults to the 'bash' shell, where older versions used 'tcsh'. Why would that bother a beginner? Step-by-step instructions written for tcsh may not work in bash, so check that the material you're using has been updated.

Scissors and glue
Text used in Terminal can be moved into and out of the Mac clipboard using the Cut, Copy, Paste commands. Note: items can be dragged into Terminal from a Finder (this is especially useful to save typing path names, but text cannot be dragged out of the Terminal windows.

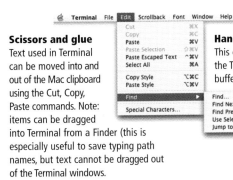

Handy find
This command searches the Terminal window buffer for specified text.

Keep for later
Store settings of one or more open Terminal windows using Save, move your session or selection to a text file using the Save Text As and/or Save Selected Text As commands.

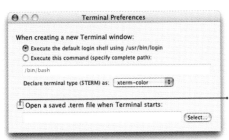

Back to Begin
By checking this option you can save desired terminal file to open at Terminal commencement.

Out of here
If you are already at the command prompt, leave the Terminal session by either closing the window **(2)** or quitting Terminal **(1)**.
If you try this and a program is still running within Terminal, you'll be warned. Terminating it in this way *might* cause loss of data, so it's a habit better avoided. It's better to close the program properly.

Terminal preferences

Mac OS X provides a range of options for using shell commands and terminal emulation which are convenient and easy to use. These allow you to: • select text and drag it to another application or to the desktop as a clipping; • apply transparency to terminal window/s; • turn anti-aliasing on or off; and • adjust character spacing thanks to better font control. But wait! There's more ...

Terminal

Source for preference
Set general Terminal Preferences from the Terminal menu to select which shell to use and execute a login script at shell start up. To control more specific preferences go to File > Show Info or to Terminal > Window Settings. In either case, the Terminal Inspector will appear, complete with a pull-down list of preferences (namely Shell, Processes, Emulation, Buffer, Display, Color, Window, and Keyboard).

1. Verbosity
The default scrollback buffer of 10,000 lines is more than enough to let most people see what they've been doing. If you want more, the option's there.

2. Wrap up
Keep these wrap options checked so you'll be able to read long lines both as you type them in and when you scroll back after making the window narrower.

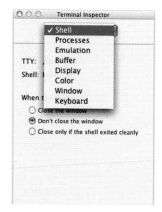

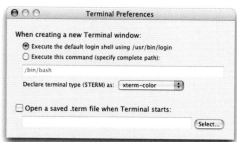

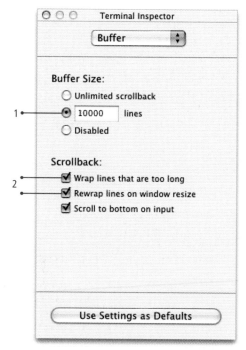

Improved functionality
Preferences seen here fine-tune Terminal's emulation of a VT100/VT220 device. (If you are using Telnet, you may need to adjust the settings in this window. If you do not know what these settings mean, do not change them.)

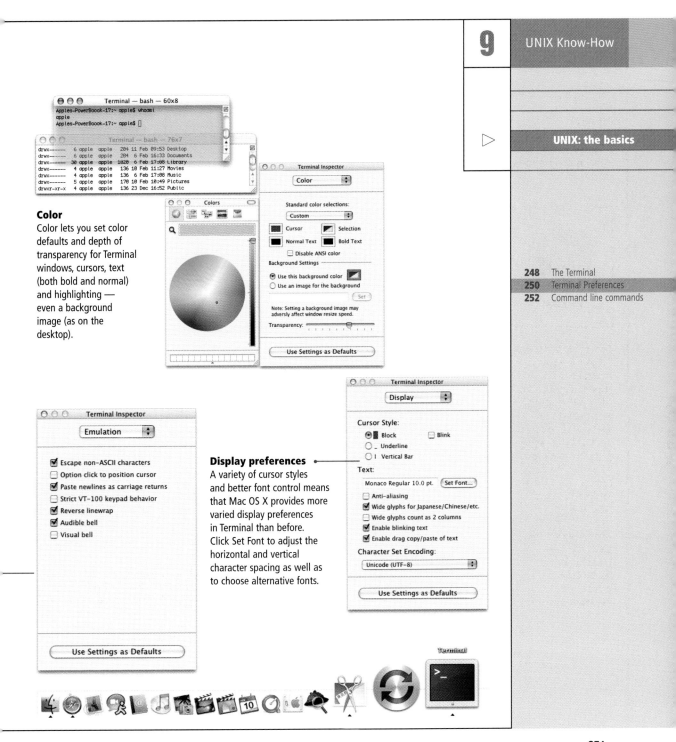

Color
Color lets you set color defaults and depth of transparency for Terminal windows, cursors, text (both bold and normal) and highlighting — even a background image (as on the desktop).

Display preferences
A variety of cursor styles and better font control means that Mac OS X provides more varied display preferences in Terminal than before. Click Set Font to adjust the horizontal and vertical character spacing as well as to choose alternative fonts.

Common line commands

Darwin provides commands for navigating and manipulating the contents of your hard disk, which carry out similar functions established by the Mac Finder, such as moving folders as well as copying, pasting and deleting files and directories. For the purposes of this 'Visual Companion', we have chosen not to blind you with 'command' science. Instead, we will give you just a bit of the basics here ...

Terminal

Gateway to shell
An alternative to interacting with your Mac via the Aqua interface, a shell displays the command line prompt and accepts input. Running a single shell command or opening a Terminal window into which you can type several commands is just an alternative way of telling your Mac what to do.

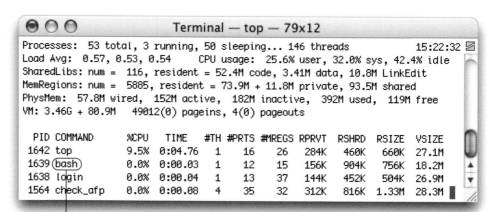

Shell's your oyster
The shell is an application that interprets entered commands to Mac OS X's UNIX kernel. One of the first UNIX shells to be developed and still currently in active use is 'sh'. A number of backward compatible shells have since been developed. (This means that anything that works in 'sh' should work in any shell developed thereafter.) Darwin's current default shell, 'bash' is derived from 'sh'. Earlier versions used 'tcsh', which is derived from 'csh' (the C shell). 'tcsh' is still available if you prefer it. (See previous page, Terminal Preferences.) Either way, use the up-arrow key to recall previous commands and then use the left and right-arrows to fix typing errors or change commands.

Finger fun
Commands typed on the command line will appear after the prompt. Pressing Return tells the system to execute the command. Note: most commands are names of programs and when typed, will be launched by Darwin (an alternative to double-clicking a program in the OS X Finder.)

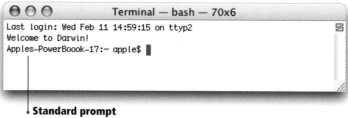

Standard prompt
When Terminal is launched, it displays your Mac's name, the directory you're in and your username.

Shortcut commands to get you going

Note: *type bind -P at the command-line prompt for a comprehensive list of command shortcuts. To get you started, "\M-b" means type esc followed by b; "\C-l" means hold down the ctrl key and press l.*

Directory commands

~	home directory
.	current directory
..	parent directory of current directory
/	topmost or root directory

Command	Details
cal	prints a calendar for any year specified (1 to 9999)
cat	displays text file
cd	sets current default directory
cp	copies file
df	displays free-space
diff	compares two files
du	disk utilisation
find	locates files in directory
grep	searches for strings or patterns

Command	Details
head	displays the first 20 lines of a file
ls	lists a directory,
man	extensive Darwin manual
mkdir	creates a directory
mv	moves/renames file or patterns
pwd	informs user of current directory
rm	deletes file
rmdir	removes a directory
tail	displays the last 20 lines of a file

FREE OPEN-SOURCE APPLICATIONS

Thanks to open source technology, developers can customise and enhance relevant applications using Darwin. Some — such as the Apache web server and the Samba Windows-style fileserver — are a standard part of Mac OS X. Others are freely available for download, such as:

- analog (for Web logs analysis);
- mrtg to monitor and graph network activity; and
- PHP for server-side scripting.

SUMMARY

Terminal

AppleScript automation

Whenever you find yourself completing simple tasks over and again, you can ask AppleScript — your Mac's autopilot—to take the controls. Just write a short script using AppleScript (which looks more like English than a programming language), or grab a free script that does exactly what you're looking for from a site like ScriptBuilders: www.macscripter.net/script-builder.t

Find fabulous fonts
Type 'The quick brown fox...' a few hundred times, and format each line with a different font so you can compare all your typefaces. Sound useful? Sounds boring and repetitive. Sounds like a job for AppleScript! Check out Apple's Font Sampler script, which is in the Info Scripts folder in Example Scripts in AppleScript in Mac OS X's Applications folder.

Revisionism
What were you thinking? You didn't holiday in Tahiti in 1999—it was 2000. No problem, you can instantly change the name of every digital photo in a folder on your Mac using AppleScript. And this is just one of many uses for the handy 'Replace Text In Items Name' script, which is in Finder Scripts within the Example Scripts folder.

From scripting to programming
AppleScript is a very simple scripting language. In fact, many AppleScript scripts look like ordinary English sentences, and creating a new AppleScript using Script Editor is simpler than creating a new resume in Microsoft Word. But that doesn't mean that AppleScript is not powerful. If you install the contents of the optional Xcode Tools CD-ROM that came with Mac OS X or your Macintosh (Developer Tools in earlier versions), you'll find that AppleScript is one of the languages that you can use with Project Builder—Apple's fully fledged programming environment for the Macintosh. Apple calls this combination AppleScript Studio. If and when you are ready, you can use AppleScript Studio to turn your scripts into sophisticated programs, complete with dialog boxes and pull-down menus.

AppleScript online
AppleScript and XML Web Services can exchange information over the Internet—an ability that's exploited by Apple's Stock Quote script, which you'll find in the Internet Services section of the Script Menu. The default ticker code is AAPL (Apple Computer).

Give it a go
After taking Apple's sample AppleScripts for a spin, you're probably keen to create some scripts of your own. Just open Script Editor (in the AppleScript folder, in Mac OS X's Applications folder), type what you see here (without the colours or indentation), and click the Run button. Your new script will open Safari and then go to Apple's 'AppleScript— Mac OS X' Web page.

In the red
Individual programs often come with their own handy AppleScripts. For example, if your Mac came with AppleWorks, you can open the program, create a spreadsheet, insert some data, and then run the Negative Cells Red script (by selecting it from AppleWorks' Script menu, in the menu bar). This script will show you if and where you're 'in the red'.

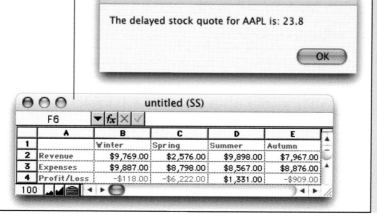

Write your own AppleScripts

Write your own AppleScripts using Script Editor, which is in the AppleScript folder in the Applications folder. You can also use Script Editor to modify other people's scripts—like this version of a script from Apple, which creates two parallel Finder windows to help you quickly moving files around you hard disk. If you catch the AppleScript bug, look to AppleScript Studio for greater possibilities including interface building tools.

Start at the start (5)
This Finder window will show the startup disk – rather than, say, a CD-ROM or a particular folder.

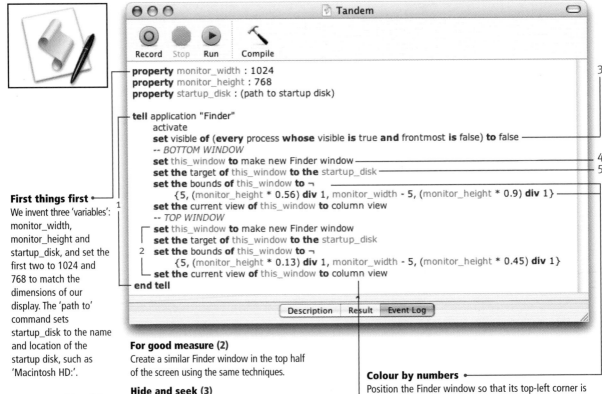

First things first
We invent three 'variables': monitor_width, monitor_height and startup_disk, and set the first two to 1024 and 768 to match the dimensions of our display. The 'path to' command sets startup_disk to the name and location of the startup disk, such as 'Macintosh HD:'.

Straight talking (1)
All the commands between the 'tell' and 'end tell' statements are directed to the Finder. The first such command, 'activate', makes the Finder the front-most, active program.

For good measure (2)
Create a similar Finder window in the top half of the screen using the same techniques.

Hide and seek (3)
We hide ('set visible to false') every visible program ('every process whose visible is true') other than the front-most program ('and frontmost is false'), which is the Finder (see 'Straight talking').

Wish for a window (4)
We create a new Finder window, and decide that for the purposes of this AppleScript we will call it 'this_window'.

Colour by numbers
Position the Finder window so that its top-left corner is five pixels from the left edge of the screen and slightly more than half way down (56%). The bottom-right corner is five pixels from the right edge and 90% of the way down the screen. The "div 1" ensures the result of the calculation is a whole number, and the "¬" breaks the statement over two lines.

Neat, little rows
Tell the Finder window to use Column view.

The rulebook
Select Open Dictionary from Script Editor's File menu to read a 'dictionary' of the commands available within any AppleScript-aware program. For example, the Finder's dictionary tells us that the property 'frontmost' is boolean. This means that it's either true or false—rather than being a number between 1 and 100, for example. Either the Finder is in front of all other programs, or it is not.

Essential reading
The complete AppleScript Language Guide is online via developer.apple.com/documentation/AppleScript/AppleScript.html — the direct URL is even longer!
This is not for beginners. There's a link to a gentler introduction to AppleScript on the same page — look for AppleScript for Mac OS X. An outline of the changes to AppleScript in Mac OS X 10.3 is online at: www.apple.com/applescript/macosx/

Launching AppleScript

There are many ways to launch an AppleScript in Mac OS X, and to be effective, those that you choose should be instantly accessible and easy to use. On these pages, we provide a few handy pointers and examples to choose from.

To the toolbar

You already knew you could add icons to your Finder window toolbars by selecting Customize Toolbar from the Finder's View menu, right? Well, you can drag AppleScript applications directly into the toolbar too. Remember to check the Run Only option when you save your script as an application.

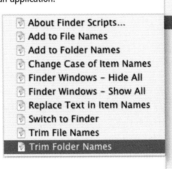

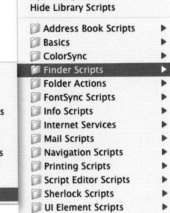

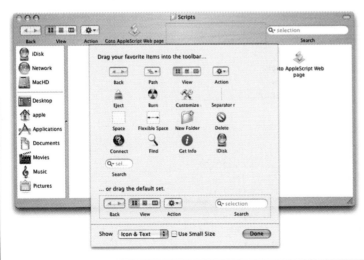

Pop-up pleasure

Add Script Menu to your menu bar for access to compiled AppleScripts as well as Perl and UNIX shell scripts. Run Install Script Menu (in the AppleScript folder in the Applications folder) to install this utility. If you later decide to remove it, run Remove Script Menu. From the Script menu, choose Open Scripts Folder to go to the folder where you should put compiled scripts for your personal use. Or, add compiled scripts to the Scripts folder in the Library folder at the root level of your hard disk to make them available to anyone who uses your Mac.

Special service
Smart programs include their own script menu where you can launch compiled scripts designed to work with that program in particular. Some programs will even let you attach an AppleScript to a keyboard shortcut. One of the Microsoft Entourage scripts shown here will automatically turn an email message into an event in your calendar.

AppleScript speed
Running an AppleScript as a compiled script is faster than running it as an application, because you don't have to wait for the application to launch. To turn an AppleScript application into a compiled script, open it in Script Editor, choose Save As, and then choose 'Script' in the File Format pop-up menu. To turn a compiled script into an application, choose Application from this pop-up menu and put a tick in the Never Show Startup Screen checkbox. You will only be able to do this if the script's author has not saved it as Run Only.

Ready, Set, Run
Script Editor, the program you use to write and edit AppleScripts, also includes a Run button for running scripts.

Drag and drop
Many AppleScripts that you have saved as double-clickable applications can also function as 'droplets' — AppleScripts that act on the files and folders that you drag onto them. Here, we are adding the Documents, Library, Movies, Music, Pictures, Public and Sites folders to our Favorites menu by dragging them onto Apple's '+favs' script, a free download from: www.apple.com/applescript/macosx/toolbar/

Image manipulation using Scripts

AppleScript is the ideal tool for manipulating hundreds of images in the same way — cropping or scaling them all to the same size, changing them all to black-and-white, or compressing them all for the Web. Here's how to get started with Photoshop, GraphicConverter and AppleScript.

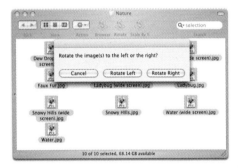

Built right in
Mac OS X 10.3 Panther introduced Image Events, which allow AppleScripts to carry out simple manipulations of images(flip, rotate, pad, crop, scale and convert file format) using an application that runs unobtrusively in the background.
See www.apple.com /applescript/imageevents/ for more examples of how Image Events can be used.

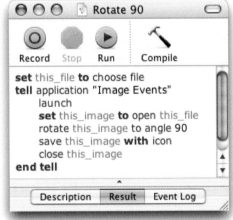

```
set this_file to choose file
tell application "Image Events"
    launch
    set this_image to open this_file
    rotate this_image to angle 90
    save this_image with icon
    close this_image
end tell
```

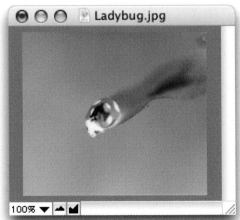

Ghostly thumbnails
Imagine that your Web site uses dark, brooding, thumbnail images to link to each page. It took just seconds to write this script, which tells the shareware program GraphicConverter to turn a photograph into an inverted, black-and-white, thumbnail. Write this script in Script Editor and then save it in the Scripts folder in the GraphicConverter folder, in Application Support, in Library, in your home directory. Restart GraphicConverter, and then open your image and select this script from the script menu whenever you want to use it. Other free AppleScripts for GraphicConverter can be found at: www.lemkesoft.com/en/ graphscripts.html

Image editing ability
In earlier versions, similar functions were provided by Image Capture. If you download Apple's free Window Contents scripts (www.apple.com/ applescript/toolbar/) and install them in your Finder window toolbar, you can easily scale or rotate all photographs in a folder. The scripts do this by harnessing Image Capture's basic image editing abilities.

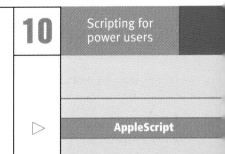

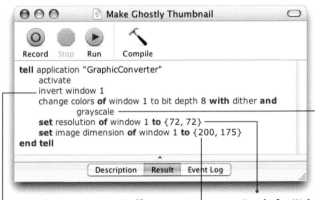

Fade to gray
Convert the front-most image from color to grayscale.

See a ghost
'Invert' the colors in the front-most image, so that black becomes white.

Uniform rows
Scale the front-most image to 200-by-175 pixels, so it will be the same size as the other thumbnails.

Ready for Web
Reduce the front-most image's resolution to 72dpi, for publication on the Web.

Power to Photoshop
The granddaddy of all image-editing programs, Adobe Photoshop, has a built-in tool called Actions for automating repetitive tasks. Actions are great if you only need to automate Photoshop, because you can easily 'record' Actions using the Actions palette and convert them to droplets.

But if your scripts must do anything that involves Photoshop co-operating with another program, then you will have to use AppleScript for your scripting. Luckily, the free Photoshop 7.0 Scripting Plug-in for Macintosh (www.adobe.com/support/ downloads/detail.jsp? ftpID=1477) brings AppleScript support to

Photoshop 7. To combine the simplicity of Actions with the power of AppleScript, try creating an Action in Photoshop and then adding the 'do action' command to your AppleScript script. This command only requires you to name the Action you wish to use and the Action group to which it belongs.

APPLESCRIPT AID
A convenient way to learn about AppleScript essentials is to launch Script Editor and go to the Help menu. (You will find that it's perfect for specific enquiries and easy to find your way around!)

TECH TIP

AppleScript & UNIX shell scripting

The two most popular scripting systems for Mac OS X—AppleScript and UNIX shell scripting—can 'talk' to each other. Experienced AppleScript and UNIX users will instantly realize how powerful this combination could be. The UNIX command cron, which can be set to trigger any command at any time of the day, including a command that runs an AppleScript application — provides a gentle introduction to this awesome combination. To control 'cron', edit the crontab file.

Root of the problem
A crontab file tells your Mac when to automatically run certain UNIX commands. The system's crontab file belongs to the all-powerful root user, which is why we had to use the 'sudo' command to open it. If you don't want to execute these commands when other users are logged into your Mac, edit your own crontab file, not the system's file.

Take a Pico
Open the system's crontab file by launching Terminal (Applications > Utilities folder), typing 'sudo pico /private/etc/crontab', giving your admin password when required. This opens the file in Pico, which is a very basic text editor for UNIX—like TextEdit is a text editor for Mac OS X.

Synchronize watches
Tell UNIX to execute the command at 1.10pm (24-hour clock) on every day of every month (as shown here), or on any other days or times that you choose. Press the Tab key to jump from column to column.

```
000                    Terminal — pico — 91x27
 UW PICO(tm) 2.5            File: /private/etc/crontab            Modified

# /etc/crontab
SHELL=/bin/sh
PATH=/etc:/bin:/sbin:/usr/bin:/usr/sbin
HOME=/var/log
#
#minute hour    mday    month   wday    who     command
#
#*/5    *       *       *       *       root    /usr/libexec/atrun
#
# Run daily/weekly/monthly jobs.
10      13      *       *       *       root    /usr/bin/open /Library/Scripts/plastic
15      3       *       *       *       root    periodic daily
30      4       *       *       6       root    periodic weekly
30      5       1       *       *       root    periodic monthly




^G Get Help   ^O WriteOut   ^R Read File   ^Y Prev Pg   ^K Cut Text    ^C Cur Pos
^X Exit       ^J Justify    ^W Where is    ^V Next Pg   ^U UnCut Text  ^T To Spell
```

Perfect placement
Go to the Emulation panel in Terminal's Terminal Inspector dialog box and turn on the ability to place the cursor by Option-clicking. Then, hold down the Option key and click here to place the cursor. Press the Return key once, and start typing on a new line to create your new crontab entry.

Privileged few
Keep in mind the consequences of asking cron to run your script as the root user, or for that matter, as any other user.

Keyboard commands
When you have typed your new crontab entry, press Control+O (that is, hold down the Control key while you press the O key) to WriteOut the file, then press the Return key when Pico's asks for confirmation. Last, press Control+X to Exit from Pico.

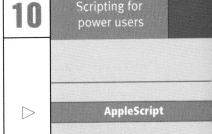

```
/private/etc/httpd/httpd.conf
/private/etc/httpd/httpd.conf.bak
/private/etc/httpd/httpd.conf.default

                              Cancel        OK
```

```
Record   Stop   Run   Compile

do shell script "locate /private/etc/httpd/http"
display dialog the result


        Description   Result   Event Log
```

Saving your script

For simplicity's sake, save your script as an AppleScript application (not a compiled script) in the Scripts folder in Mac OS X's Library folder. (Our demonstration script is called 'plastic'.) Then, edit crontab so that it will use the Open command to launch this application at the times entered earlier. The '/usr/bin/' suffix is insurance against the possibility that cron won't know where to find the Open command.

Backchat

The conversation can flow in the other direction, too. AppleScript's 'do shell script' command allows an AppleScript to execute any UNIX command and to receive the result. Here, the AppleScript has executed the UNIX command 'locate private/etc/httpd/http' and sent the result to a dialog box. NB: If instead you get an AppleScript error "locate: no databse file /var/db/locate.database", you need to run the Terminal command 'sudo /usr/libexec/locate.updatedb'. This takes quite some time to complete.

Simplicity itself

Getting cron to automatically run a compiled AppleScript script is a challenge, which is why we saved our demonstration script 'plastic' as an AppleScript application. However, executing a compiled script from the command line is simple. Just resave the AppleScript application 'plastic' as a compiled script (in the same location), then open Terminal and type 'osascript /Library/Scripts/plastic'.

Backup

Your data is too important for you not to protect it with Plan B—Plan Backup, that is. Apple's own Backup utility is a convenient choice for .mac subscribers and includes the option of off-site backup. There are various alternatives including the well-known Dantz Retrospect — the Express (personal) version is also available as part of the Norton SystemWorks bundle.

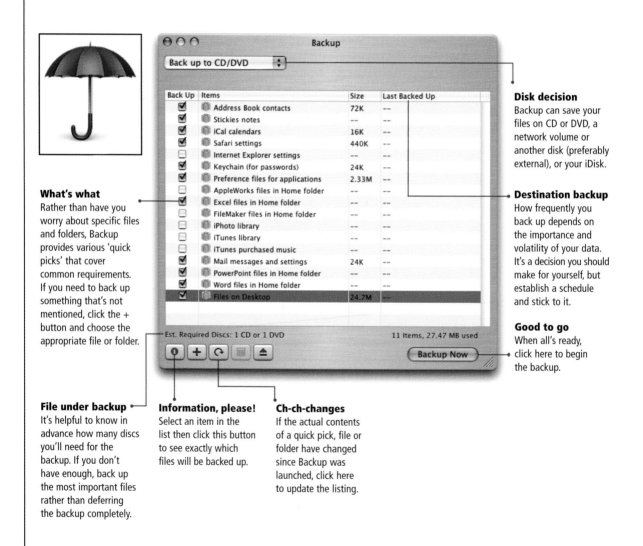

Disk decision
Backup can save your files on CD or DVD, a network volume or another disk (preferably external), or your iDisk.

Destination backup
How frequently you back up depends on the importance and volatility of your data. It's a decision you should make for yourself, but establish a schedule and stick to it.

What's what
Rather than have you worry about specific files and folders, Backup provides various 'quick picks' that cover common requirements. If you need to back up something that's not mentioned, click the + button and choose the appropriate file or folder.

Good to go
When all's ready, click here to begin the backup.

File under backup
It's helpful to know in advance how many discs you'll need for the backup. If you don't have enough, back up the most important files rather than deferring the backup completely.

Information, please!
Select an item in the list then click this button to see exactly which files will be backed up.

Ch-ch-changes
If the actual contents of a quick pick, file or folder have changed since Backup was launched, click here to update the listing.

Backup where?

Backing up to iDisk is useful for smaller amounts of data, especially when you need the reassurance of off-site backup (eg, for financial records). Backup presents a smaller set of quick picks when you are using iDisk. An external or networked drive has the advantage of speed. Using the built-in CD or DVD burner is cheap and convenient. The use of write-once media means you retain each day's (or week's) versions of the files, which is handy if you ever need to go back to an old version (eg, following file corruption). Rewritable media works out cheaper in the long run, and reduces landfill.

Good to go

There appears to be plenty of space on this iDisk, but it has less than one-sixth of the capacity of a CD. The upside is that if your office burns down, your data's safe on Apple's server.

While you were sleeping

Backup can automatically keep your backups up-to-date (unless you're backing up to CD or DVD). To schedule backups, click on the Calendar button at the lower left of the Backup window, and then set the times. Bear in mind that you must be logged in at the specified time.

The command line

Usually, we control our Macs with the mouse. We point and click, drag and drop, and enter commands by choosing them from menus. But Mac OS X also has an optional 'command line', where you can type sophisticated instructions. It's not as easy as using the mouse, but it's a lot more powerful and it can be faster too. What's more, mastering the command line is the only way to use many handy Unix programs, and sometimes it's the only way to fix a flaky Mac.

The open desktop.

Down in the depths
'Underneath' Mac OS X sits a UNIX-based operating system, called Darwin. You can access Darwin's command line directly by running Terminal, which is in Utilities in Mac OS X's Applications folder.

Prompt service
Darwin presents you with a 'prompt' (everything up to and including the '$') to tell you that it's ready for you to start typing. The 'Apples-PowerBook-17' in the prompt is the name of the Mac (set in the Sharing system preference), 'apple' is the short version of the Mac OS X username, '~' means that you are currently in your home directory, and '%' means that you are a normal user, not the all-powerful 'root' user. Now type 'pwd' (no quotes) and press the return key. This command tells Darwin to show you the 'path'

```
Last login: Fri Feb 13 18:04:19 on ttyp2
Welcome to Darwin!
Apples-PowerBook-17:~ apple$ pwd
/Users/apple
Apples-PowerBook-17:~ apple$ cd documents/test
Apples-PowerBook-17:~/documents/test apple$ ls -l
total 0
-rw-r--r--  1 apple  apple  0 13 Feb 17:41 document1
-rw-r--r--  1 apple  apple  0 13 Feb 17:41 document2
-rw-r--r--  1 apple  apple  0 13 Feb 17:41 document3
Apples-PowerBook-17:~/documents/test apple$ sudo chown www:www document1
Password:
Apples-PowerBook-17:~/documents/test apple$ chmod 711 document2
Apples-PowerBook-17:~/documents/test apple$ rm document3
Apples-PowerBook-17:~/documents/test apple$ ls -l
total 0
-rw-r--r--  1 www    www    0 13 Feb 17:41 document1
-rwx--x--x  1 apple  apple  0 13 Feb 17:41 document2
Apples-PowerBook-17:~/documents/test apple$
```

Terminal — bash — 80x19

End result
Use the 'ls' command again. document1 is now owned by 'www'. document2 now has 'rwx--x--x' privileges. document3 no longer exists.

Change directory
Type 'cd' (the change directory command) followed by the path to the folder to which you want to move. There's no 'preceding slash' because you are starting from your home folder. The prompt changes to show your new location.

Easy street
Use TextEdit to create blank plain-text files called document1, document2 and document 3 in a folder called test in your Documents folder if you want to take these Terminal commands for a spin. These files will be owned by you and have 'rw-r--r--' privileges. You'll need to 'cd documents/test' at the command prompt — there's no initial '/' because you're starting from your home directory, not the root directory.

Superuser do
Use the 'chown' command to change the owner of document1 to 'www' (a hidden user that runs your Mac's web server, and which belongs to a group called 'www'). Type 'sudo' before the 'chown' command to give yourself 'superuser' abilities, such as the ability to change the file's owner. Give your password when prompted. Use the 'chmod' command to give 'read/write/execute' privileges (indicated by the number 7) to document2's owner, and 'execute only' privileges (indicated by the number 1) to everyone else. Use the 'rm' command to delete document3. You don't need to use 'sudo' to delete your own files or change their permissions.

READ THE MANUAL
The UNIX layer included with Mac OS X comes with an extensive manual, called 'the man pages'. Access the manual with the 'man' command. For example, type 'man rm' to read the manual for the rm command.

HOT TIP

List directory contents
The 'list directory contents' command ('ls') shows all the files in the current directory. The '-l' flag requests additional information about these files. If we saw 'drwxrwxrwx' in the first column of our listing, we'd know that the file was actually a directory ('d'); that the file's owner was permitted to read the file (the first 'r'), write to it (the first 'w'), or execute it as a script or program (the first 'x'); that every member of the owner's group had the same freedoms (the next 'rwx'); and that everyone else had these freedoms (the last 'rwx'). By way of contrast, the first column of our directory listing shows that document1 is a file not a directory – only the file's owner may read it, no-one may write to it, and anyone may execute it. User 'apple' owns all three files.

Virus protection

When the Internet catches a cold, the whole world sneezes. Fortunately, very few viruses affect Mac OS X, but it is still advisable to use antivirus software to reduce the risk of passing on an infected document to a Windows user.

Virus Protection

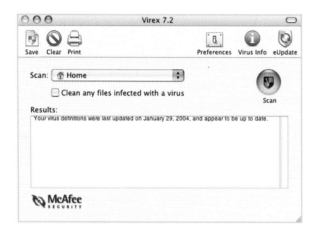

Mind your malware
Hostile programs—or 'malware'—come in many forms, including viruses, worms and trojan horses, though the term 'virus' is often used to describe all hostile software. Virus writers continually release new threats into the wild, which is why it's vital to keep your virus definition file up-to-date. Vendors typically provide new definitions on a weekly or monthly cycle if you use the automatic update feature (eg, eUpdate), but you may find more frequent updates are available for manual downloading and installation.

Shields up
Virex lacks the ability to automatically scan downloaded files, but this can be overcome by using an AppleScript folder action. Download Virex Auto-Scan FA from macscripter.net. Nor does it support scheduled scanning (the closest it comes is automatic scan at login). Again, there's a workaround: www.ucs.ed.ac.uk/usd/scisup/faq/virexschd.html gives step-by-step instructions for scheduling Virex scanning using cron.

Beyond the brand

We've described Virex as it is included with a .mac subscription, but other companies produce software to help protect your Mac. For example, Sophos AntiVirus can automatically scan files as they are opened (just as Mac OS 9 antivirus programs did), though a Mac OS X 10.3-compatible version had not been released at the time of writing. Norton AntiVirus supports on-schedule scanning and downloading of updates.

Not all security measures require special software—eg, don't open email attachments unless you know who sent them. (But you should scan attachments for viruses regardless of their source.) The Secure Mac site can help you survey all your security options: securemac.com

Don't defrag

Most experienced Mac and PC users are used to periodically defragmenting their disk drives to improve performance. Mac OS X 10.3 Panther is far less susceptible to fragmentation and it optimizes the placement of some files. Apple suggests defragmentationwill only be useful if your disks are almost full and you often modify or create large files.

Always on, always vulnerable

If you have a broadband Internet connection (cable, DSL or satellite), viruses are not your only concern. You are always connected to the Internet, so you are always exposed to hackers. A firewall is your first line of defence. Luckily, Mac OS X includes a firewall. Basic settings are available in the Sharing system preference, but to learn about detailed configuration from the command line, open Terminal and type 'man ipfw' (no quotes). A halfway house is to control the firewall via utilities such as Norton Personal Firewall, BrickHouse (brianhill.dyndns.org), or SunShield (www.sunprotectingfactory.com)

Field Guide
search

A

P